Criminal Law

GW00728997

T.J. MCINTYRE, B.C.L., LL.M, B.L.

Portobello College, Dublin

SINÉAD MCMULLAN, LL.B, B.C.L. (OXON), B.L.

Trinity College Dublin

DUBLIN
ROUND HALL LTD
2001

Published in 2001 by
Round Hall Ltd.
43 Fitzwilliam Place
Dublin 2
Ireland

Typeset by
Devlin Editing, Dublin

Printed and bound by
Antony Rowe Ltd, Eastbourne

A CIP catalogue record for this book is available from the British Library

ISBN 1-85800-252-1

© Round Hall Ltd 2001

ABOUT THE AUTHORS

T.J. McIntyre, B.C.L., LL.M, Barrister at Law, is a lecturer in law at Portobello College, Dublin and was formerly a Judicial Research Assistant to the High Court and Supreme Court.

Sinéad McMullan, LL.B, B.C.L. (Oxon) is a practising barrister and lecturer in law at Trinity College Dublin. She has also lectured at Dublin Institute of Technology.

To Clodagh
T.J.M.

CONTENTS

TABLE OF CASES

TABLE OF STATUTES

CONSTITUTION OF IRELAND

TABLE OF EU LEGISLATION

TABLE OF INTERNATIONAL LAW

1. INTRODUCTION TO FUNDAMENTAL PRINCIPLES AND CONCEPTS

1.1 Distinction between criminal and civil matters

At first, discussion of the nature of a crime might seem to be of purely academic interest. In practical terms, however, it is important to be able to distinguish crimes from other legal wrongs. The trial of criminal offences is governed by Article 38 of the Constitution, which confers special protections on those accused of such offences. In particular, paragraphs 1, 2 and 5 of Article 38 provide that:

> "1. No person shall be tried on any criminal charge save in due course of law.
>
> "2. Minor offences may be tried by courts of summary jurisdiction."
>
> "5. Save in the case of trial of offences under section 2, no person shall be tried on any criminal charge without a jury."

In addition, Article 38 must be read in conjunction with Article 37.1, which allows for limited powers and functions of a judicial nature to be carried out by persons who are not judges appointed under the Constitution, or bodies which are not courts established under the Constitution (*e.g.* the Employment Appeals Tribunal, or the Labour Court). However, Article 37.1 is limited to "matters other than criminal matters".

The net effect of these two articles is, therefore, that once we determine that a matter is criminal, it must be tried before courts established under the Constitution, with a jury unless the matter is minor, and in due course of law. We will see that this last phrase encompasses certain rules of law, such as the right to silence and the presumption of innocence, which are not applicable to civil trials. How, then, do we determine when a matter is criminal?

From a theoretical point of view, the criminal law is a branch of public law, and concerns itself with public wrongs. It is thus distinct from branches of private law, such as contract or tort. If a person commits a tort, or a breach of contract, this is a matter solely for the person injured. Only that person may sue, and he may settle or discontinue those proceedings freely. The criminal law, by contrast, deals with conduct which is felt to be injurious to the community as a whole. For that reason, enforcement is not left to the victim of a crime but is carried out by public bodies. (However, it is possible for prosecutions to be brought by ordinary members of the public in some circumstances.) For the same reason, if the prosecution succeeds, the victim cannot pardon the offender; this power is reserved to the State. In short, the offence is not merely the concern of the victim.

Another general characteristic of the criminal law is that it deals with moral wrongs, although this fact is not particularly helpful in defining what is or is not a crime. Many crimes bear little moral stigma, while many immoral acts are perfectly legal. Moreover, the perceived moral quality of crimes varies from time to time. For example, drink driving was for a long time regarded as a trivial offence and not a real crime and only quite recently have attitudes begun to harden against it.

A third identifying feature of the criminal law is that the sanctions imposed are punitive rather than compensatory. In the law of contract or tort, damages are measured by reference to the position of the injured party, to compensate the victim for the loss suffered. In the criminal law, however, the sanction is primarily measured having regard to the blameworthiness of the offender and if a monetary fine is imposed it does not go to the victim. This reflects the wider scope of the criminal law; while the civil law confines itself to the position of the wrongdoer and the injured party, the criminal law also seeks to deter others by punishing the wrongdoer.

The main Irish case applying these criteria is *Melling v. O Mathghamhna* (1962). In this case, the conduct penalised was the smuggling of butter, which was made subject to a penalty of £100 or treble the value of the goods. This was held by the Supreme Court to amount to a criminal charge for the purposes of Article 38, with each of the judgments taking a slightly different approach to determining whether a matter was criminal. Lavery J. looked primarily to the practical effect of the proceedings:

> "It seems to me clear that a proceeding, the course of which permits the detention of the person concerned, the bringing of him in custody to a Garda station, the entry of a charge in all respects appropriate to the charge of a criminal offence, the searching of the person detained and the examination of papers and other things found upon him, the bringing of him before a District Justice in custody, the admission to bail to stand his trial and the detention in custody if bail be not granted or is not forthcoming, the imposition of a pecuniary penalty with the liability to imprisonment if the penalty is not paid has all the *indicia* of a criminal charge." (At page 9.)

Kingsmill Moore J. took a more theoretical approach, holding that a criminal charge was distinguished by three elements: its nature as an offence against the community at large, the punitive nature of the sanction, and the requirement of *mens rea*. Ó Dálaigh J. took a similar approach to Lavery J., looking primarily to the practical effect of the proceedings.

The tests set out in *Melling* have since been applied by the Supreme Court in *McLoughlin v. Tuite* (1989). This case also involved a revenue matter, concerning various sections of the Income Tax Act 1967, imposing a fixed penalty on any person failing to comply with a notice to make income tax returns and allowing the penalty to be recovered by civil proceedings. The taxpayer claimed that this section was invalid as it imposed a criminal penalty other than in accordance with Article 38. The Supreme Court, however, rejected this argument, holding that although the penalty payment was punitive in effect, the proceedings did not otherwise have the indicia of a criminal offence. In particular: *mens rea* was not required, no question of detention or arrest arose and imprisonment could not be imposed in default of payment. In addition, the sum could be recovered from the estate of a deceased taxpayer, in a way which was characteristic of a civil debt, but entirely inconsistent with a criminal penalty.

Another, more recent case which applied the *Melling* principles is *Goodman v. Hamilton (No 1)* (1992). This case involved the Beef Tribunal, set up to investigate allegations of misconduct, including criminal activity, in the beef industry. The plaintiff, who controlled companies accounting for a large part of the industry, alleged that this would amount to the trial of a criminal charge. This argument was, however, rejected by the Supreme Court, which held that although the Tribunal was investigating allegations of criminal misconduct, it was not conducting a criminal trial. In particular, Finlay C.J. stated:

> "The essential ingredient of a trial of a criminal offence in our law, which is indivisible from any other ingredient, is that it is had before a court or judge which has got the power to punish in the event of a verdict of guilty. It is of the essence of a trial on a criminal charge or a trial on a criminal offence that the proceedings are accusatorial, involving a prosecutor and an accused, and that the sole purpose and object of the verdict, be it one of acquittal or of conviction, is to form the basis for either a discharge of the accused from the jeopardy in which he stood, in the case of an acquittal, or for his punishment for the crime which he has committed, in the case of a conviction.

The proceedings of the inquiry to be held by this Tribunal have none of those features. The Tribunal has no jurisdiction or authority of any description to impose a penalty or punishment on any person. Its finding, whether rejecting an allegation of criminal activity or accepting the proof of an allegation of criminal activity, can form no basis for either the conviction nor acquittal of the party concerned on a criminal charge if one were subsequently brought, nor can it form any basis for the punishment by any other authority of that person." (At page 588.)

The effect of this judgment is that if a proceeding deals with criminal matters, this will not necessarily make it a criminal trial. For example, if A hits B, causing injury, this may amount to a criminal act. Prosecution of A for this act by the D.P.P. would clearly be a trial of a criminal charge within the meaning of Article 38.1, and all the relevant constitutional safeguards would apply. If, however, B sues A seeking compensation for the injury suffered, then this is not the trial of a criminal charge. A may be liable to pay compensation; he is not, however, liable to be punished. *Mens rea* is not an issue, nor is there any question of detention or arrest.

Finally, the most recent case on this point is *Gilligan v. Criminal Assets Bureau* (1998). This case concerned the Proceeds of Crime Act 1996. The plaintiff claimed that the scheme of the Act, which provides for the forfeiture of property which constitutes the proceeds of crime, violated his Article 38.1 right to a trial on any criminal charge in due course of law, since the proceedings were in essence criminal rather than civil yet lacked the constitutional safeguards applicable to a criminal trial. It was argued by the defendants that forfeiture proceedings under the act were civil and not criminal in nature, although they necessarily involved the determination of some matters which may constitute elements of criminal offences.

In resolving this issue, McGuinness J. looked to the earlier case law setting out the *indicia* of a criminal offence. Applying that caselaw, she first noted that the procedure under the Act was *in rem* rather than *in personam* (meaning that the action dealt with the status of property rather than the status of an individual). There was no question of the detention of a party to proceedings under the Act, nor the infliction of any specific penalty, whether imprisonment or fine. Although money or property could be removed from a party to the proceedings, if the property was shown to be the proceeds of crime, then "its removal could well be viewed in the light of reparation rather than punishment or penalty." As for the determination of whether a crime had been committed, McGuinness J. accepted that civil actions could validly make determinations in respect of matters which may also constitute the elements of a crime.

1.1.1 Criminal v. civil - summary

Criminal Law	Civil Law
Harm caused to public	Harm restricted to individual
Action brought by State	Action brought by individual
Deals with moral wrongs	Does not concern itself with moral guilt
Proof beyond reasonable doubt	Proof on the balance of probabilities
Presumption of innocence, right to silence	n/a
Procedure includes arrest, search, admission to bail	n/a
Tried before judge and jury (except in the case of minor offences)	Tried before judge alone (except in some cases - for example defamation)
Outcome is punishment of offender	Outcome is compensation of plaintiff

Further reading: Kelly, *The Irish Constitution* (3rd ed., Hogan and Whyte (eds.), Butterworths, 1994), pp.621-623; *O'Keeffe v. Ferris* (1997).

1.2 Presumption of innocence

The presumption of innocence is not explicitly stated in the Constitution, but is implicit in the requirement of Article 38.1 that "no person shall be tried on any criminal charge save in due course of law". It is fundamental to the Irish legal system, and is internationally recognised as an essential safeguard. For example, the European Convention on Human Rights, to which Ireland is a party, requires in Article 6(2) that "everyone charged with a criminal offence shall be presumed innocent until proved guilty according to law".

The application of the presumption of innocence can be seen in *Woolmington v. DPP* (1935). This case is the authoritative statement of the presumption in the UK and in a number of Commonwealth countries: while there is a distinct constitutional foundation for the presumption in this jurisdiction, *Woolmington v. DPP* (1935), remains an oft-cited and persuasive authority. The charge was murder. The accused admitted killing the deceased, but claimed that the gun went off accidentally. The trial judge directed the jury that once the prosecution proved that the deceased was killed by the accused, the burden then shifted to the accused to prove the facts alleged to constitute a defence. This direction was held by the House of Lords to be incorrect, and a definitive statement of the law was given: the burden at all times remains on the prosecution, and once a defence is raised, then the accused is entitled to be acquitted unless the prosecution disproves that defence. Viscount Sankey emphasised, at page 481, that:

> " ... it is not for the prisoner to establish his innocence but for the prosecution to establish his guilt ... while the prosecution must prove the guilt of the prisoner there is no such burden placed on the prisoner to prove his innocence and it is sufficient for him to raise a doubt as to his guilt; he is not bound to satisfy the jury of his innocence ... Throughout the web of the English criminal law one golden thread is always to be seen, that it is the duty of the prosecution to prove the prisoner's guilt ... the principle ... is part of the common law of England and no attempt to whittle it down can be entertained."

The Supreme Court has recently discussed the presumption of innocence in two cases. The first is the case of *Hardy v. Ireland* (1994). This case concerned section 4(1) of the Explosive Substances Act 1883, which criminalises possession of explosives (here mercury tilt switches) under circumstances giving rise to "a reasonable suspicion that [the defendant] does not have it in his possession ... for a lawful object", unless the defendant "can show that he ... had it in his possession ... for a lawful object". The defendant claimed that the effect of this was to impermissibly undermine the presumption of innocence. This was rejected by the Supreme Court, but in a way which showed that it was divided as to what the presumption of innocence required. All the members of the Court accepted that the presumption of innocence was a necessary component of a trial in due course of law pursuant to Article 38.1. However, the judges differed on whether the burden of proof can be shifted in a way which is compatible with the presumption of innocence.

The majority judgment, delivered by Hederman J., solved the problem by reading the section narrowly, so that it required the prosecution to prove beyond reasonable doubt that the accused did not have the items in his possession for a lawful purpose. He stated, at page 564, that:

> " ... the prosecution has to prove beyond reasonable doubt ... (1) that the accused knowingly had in his possession a substance which it proves is an explosive substance; (2) that he had it under such circumstances as to give rise to a reasonable suspicion that he did not have it in his possession for a lawful object and that, in turn, means that there is an onus on the prosecution to prove that the accused could not show that he had it in his possession for a lawful object. Once those ingredients are in place, it is still open to the accused to demonstrate in any one of a number of ways, such as by cross-examination, submissions or by giving evidence, that a prima facie situation pointing to his guilt should not be allowed to prevail ... this analysis ... protects the presumption of innocence; it requires that the prosecution should prove its case beyond all reasonable doubt; but it does not prohibit that, in the course of the case, once certain facts are established, inferences may not be drawn from those facts ..."

This reading essentially side-stepped the issue of whether a statute may require an accused to prove a particular defence on the balance of probabilities, from which it may be inferred that this issue presented some difficulties for the majority.

By contrast, the judgments of Murphy and Egan JJ. accepted that the section imposed an onus on the accused to prove on the balance of probabilities that he had the explosives in his possession for a lawful purpose, but held that such a shifting of the burden of proof with regard to a defence did not violate Article 38.1. Egan J. remarked, at p.566, that "There is nothing in the Constitution to prohibit absolutely the shifting of an onus in a criminal prosecution or to suggest that such would inevitably offend the requirements of due process." Murphy J. reasoned as follows, at page 568:

> "... the second limb of the section deals not with the charge but with a statutory exoneration or exculpation from a charge already made and sustained beyond reasonable doubt. I am convinced that the burden which the accused must discharge if he is to avail of that procedure is a duty to satisfy the jury of the statutory condition, that is to say, the existence of a lawful object on the balance of probabilities ... I do not see that there is any inconsistency between a trial in due course of law as provided for by Article 38(1) of the Constitution and a statutory provision such as is contained in s.4 of the Explosive Substances Act,

1883, which affords to an accused a particular defence of which he can avail if, but only if, he proves the material facts on the balance of probabilities.".

The second case is *O'Leary v. Attorney General* (1995). Here, the plaintiff challenged the constitutionality of two sections of the Offences Against the State Act 1939, which provided that the possession of an "incriminating document" (in this case, a poster saying "IRA calls the shots") would be evidence of membership of an unlawful organisation, as would the belief of a chief superintendent to this effect. The plaintiff claimed that the effect of these sections was to reverse the presumption of innocence, requiring him to prove that he was not a member of an unlawful organisation.

The Supreme Court rejected this argument, however, holding that these sections provided for *evidence* of membership, but not *proof* of membership; the onus always remained on the prosecution to prove the accused's membership, and possession of an incriminating document or the belief of a chief superintendent would not necessarily constitute proof of membership. The section did not pass a legal burden of proof onto the accused to prove that he was not guilty of the offence, but an evidential burden only. The probative value of the evidence might be shaken in many ways, for example by cross-examination, by pointing to the mental capacity of the accused or the circumstances by which he came to be in possession of the document.

1.3 Burden of proof

It can be seen from the two cases discussed above that a necessary consequence of the presumption of innocence is the placing of the burden of proof on the prosecution. It is, therefore, the responsibility of the prosecution to establish the guilt of the accused. An important consequence flows from this: if a defence is raised by the accused, then it is the responsibility of the prosecution to disprove the defence, not the responsibility of the accused to prove the defence.

There are, however, two qualifications to this principle. First, there is the special case of the defence of insanity, which will be dealt with later. This common law defence must be proved by the accused on the balance of probabilities. Second, we have seen that the minority judgments in *Hardy v. Ireland* (1994) accept that a statute may place similar requirements on an accused when raising a statutory defence. An example of this is provided by the decision of the Court of Criminal Appeal in *People (DPP) v. Byrne* (1998). Section 29(2) of the Misuse of Drugs Act 1977 provides that:

> "[Where] it is proved that the defendant had in his possession a controlled drug ... it shall be a defence to prove that –
>
> (i) he did not know and had no reasonable grounds for suspecting that –
>
> (ii) that what he had in his possession was a controlled drug ... or
>
> that he was in possession of a controlled drug ...".

In this case the defendants were arrested in possession of packages containing drugs, but claimed not to be aware of their contents. It was held, however, that once *possession* of the packages was proved, the onus shifted to the defendants to prove lack of knowledge of the contents of the packages. The prosecution was obliged to prove that an accused had, and knew that he had, a package in his control and that the package contained something. The prosecution must also prove that the package contained the controlled substance alleged. The burden of proof then rested on the defendants to bring themselves within the defence in section 29(2)(a).

1.4 Right to silence and privilege against self-incrimination

We now turn to the principles of law which are usually described as the right to silence and the privilege against self-incrimination. These are closely related to the presumption of innocence; if it is the role of the prosecution to prove that an offence has been committed, then it should not be incumbent on the suspect or accused person to facilitate the prosecution by being compelled to speak.

What specific issues are covered under this heading? One Australian study gave the following list:

> "the right of a suspect to refuse to answer questions put to him or her by criminal investigators; and
>
> the right of an accused person to choose whether or not to testify at his or her trial; and
>
> the consequences for the accused of exercising either or both of these rights; in particular, the question of whether adverse inferences can be drawn from, or adverse comments made about, the exercise of the right

to refuse to answer questions and / or the right to not testify." (*The Right to Silence: An Examination of the Issues* (Parliament of Victoria, 1998), Ch. 1).

To this, we can add the right not to have compelled answers used in evidence in a criminal matter (the privilege against self-incrimination). We will look at each of these rights in turn.

1.4.1 Pre-trial right to silence

First we will look at the right to silence at the pre-trial stage, that is, while a crime is being investigated, but before a person has been charged with that crime. At common law, it was clear that suspects enjoyed a right to refuse to answer police questions. However, recent legislation has increasingly tended to require answers to be given in specific circumstances, or to allow a court to draw an adverse inference from the failure to give answers. Consequently, we must ask whether there is a constitutional right to silence which could be asserted against such legislation.

This issue came before the Supreme Court in *Heaney v. Ireland* (1996). This case dealt with section 52 of the Offences Against the State Act 1939, which requires suspects to give accounts of their movements around the time at which a crime is alleged to have taken place. Failure to give such an account is an offence. The two defendants challenged the constitutionality of this provision, claiming that it infringed their constitutional right to silence.

The Supreme Court accepted that there is a constitutional right to silence at the pre-trial stage, stating that such a right exists as a corollary of the right to freedom of expression under Article 40 of the Constitution. However, the court went on to hold that this right was not absolute and that the State was entitled to encroach on it in the interests of maintaining public peace and order, provided that the limitation of the right was proportionate to the purpose of the legislation. In this case, the court took the view that section 52 struck an acceptable balance between "any infringement of the citizen's rights with the entitlement of the State to defend itself", so that the section was constitutional.

A similar conclusion was reached by the Supreme Court in the next case to come before it on this issue, *Rock v. Ireland* (1997). In that case, the validity of sections 18 and 19 of the Criminal Justice Act 1984 was challenged. These sections apply where a person is arrested without a warrant and permit a court to draw adverse inferences from a failure by that person to account for their possession of any object, or the presence on their person of any mark, or their presence at a particular place, which a garda believes may be related to the offence for which they have been arrested. These inferences may amount to corroboration of other evidence — however, a person may not be convicted solely on the basis of such an inference. In short, therefore, under sections 18 and 19 a person's silence when arrested may be used in evidence against that person at trial.

Here, the applicant was arrested while in possession of a quantity of banknotes, which proved to be forged US dollars. After his arrest, he was invited to account for his possession of these, which he declined to do, so that sections 18 and 19 came into play. He sought a declaration that sections 18 and 19 were repugnant to the Constitution. This was, however, refused by the Supreme Court, which reiterated that the constitutional right to silence was not absolute. The court went on to apply a test of proportionality in deciding whether this limitation of the right was constitutional. It pointed out that the restriction on the right to silence was limited, and in particular emphasised that: an adverse inference could not form the basis for a conviction without other evidence being present; an adverse inference could only be drawn where the court deemed it proper to do so; and the weight or value of any such adverse inference could be challenged by the accused. Consequently, the court found that the restriction of the right to silence was justified, and upheld sections 18 and 19.

It is clear from these two decisions that legislation can validly restrict the right to silence at the pre-trial stage. Recent examples of such legislation include section 7 of the Criminal Justice (Drug Trafficking) Act 1996 and sections 2 and 5 of the Offences Against the State (Amendment) Act 1998, which in each case allow adverse inferences to be drawn against a defendant who remains silent when questioned. The effect of these provisions is that an accused person will have to decide what facts he will be relying on during his trial and to decide whether to bring such facts to the attention of the gardaí at an early stage.

However, it is important to note that, where no such legislation has been enacted, then the right to silence remains available. An example of this can be seen in *People (DPP) v. Finnerty* (1999). In this case, the defendant was accused of rape, and put forward an alternative account of the events on the night in question. In response, the prosecution sought to put it to the defendant that he had not given any such account when arrested and questioned. The implication of this would, of course, be that the defendant's account was a recent fabrication.

The trial judge allowed the prosecution to question the defendant on his silence when arrested, and the defendant was thereafter convicted. On appeal, the Court of Criminal Appeal upheld this decision, stating that it did not impinge on the defendant's right to silence, inasmuch as it was limited to the credibility of the defendant's account of events and was not in itself evidence of guilt. On further appeal, however, the Supreme Court disagreed and quashed the conviction, stating that, while legislation might validly allow adverse inferences to be drawn from silence, in this case no such legislation existed. Consequently, since there was no statutory provision allowing adverse inferences to be drawn, the defendant's constitutional right to silence applied, and that right could not be undermined by informing the jury that the defendant had remained silent when questioned.

1.4.2 At-trial right to silence

Moving to the trial itself, it is clear that there is a constitutional right of an accused person, arising from Article 38.1, to refuse to testify (see the decision of Costello J., in the High Court, in *Heaney v. Ireland* (1994)). However, where an accused person does choose to testify, he or she must answer questions put to him or her by the prosecution, and cannot decline to do so on the basis that the answers would incriminate him or her: Criminal Justice (Evidence) Act 1924, section 1(e).

1.4.3 Privilege against self-incrimination

We have seen that legislation may validly require a person to answer questions connected with a criminal investigation. However, the fact that a person may be compelled to answer does not necessarily mean that any information which they give can be used in evidence against them at trial, and the question must be asked as to whether the privilege against self-incrimination will prevent such use.

This issue recently came before the Supreme Court in *Re National Irish Bank* (1999). This case concerned section 10 of the Companies Act 1990, which imposes an obligation on company officers and agents to co-operate with inspectors investigating a company by, amongst other things, answering questions posed by the inspectors. Here, National Irish Bank was being investigated in connection with a number of criminal offences, including tax evasion and fraudulent charging of customers. Employees of the bank refused to answer questions put to them by the inspectors, stating that they constituted an infringement of their right to silence and potentially required them to incriminate themselves.

On the matter coming before the Supreme Court, the court (Barrington J.) accepted that the employees enjoyed a right to silence under *Heaney v. Ireland* (1996). However, the powers given to the inspectors were proportional and no greater than required by the public interest, and therefore the right to silence had been validly restricted. The employees could, therefore, be required to answer questions put by the inspectors, notwithstanding their right to silence.

Could the answers to such questions be used in evidence against the employees? In considering this point, Barrington J. looked to case law dealing with the privilege against self-incrimination and in particular whether involuntary confessions could be admitted against an accused person, and came to the conclusion that:

> "It appears to me that the better opinion is that a trial in due course of law requires that any confession admitted against an accused person in a criminal trial should be a voluntary confession and that any trial at which an alleged confession other than a voluntary confession was admitted in evidence against the accused person would not be a trial in due course of law within the meaning of Article 38 of the Constitution and that it is immaterial whether the compulsion or inducement used to extract the confession came from the executive or from the legislature." (At page 359.)

It follows, therefore, that while legislation may validly restrict the pre-trial right to silence, it may not limit the privilege against self-incrimination. In other words, while a criminal suspect may in some circumstances be required to answer questions before trial, the answers to such questions may not be used in evidence against him or her at trial.

1.4.4 Offence of withholding information

One special case which must be mentioned relates to section 9 of the Offences Against the State (Amendment) Act 1998, which introduces a new offence of withholding information which a person knows or believes might be of material assistance in "(a) preventing the commission by any other person of a serious offence, or (b) securing the apprehension, prosecution or conviction of any other person for a serious offence". Where a person is aware of such information, they come under a duty to report it to a member of the Garda Síochána; failure to do so, without reasonable excuse, is a criminal offence. It will be clear that this represents a remarkable inroad on the right to silence, and this provision has yet to be considered by the courts.

1.4.5 Influence of the European Convention on Human Rights

Article 6 of the European Convention on Human Rights guarantees the right to a fair trial, and the question must therefore be asked as to whether limitations on the right to silence or the privilege against self-incrimination infringe this right.

As regards drawing adverse inferences from pre-trial silence, the most recent decision is *Averill v. United Kingdom* (2000). Here it was held that the drawing of an adverse inference could infringe Article 6, depending on all the circumstances of a particular case. Relevant factors included the situations where inferences may be drawn, the weight to be attached to them by national courts, the degree of compulsion inherent in the situation (for example, whether a person could be penalised for failure to answer), and whether an accused person had access to a lawyer during questioning.

In this case, the defendant was arrested and questioned in connection with a murder in Northern Ireland. He was initially refused access to a solicitor but was later allowed to consult with one. He was warned by police that an adverse inference could be drawn from silence, but refused to answer any questions relating to the offence. At trial, he put forward an alibi for the date of the murder. The trial judge drew what he stated to be "a very strong adverse inference" from the defendant's silence when arrested, and the defendant was convicted. The defendant then applied to the European Court of Human Rights, alleging that this adverse inference amounted to an interference with his right to a fair trial under Article 6.

However, the court rejected this application, stating that the drawing of an adverse inference was not, in itself, a breach of Article 6. In this case there was no obligation on the trial judge to draw an adverse inference, and the trial judge was free to consider if there was an excuse or a justification for the failure to speak. In deciding to draw an adverse inference, the trial judge provided detailed reasons for his decision, which were subject to review on appeal. In addition, the inferences had not been the sole reason for the conviction, which was supported by other evidence. In light of all these factors and safeguards, the court found that the drawing of an adverse inference did not interfere with the accused's right to a fair trial.

Turning to the question of compelled answers to police questioning, this issue recently came before the European Court of Human Rights in Heaney and *McGuinness v. Ireland* (2000). This case arose from the facts of *Heaney v. Ireland* (1996), discussed above, and was brought by the two applicants following the dismissal of their Supreme Court appeal. Here they alleged that their conviction for failure to answer questions under section 52 was a breach of their right to a fair trial under Article 6, in that it amounted to punishment for invoking their rights to silence and against self-incrimination. The court upheld this argument, finding that:

> "the 'degree of compulsion', imposed on the applicants by the application of s. 52 of the 1939 Act with a view to compelling them to provide information relating to charges against them under that Act, in effect, destroyed the very essence of their privilege against self-incrimination and their right to remain silent." (Para. 55.)

Applying a test of proportionality, it went on to find that the national security concerns expressed by the Irish Government did not amount to a sufficient justification for this measure, so that there had been a violation of the applicants' rights to silence and against self-incrimination, under Article 6. It would appear, therefore, that section 52 will have to be amended or repealed in order for the State to comply with the decision of the court, and there must now be a question mark over any other legislative provisions which require criminal suspects to answer questions put to them by the police.

1.5 Standard of proof

Having dealt with the burden of proof, we turn to the standard of proof the prosecution must meet to secure a conviction. In civil law matters, the standard of proof is *on the balance of probabilities*. That is, the plaintiff will succeed if he can establish that his version of events is more likely than not. However, a higher standard applies in the criminal law, where guilt must be proven *beyond a reasonable doubt*. This standard requires that the accused be acquitted, even if the jury think it possible or even likely that he committed the crime charged, so long as they have a reasonable doubt as to his guilt. It has been explained by Denning J. in *Miller v. Minister of Pensions* (1947), as follows:

> "Proof beyond reasonable doubt does not mean proof beyond the shadow of doubt. The law would fail to protect the community if it admitted fanciful possibilities to deflect the course of justice. If the evi-

dence is so strong against a man as to leave only a remote possibility in his favour which can be dismissed with the sentence "of course it is possible but not in the least probable" the case is proved beyond reasonable doubt, but nothing short of that will suffice." (At page 373.)

The standard is constitutionally required in this jurisdiction, and has been authoritatively defined by Kenny J. in the Court of Criminal Appeal, in *People (AG) v. Byrne* (1974):

> "The correct charge to a jury is that they must be satisfied beyond reasonable doubt of the guilt of the accused, and it is helpful if that degree of proof is contrasted with that in a civil case. It is also essential, however, that the jury should be told that the accused is entitled to the benefit of the doubt, and that when two views on any part of the case are possible on the evidence, they should adopt that which is favourable to the accused unless the State has established the other beyond reasonable doubt." (At page 9.)

Applying that standard, the Court of Criminal Appeal held that a charge to the jury was defective in that it told the jury they could convict if "satisfied" of the guilt of the accused, without making it clear that they must be satisfied *beyond a reasonable doubt*.

Further reading: Ní Raifeartaigh, "Reversing the Burden of Proof in a Criminal Trial" (1995) 5 *Ir. Crim. L.J.* 135; Law Reform Commission, *Report on the Confiscation of the Proceeds of Crime* (LRC 35-1991), pp. 52-55; Dillon-Malone, "Voluntariness, the Whole Truth and Self-Incrimination after In Re NIB" (1998/99) 4 *Bar Review* 237; McCutcheon & Walsh, "Seizure of Criminal Assets: An Overview" (1999) *I.C.L.J.* 127; Ní Raifeartaigh, "The Criminal Justice System and Drug Related Offending: Some Thoughts on Procedural Reforms" (1998/99) 4 *Bar Review* 15; Editorial, "Offences Against the State (Amendment) Act, 1998 – Two Views" (1998/99) 4 *Bar Review* 5; McDermott, "Evidence and Procedure Update" (2000) *I.C.L.J.* 18.

1.6 Classification of crimes

1.6.1 Felony v. misdemeanour

Until 1997 crimes were primarily classified as being either felonies or misdemeanours, and depending on this classification, different rules applied as regards, *inter alia*, powers of arrest and the liability of accomplices. The Criminal Law Act 1997 abolished this distinction (section 3) and provided detailed rules governing powers of arrest (sections 4, 5 and 6) and the liability of accomplices (sections 7 and 8) which do not depend on this classification.

1.6.2 Minor v. non-minor

However, other distinctions between crimes remain significant. The most important is the distinction between minor and non-minor offences. This is of significance having regard to Article 38.2, which provides that minor offences may be tried without a jury. It follows that whether an offence is minor determines whether an accused has a right to trial by jury.

How do we determine if an offence is minor? The main case on this point is the case of *Melling v. O Mathghamhna* (1962), which we have already looked at in connection with determining whether a particular matter is a criminal matter. The issue also arose in that case as to whether the offence of smuggling butter was a minor offence, and the Supreme Court held that in making that decision, one must look primarily to the severity of the penalty involved and to the moral quality of the offence. As a rule of thumb, it is generally taken that an offence is minor if the maximum penalty possible is a fine of £1500 and/or 12 months' imprisonment.

1.6.3 Indictable v. summary

Another distinction is that between indictable and summary offences. This distinction is related to the distinction between minor and non-minor offences, and again hinges on mode of trial. An indictable offence is one which may or must be tried before a jury, while a summary offence is one which can only be tried before a judge sitting without a jury.

1.6.4 Serious v. non-serious

A new distinction has been created by the Bail Act 1997, which we will deal with later. At the moment, it is enough to note that the 1997 Act allows bail to be refused where an accused is charged with a serious offence, and it is established that if released on bail he is likely to commit further serious offences. The Act defines a serious offence as one of a number of specified offences for which a person, if convicted, could face five or more years imprisonment.

1.6.5 Arrestable v. non-arrestable

Similarly, the Criminal Law Act 1997 creates a new category of arrestable offences. Since the Act abolished the felony/misdemeanour distinction on which powers of arrest hinged, it was necessary to specify when the gardaí would enjoy powers of arrest without warrant, and the Act does so by providing (section 4) that a Garda may arrest without warrant any person he believes to be guilty of an arrestable offence. The Act goes on to define an arrestable offence as an offence for which a person could be punished by imprisonment for five or more years.

2. CRIMINAL PROCEDURE

2.1 Arrest and detention

The original purpose of arrest was to enable a suspect to be charged with a criminal offence. The traditional objective of detention was to ensure the attendance of an accused in court. Indeed, the Garda Síochána was expected to have completed the investigation of an alleged offence before arresting a suspect. This approach has been broadened in recent times and arrest and detention are increasingly being used to question suspects and investigate crimes.

Prior to 1997, a police officer had a common law power to arrest without warrant where he reasonably suspected that a felony had been committed. In contrast, arrest warrants were necessary in the case of misdemeanours. The Criminal Law Act 1997 abolished the distinction between felonies and misdemeanours and a new category of offence, an arrestable offence, was created. This is defined as an offence punishable by imprisonment for five years or more. Section 4 permits an arrest to be effected without warrant by any person who, with reasonable cause, suspects another to be committing or to have committed an arrestable offence.

A controversial power of arrest is contained in section 30 of the Offences Against the State Act 1939. This exists in respect of any offence under the Offences Against the State Acts 1939-1998 and any scheduled offence. The power of arrest also extends to any person suspected of being in possession of information relating to the commission or intended commission of, an offence under the Acts or a scheduled offence.

Sections 4 to 10 of the Criminal Justice Act 1984 contain powers of detention. A person must be taken to a garda station without undue delay after arrest as a suspect's rights will not be set in motion until his arrival in the garda station. A suspect may only be detained for an initial six hours beginning from the time of arrest. He must only be detained where there are reasonable grounds for believing that the detention is necessary for the proper investigation of the offence. This opinion must be formed at the time the suspect is brought to the station by the member in charge, who should not be one of the arresting gardaí. If a garda, not below the rank of superintendent, believes that it is necessary for the proper investigation of the offence to detain the suspect for a *further* six-hour period, this may be directed under section 4. Alternatively, at the end of the first six-hour period the suspect must either be released or charged and brought before a court as soon as possible.

Powers of detention are also to be found in section 2 of the Criminal Justice (Drug Trafficking) Act 1996. These powers are very extensive, allowing a suspect to be detained for up to a maximum of seven days. However, after two days of detention, an application must be made to a district judge for an extension of up to 72 hours. The suspect must be brought before the court for the application. After this period has expired, a further extension of up to 48 hours may be applied for.

The Offences Against the State (Amendment) Act 1998 increases the powers of detention, in relation to persons arrested under section 30 of the Offences Against the State Act 1939, from 48 hours to 72 hours. The extension from 48 to 72 hours may only be granted by a district judge and the suspect must be brought before the court when the application is being made.

Further reading: Ryan, "Arrest and Detention: A Review of the Law" (2000) 10 I.C.L.J. 2.

2.2 Preliminary examination

The following describes the preliminary examination procedure as it stands at the time of writing. The Criminal Justice Act 1999 will, when implemented, replace that procedure and is described below. [Since this was written, the relevant provisions of the 1999 Act have been brought into force by S.I. No. 193 of 2001. The new procedures will, therefore, apply as and from October 1, 2001.]

In the case of summary offences, trial usually follows charge with few intervening procedural formalities. In the case of indictable offences, however, the procedure of preliminary examination must generally be followed before an accused can be sent forward for trial. The preliminary examination procedure is contained in Part II of the Criminal Procedure Act 1967 and is designed to see if there is enough evidence against an accused to justify his being put on trial. The rationale for such a procedure was examined by the Supreme Court in *Glavin v. Governor of Mountjoy Training Unit* (1991), which stated that it had two functions: it protected an accused from being put on trial when there was no sufficient case against him, and it enabled an accused to fully consider the case which was to be made against him, ensuring that he would not be caught by surprise at trial.

The accused has a right to a preliminary examination, by virtue of the 1967 Act but this right is statutory only and not constitutional (*O'Shea v. DPP* (1988)). The accused is entitled to waive this right, in which case he will be sent forward for trial without further ado. If the accused does not waive this right, the procedure to be followed is set out in the 1967 Act. First, the prosecution must serve the accused with the "book of evidence". This is the colloquial term for the bundle of documents which the Act requires to be served on the accused, which includes a statement of charges, a list of all witnesses who will be called at trial, a statement of the evidence which each will give, and a list of all exhibits.

This having been done, the preliminary examination itself can proceed. This takes place before the District Court, and both the prosecution and the defence are entitled to call any witness, who will be examined on oath. At this point, submissions can be made by the defence that the accused has no case to answer, as for example where the prosecution has failed to prove an essential ingredient of the offence. If the offence charged is that of handling stolen property, for example, then an essential proof is that the property is in fact stolen. If the prosecution fails to include such a proof in the book of evidence, then the accused is entitled to a finding that there is not a sufficient case against him to justify his being put on trial. At the end of this hearing, and having considered all the evidence, including the contents of the book of evidence, the district judge will make a determination whether (in the words of the statute) "there is a sufficient case to put the accused on trial". If there is, then the accused will be returned for trial before either the Central Criminal Court or the Circuit Court; if not, then the accused will be discharged.

If a preliminary examination is flawed, and the accused is nevertheless sent forward for trial, then the subsequent proceedings will be rendered a nullity by that initial defect. The right to a preliminary examination is so inextricably linked with the trial on indictment that failure to hold a valid preliminary examination means failure to observe the requirements of trial in due course of law under Article 38.1: (*Glavin v. Governor of Mountjoy Training Unit* (1991)).

The Criminal Justice Act 1999 brings about the abolition of the system of preliminary examinations. Instead, the Act puts in place a procedure under which persons accused of indictable offences will automatically be sent forward for trial, unless the case is being tried summarily, the accused pleads guilty before the District Court, or the accused is unfit to plead. However, no person shall be sent forward for trial on indictment without the consent of the D.P.P. (or the A.G., when proceedings would otherwise require the consent of the A.G.).

A book of evidence shall then be served on the accused within 42 days of the accused first appearing in the District Court charged with the relevant offence; the District Court does, however, have power to extend that time where it is in the interests of justice to do so.

A safeguard remains in place for an accused where the evidence is insufficient to justify a trial: it is open to an accused person to apply to the trial court to dismiss one or more of the charges against the accused on the ground that there is not "a sufficient case" to put the accused on trial in respect of the relevant charge. This is, of course, the same test which was formerly used at the preliminary examination stage. Where a charge is so dismissed by the trial court, it is open to the prosecution to appeal to the Court of Criminal Appeal.

The prior system of depositions is replaced as follows: it is now open to either the prosecution or the accused to apply to the trial court to have the evidence of a person taken before trial by way of sworn deposition. The trial court will grant such application if satisfied that it would be in the interests of justice to do so: there is no automatic right to take evidence in this way. Evidence taken by way of deposition will be admissible at trial if the witness is unavailable at trial (due to death, inability to attend, being prevented from attending, or being subjected to fear or intimidation) and the accused was present at the taking of the evidence and was given an opportunity to cross-examine the witness.

As was the case with preliminary examinations, the power of the press to report is restricted. In any proceedings under the new procedure, the press can report only that the proceeding has been brought by a named person in relation to a specified charge against a named person, and the decision resulting from the proceeding.

Further reading: Osborne, "The Preliminary Examination of Indictable Offences" (1995) 5 I.C.L.J. 1.

2.3 Bail

Bail can be defined as the setting at liberty of an accused pending trial, and is granted by way of a recognisance: an undertaking that the accused will appear for trial, and that a certain sum of money will be forfeited if he does not. (Bail is also available while an appeal is pending, but this situation raises different considerations and will not be dealt with). An accused can be released on his personal recognisance, but in serious cases independent sureties will be required.

Before 1996, the law concerning bail was largely contained in successive Supreme Court decisions which laid down when it was or was not constitutionally permissible to refuse bail. Roughly speaking, bail could be refused only where an accused was likely to fail to appear for trial, or likely to interfere with the conduct of the trial. Dissatisfaction with this regime led to the Bail Referendum in 1996, which inserted into the Constitution what is now Article 40.4.7°. This Article was implemented by the Bail Act 1997.

Our starting point is the decision of the Supreme Court in *People (AG) v. O'Callaghan* (1966). In this case, the grant of bail was opposed on the grounds that the accused would interfere with witnesses, and that, if released, the accused would commit further offences while on bail. The first ground was largely unsupported by evidence, and the Supreme Court unanimously held that the second ground could not be taken into account in deciding whether to grant bail. *Per* Ó Dálaigh C.J.:

> "[The second ground is] a denial of the whole basis of our system of law. It transcends respect for the requirement that a man shall be considered innocent until he is found guilty and seeks to punish him in respect of offences neither completed nor attempted." (At pages 508-509.)

And, *per* Walsh J.:

> "[I]t would be quite contrary to the concept of personal liberty enshrined in the Constitution that any person should be punished in respect of any matter upon which he has not been convicted or that in any circumstances he should be deprived of his liberty upon only the belief that he will commit offences if left at liberty." (At 516-517.)

The Supreme Court instead stated that the only test in deciding whether to allow bail was the probability of the accused attempting to evade justice, whether by failing to appear for trial, or by interfering with the trial (by interfering with witnesses, destroying evidence, and so on). In applying this test the Supreme Court stated that regard could be had to the following factors:

1. The seriousness of the charge.

2. The nature of the evidence in support of the charge.

3. The likely sentence to be imposed on conviction.

4. The possibility of disposal of illegally acquired property.

5. The possibility of interference with prospective witnesses and jurors.

6. The accused's failure to answer to bail on a previous occasion.

7. The fact that the accused was caught red-handed.

8. The objections of the Attorney General or of the police authorities.

9. The substance and reliability of the sureties offered.

10. The possibility of a speedy trial.

Some comments on each of these factors must be made. Numbers 1, 2, 3, 6 and 7 each go to the likelihood that an accused will fail to appear for trial: clearly, an accused is less likely to appear where he faces a solid prosecution case, and a substantial sentence if convicted. It should be noted that 7 is really just an aspect of 2, the nature and strength of the evidence against the accused. Number 4 (disposal of illegally acquired property) is only relevant insofar as this amounts to interference with evidence. Equally, number 8 (prosecution objections) is only relevant insofar as the objections relate to the accused attempting to evade justice. Finally, number 10 (prospect of a speedy trial) was stated by the Supreme Court to be a factor in favour of refusing bail where otherwise it might be granted (if extensive delays were likely before the charge was heard). However, it was stressed that the availability of a speedy trial could not justify the refusal of bail where otherwise it would be granted.

In *Ryan v. DPP* (1989), the Supreme Court was invited to reconsider its decision in *People (AG) v. O'Callaghan*, on the basis that the right to liberty of the accused must be balanced against the rights of other citizens who might be the victims of further crimes. This argument was, however, rejected in pithy terms:

> "The criminalising of mere intention has usually been a badge of an oppressive or unjust legal system. The proper methods of preventing crime are the long-established combination of police surveillance, speedy trial and deterrent sentences." (*Per* Finlay C.J. at page 407.)

The net result of *Ryan v. DPP* and *People (AG) v. O'Callaghan* was, therefore, that bail could not be refused on the ground of likelihood to commit further crimes. However, a serious problem did exist with regard to offences being committed while the accused was free on bail, and section 11 of the Criminal Justice Act 1984 attempted to deter the commission of such offences, by providing for mandatory consecutive sentences for offences committed while on bail.

However, as already noted, dissatisfaction with the bail regime continued, culminating in the insertion of Article 40.4.7° into the Constitution:

> "Provision may be made by law for the refusal of bail by a court to a person charged with a serious offence where it is reasonably considered necessary to prevent the commission of a serious offence by that person."

This Article is permissive only - "Provision *may be made*" - and does not in itself allow a court to refuse bail. It was given effect by the Bail Act 1997.

The primary condition of the 1997 Act is contained in section 2(1), which allows a court to refuse a bail application made by a person charged with a serious offence if reasonably considered necessary to prevent the commission of a serious offence by that person. "Serious offence" is then defined by section 1(2) as any crime specified in the Schedule to the Act for which a person of full capacity not previously convicted could be punished by 5 or more years imprisonment. The list of crimes specified in the Schedule is quite extensive, and includes for example all offences under the Larceny Acts, 1916 to 1990 as well as the more obviously serious crimes such as murder, manslaughter and rape.

Section 2(2) then requires the court to take into account factors similar to those contained in *People (AG) v. O'Callaghan* in deciding whether to refuse bail on this ground:

a. The nature and degree of seriousness of the offence charged and the likely sentence.

b. The nature and degree of seriousness of the offence apprehended as likely to be committed, and the sentence which would be likely to be imposed for that offence.

c. The strength of the evidence in support of the charge.

d. Any conviction of the accused for an offence committed while on bail.

e. Any other convictions of the accused.

f. Any other offence charged for which the accused is awaiting trial.

The court may also take into account the fact that the accused is addicted to a controlled drug. Under section 2(3) it is not necessary for the prosecution to point to the likely commission of any particular serious offence.

Bail having been refused on the ground that the accused is likely to commit a serious offence, section 3 then allows the application for bail to be renewed four months after the initial refusal, on the grounds of delay by the prosecutor, and the court may then grant bail "if the interests of justice so require".

Section 5 of the 1997 Act tightens up requirements as regards recognisances, by providing that where an accused is granted bail subject to recognisances, the accused shall not be released until at least one third, or more if the court so requires, of each recognisance has been paid into court.

Section 6 specifies conditions which a court may or must impose on the grant of bail. (The significance of these conditions being that failure to comply will result in rearrest, and forfeiture of any recognisances.) A recognisance must contain a condition that the accused will not commit any offence, and the court may impose further conditions which it considers appropriate, for example, requiring the accused to reside in a particular place, to report to a specified Garda station, to surrender his passport, to refrain from going to a particular place or to refrain from having contact with a particular person.

Finally, section 10 of the 1997 Act makes a significant change to the Criminal Justice Act 1984. While the 1984 Act required consecutive sentences to be imposed for crimes committed on bail, section 10 also requires that a greater sentence should be imposed for offences committed while on bail.

Distinct from the question of what grounds justify the refusal of bail is the question of what evidence is required to be given to establish those grounds. From a practical point of view it is vitally important to know what form of evidence is required in opposing the grant of bail: is hearsay evidence admissible, must evidence be given *viva voce* or will affidavits suffice, and so on. There was a tendency on the part of judges to refuse to grant bail on evidence which was far from ideal, but this has now been cut short by the decision of the Supreme Court in *People (AG) v. McGinley* (1998). In that case the accused was refused bail in the High Court on the basis of the hearsay evidence of a garda to the effect that the victim's family had been threatened by members of the accused's family. On appeal to the Supreme Court, it was held that as a rule an applicant for bail was entitled, as part of his right to fair procedures, to have any evidence against him given under oath and subject to cross-examination, unless there were any special factors present (such as confidential police sources) which would justify the admission of hearsay evidence.

Further reading: Bacik, "The Bail Act 1997" (June 1997) *Practice and Procedure* 7; O'Higgins, "Bail - A Privilege or a Right?" (1998) *Bar Review* 318.

2.4 Appeals

This section will be limited to the case of appeals against verdicts on indictment. Where a person is convicted after a summary trial (i.e. in the District Court) there is a statutory right of appeal to the Circuit Court and that appeal takes the form of a re-hearing of the matter. The remedy of judicial review is also available where the procedure adopted by the District Court is defective in some way. However, we will confine ourselves to the case of appeals from conviction on indictment, that is, in the case of trials taking place before the Circuit Court, Central Criminal Court, or Special Criminal Court.

2.5 The Court of Criminal Appeal

The Court of Criminal Appeal (the CCA) is not a court mentioned in Article 34 of the Constitution, and is therefore entirely a statutory creation, first established by the Courts of Justice Act 1924. It is composed of one Supreme Court and two High Court judges, with the Supreme Court judge presiding, and delivers a single judgment. It operates (in theory) a two-stage procedure, where first, one applies for *leave to appeal* (unless this has already been granted by the court of trial); having obtained leave to appeal, one proceeds to the *substantive appeal*. In practice, the court almost invariably combines the two stages, treating the application for leave to appeal as the appeal itself.

2.5.1 The "basic powers" of the Court of Criminal Appeal

What might be called its basic powers, in relation to ordinary appeals, are now set out in section 3 of the Criminal Procedure Act 1993. On the hearing of an *appeal against conviction*, the court may:

1. *affirm* the conviction;

2. *quash* the conviction, making no further order;

3. *quash* the conviction, ordering that the applicant be *re-tried for that offence*; or

4. *quash* the conviction, and *substitute a verdict of guilty for some other offence.*

Some points on each option must be made. As regards option 1, a conviction can be affirmed under section 3, even where the court would decide a point raised in the appeal in favour of the applicant, where the court considers that no miscarriage of justice has actually taken place. This is designed to deal with the situation where a trial judge makes a technical or otherwise minor mistake, which does not result in any prejudice to the accused.

As regards options 2 and 3, it will be clear that a successful appeal is not a "get out of jail free" card. The court may direct that a retrial take place, at which point the process starts over. However, the court has a discretion not to do so, and will decline to order a retrial where, for example:

- A conviction is quashed because of the weakness of the evidence against the applicant;

- The applicant has already spent such a period of time in prison that no court on a retrial would impose a further sentence; or

- No reasonable jury, properly directed, could convict the applicant on the evidence presented.

Having said that, the normal practice is that a retrial will follow the quashing of a conviction unless there are special circumstances leaning in the other direction.

Option 4, quashing the conviction and substituting a conviction for another offence, requires close scrutiny. The text of the relevant subsection states:

> "the Court may ... quash the conviction and, if it appears to the Court that the appellant could have been found guilty of some other offence and that the jury must have been satisfied of facts which proved him guilty of the other offence - (i) substitute for the verdict a verdict of guilty of the other offence, and [sentence the appellant accordingly so long as the sentence is not more severe than the original]."

The problems with this power will be obvious. In allowing the court to find a person guilty of an offence, in circumstances where he has not been convicted by a jury of that offence, this section on its face appears to fall foul of Article 38.5 of the Constitution that "no person shall be tried on any criminal charge without a jury, save in the case of minor offences, special courts and military tribunals." The constitutionality of this power must therefore be suspect, and it seems that it has never been exercised.

On the hearing of an *appeal against sentence*, the Court may let the original sentence stand, or quash the sentence and impose such sentence as it considers appropriate. This, it should be noted, includes the power to vary the sentence upwards: an appeal against sentence may, therefore, be a risky option.

It should be noted that these two forms of appeal, against conviction and sentence, can be brought only by a convicted person; appeals by the prosecution are dealt with below.

2.5.2 Prosecution appeal against sentence

The "basic powers" of the Court of Criminal Appeal, set out above, are in essence the same powers as it enjoyed until 1993. In that year, however, two fundamental changes were made to the jurisdiction of the court. The first was contained in the Criminal Justice Act 1993, section 2 of which allows the D.P.P. to apply to the court to review a sentence imposed by a court on conviction of a person on indictment, where he considers that sentence to be unduly lenient. It will then be open to the court to let the sentence stand, or to quash it and substitute a higher (or lower) sentence.

This change was prompted largely by the public outcry over two controversially lenient sentences. The first was the Lavinia Kerwick case, in which a rape victim went public over her disgust that her rapist had escaped a custodial sentence. The second was the Kilkenny incest case, where again the sentence imposed was publicly felt to be inadequate in relation to the gravity of the crime (both of these cases are discussed in the Annotation to the 1993 Act by Bird, cited below).

While it was possible for the D.P.P. to appeal against sentence in a small class of cases before the passing of this Act, this power was useless in practical terms. By convention, it was seldom exercised. In addition, it rested on the happenstance of certain offences being tried before the Central Criminal Court; if the Circuit Court or Special Criminal Court were to impose an unduly lenient sentence, then the D.P.P. was powerless. It was necessary, therefore, to create a comprehensive power capable of practical use, which the 1993 Act did.

Soon after the creation of the power, the case of *DPP v. B* (1994) came before the court. (The following is a summary taken from the detailed analysis in O'Malley's article, cited below.) This was the first prosecution application under the new section, and the court therefore took the opportunity to outline how the new power would be operated. The facts were particularly horrific, which was no doubt a reason why the case had been chosen by the DPP as a test case. The applicant had been convicted on three charges of rape, against two different victims. The two offences had been committed shortly after each other. In each case the applicant had broken into the victim's home. The first victim was a woman who was asleep in bed with her husband: she was abducted, taken to another part of the house, and raped. The second victim was an elderly widow who was assaulted, raped and buggered by the applicant at knifepoint. He confessed when arrested soon after, and pleaded guilty at preliminary examination. He had a previous conviction for indecent assault.

The applicant came to be sentenced before Hamilton P. in the Central Criminal Court, who stated that a 14-year sentence would have been appropriate but for the early guilty plea; taking the plea into account, however, he would impose concurrent sentences of 10 years each.

On appeal, the court during argument indicated that counsel should address whether the sentencing judge had failed to take into account relevant factors, or had taken into account irrelevant factors. In reply, counsel for the D.P.P. argued that a ten-year sentence for each offence was not of itself inappropriate; but it was inappropriate to make each sentence concurrent, since there was no element of additional punishment for an additional offence, particularly where the two offences were completely separate.

The court (O'Flaherty J.), in giving judgment, first set out four guidelines to be used in determining whether a sentence was "unduly lenient":

1. The Director of Public Prosecutions bears the onus of proof.

2. The decision of the trial judge should not be upset without good reason, since he or she is in the best position to assess sentence, having heard all the facts first-hand. His decision, if it balances the offence with the position of the offender, should not be disturbed.

3. The court should not ask if a more severe sentence would have been upheld on appeal; the test is not whether the trial judge could have

imposed a higher sentence, but whether the sentence he or she did in fact impose was "unduly lenient".

4. Having regard to these guidelines, the ultimate question is whether the particular sentence is a "substantial departure from what would be regarded as the appropriate sentence". If not, the court will not intervene.

The court went on to apply those guidelines to hold that the sentence imposed by Hamilton P. would not be disturbed.

It should be noted that the existence of a prosecution appeal against sentence creates an anomaly. As a matter of practice, which is codified in paragraph 9.20 of the Bar Code of Conduct, it is not considered appropriate for a prosecutor to make any submissions on the sentence which should be imposed on an accused. A prosecutor may play on gruesome facts during the trial; but after conviction, he or she is limited to a bare recital of whether the accused has any previous convictions. The defence lawyer, by contrast, is free to make submissions as to the appropriate sentence. It follows that the prosecutor is unable to guide the trial judge as to the factors to be taken into account, but if dissatisfied with the sentence imposed, is able to go before the Court of Criminal Appeal and argue that the trial judge failed to take all relevant factors into account. If the prosecutor can make these arguments at this later stage, it is hard to see why he cannot do so at the earlier stage, particularly where doing so might avoid the need for a prosecution appeal.

2.5.3 *Miscarriages of justice*

The next major change to the jurisdiction of the Court of Criminal Appeal was brought about by the Criminal Procedure Act 1993, which dealt with the position of "miscarriages of justice" — cases such as those of the Birmingham Six, where it seemed that the ordinary appeals system was inadequate to deal with lingering doubts over guilt, particularly once the normal appeals procedure had been exhausted.

Although there was a tendency to look down on the English legal system, which seemed to produce miscarriages of justice with monotonous regularity, these cases were not unknown in Ireland, with the most notorious example being the conviction of Nicky Kelly in 1978 on evidence which, he alleged, was fabricated by the guards following violent interrogation. After an unsuccessful appeal to the Court of

Criminal Appeal, he was ultimately granted a presidential pardon in 1992, some fourteen years after the event.

A commission was therefore set up in 1989 under the chairmanship of Judge Frank Martin of the Circuit Court, to examine whether there was a need for a procedure over and above the normal appeals procedure, and whether there should be restrictions on the use of confession evidence. The Commission ultimately recommended that there should be a special procedure set up to review alleged miscarriages of justice, but felt that this should not be court-based, primarily on the basis that the restrictive nature of the rules of evidence would hinder attempts by a convict to clear his name. Instead, the Commission recommended that there should be an independent body, with statutory powers to call witnesses, demand documents, and so forth, which would investigate these matters.

This recommendation was not accepted by the 1993 Act which adopts a twin-track approach instead. Those wishing to challenge an alleged miscarriage of justice have two options open to them. First, they can petition the Minister for Justice, who has the power to set up an *ad hoc* committee to inquire into that alleged miscarriage of justice. This committee will then recommend to the Government whether a pardon should be granted. Secondly, they can proceed down the court route, launching a fresh appeal to the Court of Criminal Appeal on the basis of new or newly obtained evidence. In either event, if the applicant is successful in his or her petition or appeal, and the Minister or the court is of the opinion that there has been a miscarriage of justice, then the applicant is entitled to compensation.

The Role of the Court of Criminal Appeal

The court route is provided for in section 2, which imposes a number of preconditions before an application under this section can be brought. First, the applicant must have already appealed to the Court of Criminal Appeal. Second, the proceedings in relation to the appeal must be complete: there can be no further proceedings pending. (This does not, however, seem to preclude concurrent claims before, for example, the European Court of Human Rights.) Third, and crucially, the applicant must allege that:

> "new or newly discovered facts [show] that there has been a miscarriage of justice in relation to the conviction or that the sentence imposed is excessive.". (Section 2(1)(b).)

What is a newly discovered fact? Before the 1993 Act, for an appeal to be brought on the basis of new evidence, it had to be shown that the evidence was not available at the trial. Although there was no authority on the point in this jurisdiction, it had been held elsewhere that this rule excluded evidence which with reasonable diligence could have been available to the defence at trial. The 1993 Act adopts a broader definition, by stating that:

"a newly discovered fact is ... a fact discovered by or coming to the attention of the convicted person after the relevant appeal proceedings have been finally determined *or a fact the significance of which was not appreciated* by the convicted person or his advisers during the trial or appeal proceedings." (Section 2(4)); and

"[a] new fact ... is a fact known to the convicted person at the time of the trial or appeal proceedings the significance of which was appreciated by him, where he alleges that there is *a reasonable explanation for his failure to adduce evidence* of that fact." (Section 2(3))

It will be clear from the portions in italics that the definition of new or newly discovered facts is quite wide. In particular, section 2(3) allows an appeal to be brought where there is a reasonable explanation why evidence was not tendered, which would cover for example, the situation where an accused is threatened if he should implicate another in a crime alleged to have been committed by him.

Once these preconditions for the jurisdiction of the court are met, and once the court has determined that a miscarriage of justice within the meaning of section 2 has occurred, it is then open to the court to certify under section 9 that a miscarriage of justice has taken place, so as to entitle the applicant to compensation. However, despite the fact that the same terminology is used in both sections, it is now clear that the two are distinct, and the quashing of a conviction under section 2 does not in itself entitle an applicant to compensation under section 9. This is the net result of two cases to come before the Court of Criminal Appeal, each of which has elaborated on the distinction between the two sections.

The first of these was *People (DPP) v. Pringle* (1997), in which the Supreme Court laid down certain applicable principles. In that case, the Court of Criminal Appeal had quashed the conviction of an applicant on the basis of a newly discovered fact showing a miscarriage of justice within the meaning of section 2. It refused, however, to certify that a miscarriage of justice had taken place within the meaning of section 9. On appeal to the Supreme Court, it was held that the mere fact of the quashing of a conviction under section 2 does not give rise to a right to compensation. Instead, before a section 9 certificate could be granted, it was for the applicant to establish, on the balance of probabilities, that there had been a miscarriage of justice in his case, *i.e.* that he was more likely than not innocent of the offence of which he had been convicted.

The second case was *People (DPP) v. Meleady and Grogan* (1997), which dealt with the so-called "Tallaght Two". The convictions of the applicants had been quashed by the Court of Criminal Appeal, but in that case the court had felt that compensation could not be granted unless there had been a retrial at which the applicants had been found not guilty. This decision was reversed by the Supreme Court, which held that the inquiry under section 9 as to whether a miscarriage of justice had taken place did not depend on a subsequent jury acquittal: compensation could be awarded without the need for a fresh trial to take place.

Further reading: Bird, "Annotations to the Criminal Justice Act 1993" (1993) I.C.L.S.A. 6-01 *et seq.*; Hutchinson, "Annotations to the Criminal Procedure Act 1993" (1993) I.C.L.S.A. 40-01 *et seq.*; O'Malley, "The First Prosecution Appeal Against Sentence" (1994) 4 I.C. L.J. 192.

3. MENTAL ELEMENT OF CRIMES

3.1 Definition of *mens rea*

What is *mens rea*? It is the mental or fault element of a crime, without which no crime is committed. This concept has its origins in the idea that a person should not be convicted of a crime unless he is morally blameworthy or otherwise at fault, and should not therefore be convicted unless he intended to bring about the *actus reus* of the crime charged. If a killing is accidental, then it cannot amount to murder, because there was no intention to kill or cause serious injury, and hence no (or at least less) moral culpability. This is the simplest example of the principle in action.

However, the law does not always require the same degree of moral culpability before a person can be convicted of a crime. Sometimes a crime is committed if a person intends a certain result; sometimes if a person is reckless whether a certain result occurs; sometimes if a person negligently brings about a certain result; and sometimes if a person causes a certain result regardless of any fault. It is generally accepted that there are six categories of *mens rea*. In decreasing order of moral culpability they are:

1. Intention

2. Recklessness

3. Criminal Negligence

4. Negligence

5. Strict Liability with a defence of reasonable mistake

6. Absolute Liability

The first two are the mental states required in the case of most serious crimes. The third is confined to the crime of manslaughter. The fourth to sixth are not really concerned with mental states and are essentially confined to so-called regulatory crimes, for example crimes such as pollution or trading without a licence, which tend not to be regarded as truly criminal and which might equally well be dealt with by the civil law. We will consider each type of *mens rea* separately.

3.2 Intention

What does it mean to intend to bring about a particular result or state of affairs? It does not necessarily mean to *desire* the result. If A is strapped for cash, and decides to kill B and collect on the life insurance policy, then A intends to kill B notwithstanding that A is genuinely fond of B and will regret B's death. We would not say that A desires B's death. Nevertheless, in most cases the intended result will also be the desired result.

Nor does intention require that the result is *likely*. If A shoots at B intending to kill B, then if the bullet does in fact kill B the crime of murder is committed. This is so notwithstanding that A might have been shooting from a great distance, and might have been exceptionally lucky to hit B.

Nor is intention the same as *motive*. Suppose a person commits an apparently motiveless crime. The absence of motive might make it more difficult to link the crime to A: but it remains a crime nevertheless. The position is summarised in the following quote of Dickson J. in *R. v. Lewis* (1979):

> "Motive is no part of the crime and is legally irrelevant to criminal responsibility. It is not an essential element of the prosecution's case as a matter of law ... Proved absence of motive is always an important fact in favour of the accused ... Conversely, proved presence of motive may be an important factual ingredient in the [prosecution] case."

In most cases these problems will not arise. The result will ordinarily be both desired and likely, and there will ordinarily be a motive. The difficulty arises in cases where the accused says that he intended to do one thing, foresaw another thing as a consequence, yet denies that he intended that consequence. This situation is epitomised where A puts a bomb on board a ship, intending to collect on the insurance. A certainly intends to blow up the ship. A knows that a possible or probable result will also be the death of all of those on board the ship. Does A *intend* to kill the passengers and crew, or is A merely *reckless* as to whether or not they die?

The courts have had difficulty coming to terms with these types of cases. In particular, a series of cases before the English courts illustrate the problems caused. In *Hyam v. DPP* (1975) the defendant put blazing newspaper through the letterbox of a house to frighten a woman inside. In fact, it caused the death of two of the woman's children. The House of Lords accepted that this was murder if the defendant knew that death or serious injury was a "highly probable" result of her actions, even if she did not desire that result.

In *R v. Moloney* (1985), a somewhat different result was reached. Here a man was killed by his stepson. After heavy drinking at a wedding anniversary, they played a drunken game with loaded shotguns to see who was quicker on the draw. The victim then taunted his stepson to pull the trigger, which he did, killing the victim. The stepson was charged with murder. The jury were directed that the stepson intended to kill if either (a) he desired to kill the victim whether or not he had foreseen that it would probably happen, or (b) he foresaw that his conduct was likely to kill the victim, regardless of whether he desired to kill. However, the House of Lords held that such a direction was incorrect: foresight that a result was probable was not the same as intending that result. Instead, foresight that a result was "a natural consequence" of the defendant's act was evidence from which the jury could *infer* that he intended that result.

Shortly afterwards, in *R. v. Hancock and Shankland*, the House of Lords adopted yet another position. The events in this case took place during the bitter miners' strike in England. Two miners on strike attempted to intimidate "scab" workers by pushing concrete blocks from a bridge over the road along which the workers were driving with a police escort. One block hit the windscreen of a car, killing the driver. The defendants were charged with murder, and raised the defence that they did not intend to kill or cause serious injury, but to block the road and frighten the workers. The jury was directed in accordance with *R v. Moloney* that intent could be inferred from foresight that death or serious injury was "a natural consequence" of the defendants' actions. However, this direction was found by the House of Lords to be inadequate: a jury should also be referred to the issue of *probability*, and told that they can infer intention where a result is "a natural and *probable* consequence" of the defendant's actions. In addition, the jury should be told that the more probable the result, the more likely that it was intended by the defendant.

The decision of the Court of Appeal in *R v. Nedrick* was an attempt to reconcile the effects of the previous decisions. The facts in this case were very similar to those in *Hyam v. DPP* (1975). The defendant had poured paraffin through the letter box of a woman against whom he had a grudge and set it alight. The woman's child died in the fire. The jury was directed that the defendant was guilty of murder if he knew that it was highly probable that what he did would cause serious injury to somebody in the house. His conviction was quashed by the Court of Appeal, which made the following remarks at page 3 of the report:

"It may be advisable to explain first to the jury that a man may intend to achieve a certain result whilst at the same time not desiring it to come about.

'A man who, at London Airport, boards a plane which he knows to be bound for Manchester, clearly intends to travel to Manchester, even though Manchester is the last place he wants to be and his motive for boarding the plane is simply to escape pursuit.' [quoting from the judgment of Lord Bridge in *R v. Moloney* (1985) at 926.]

When determining whether the defendant had the necessary intent, it may therefore be helpful for the jury to ask themselves two questions. (1) How probable was the consequence which resulted from the defendant's voluntary act? (2) Did he foresee that consequence?

If he did not appreciate that death or serious harm was likely to result from his act, he cannot have intended to bring it about. If he did, but thought that the risk to which he was exposing the person killed was only slight, then it may be easy for the jury to conclude that he did not intend to bring about that result. On the other hand, if the jury are satisfied that at the material time the defendant recognised that death or serious harm would be virtually certain (barring some unforeseen intervention) to result from his voluntary act, then that is a fact from which they may find it easy to infer that he intended to kill or do serious bodily harm, even though he may not have had any desire to achieve that result.

Where a man realises that it is for all practical purposes inevitable that his actions will result in death or serious harm, the inference may be irresistible that he intended that result, however little he may have desired or wished it to happen.".

Finally, the recent decision of the House of Lords in *R. v. Woolin* (1999) considers the same issue. In this case the accused was acquitted of murdering his three-month-old son by throwing him on the ground and thereby fracturing his skull. It was agreed that he did not desire to cause serious bodily harm to the infant and the issue was whether he nevertheless had intention to cause serious bodily harm. Lord Steyn disagreed with *Nedrick* that foresight of virtual certainty was merely evidence from which intention may be inferred. Instead, he held that a result seen as virtually certain was an intended result.

In summary, therefore, the position appears to be that a defendant intends those results which it is his objective to carry out, which are a necessary precondition to achieving his objective (killing another to collect on the life insurance policy) or which he knows to be a virtually certain consequence of achieving his objective (the death of passengers and crew after a plane is blown up in mid air, even though the objective is not to kill but to collect on the insurance covering the plane itself). There is, however, a grey area where intention shades into recklessness.

Where a charge to the jury is defective as regards the need for intention to be shown, then any resulting conviction will be quashed. This can be seen in the case of *People (DPP) v. McBride*. In this case, the defendant was charged with causing grievous bodily harm with intent, contrary to section 18 of the Offences Against the Person Act 1861; unlawfully and maliciously inflicting grievous bodily harm, contrary to section 20 of the 1861 Act; and assault occasioning actual bodily harm, contrary to section 47 of the 1861 Act.

The judge's charge to the jury had contained several defects. The defendant had testified to the effect that his mind had gone blank when he hit the victim. In his charge to the jury, in respect of the first offence, the judge said simply that this was no defence to the charge. This was held to be incorrect: the jury should have been told that this was something they had to consider in deciding whether the defendant had the necessary intent for the charge, notwithstanding that it was not of itself a defence to the charge. In addition, the court indicated that the jury should have been directed on the presumption that a person intends the natural and probable consequences of their actions, together with the fact that this presumption is rebuttable.

In respect of the second and third charges, the direction to the jury was also inadequate. The judge had directed the jury that, for both charges, intention was not required to be proved. This was correct insofar as it meant that it was not necessary to show an intention to cause actual or grievous bodily harm; but not insofar as it gave the impression that it was not necessary to show an intention to apply force to the body of the victim. For example, in respect of assault occasioning actual bodily harm, it was necessary to show an intention to assault, but not necessary to show an intention to cause actual bodily harm. The convictions in respect of these charges were, therefore, quashed.

3.3 Recklessness

Compared with intention, recklessness poses fewer problems. Recklessness exists where a person does not intend to bring about a particular result, but runs an unjustifiable risk of bringing that result about. By unjustifiable we mean a risk without good cause, having regard to the social value of the activity involved. For example, a surgeon who carries out an emergency operation involving a risk of the patient dying as a result of the surgery, is taking a justifiable risk. Suppose we modify the example of the bomb on board the airline, so that A now puts a bomb on board a ship, intending to collect on the ship's insurance. Suppose further that the bomb is unlikely to sink the ship immediately, but should leave plenty of time for the ship to be evacuated. A does not intend to kill the passengers; nevertheless, he has subjected them to an unjustifiable risk of injury or death.

But suppose that a person creates an unjustifiable risk in circumstances where it is not clear whether he is aware of that risk. If he is aware, then he is clearly reckless. But suppose that, despite the risk being obvious, he fails to recognise it, and is blissfully unaware of the risk his conduct poses. Is that person reckless?

In English law, the answer would be yes. The leading English case is *R. v. Caldwell*. In that case, the defendant set fire to a hotel, avenging a grievance against the proprietor. He was charged with arson for which the *mens rea* (in English law) was intention to endanger the life of another, or recklessness as to whether the life of another would be endangered. His defence was intoxication. In dealing with this defence, it was necessary for the House of Lords to decide whether a person could be said to be reckless where he fails to recognise the risk which he is creating. The House of Lords held that a person in those circumstances was reckless. *Per* Lord Diplock at page 353:

> "Reckless ... is an ordinary English word. It had not by [the date of the legislation] become a term of legal art with some more limited esoteric meaning than that which it bore in ordinary speech, - a meaning which surely includes not only deciding to ignore a risk of harmful consequences resulting from one's acts that one has recognised as existing, but also failing to give any thought to whether or not there is any such risk in circumstances where, if any thought was given to the matter, it would be obvious that there was."

In reaching this conclusion, Lord Diplock seemed to be heavily influenced by the moral judgment that a person who failed to appreciate an "obvious risk" should not be allowed to escape liability. He stated, at page 352:

> "Neither state of mind [appreciating or failing to appreciate a risk] seems to me to be less blameworthy than the other; but if the difference between the two constituted the distinction between what does and what does not in legal theory amount to a guilty state of mind ... it

would not be a practicable distinction for use in a trial by jury. The only person who knows what the accused's mental processes were is the accused himself ... If the accused gives evidence that because of his rage, excitement or drunkenness the risk of particular harmful consequences of his acts simply did not occur to him, a jury would find it hard to be satisfied beyond reasonable doubt that his true mental process was [that he recognised a risk]."

Immediately after this decision, the House of Lords decision in *R. v. Lawrence* (1981) confirmed the application of this standard of recklessness to the crime of reckless driving.

The objective standard of recklessness can be criticised where the particular accused cannot be classed as a reasonably prudent person by reason of age, disability, lack of experience or understanding. In *Elliott v. C. (a minor)* (1983), a fourteen-year-old girl set fire to a shed by pouring white spirit onto the floor and throwing a lighted match onto the spirit. She suffered from a slight mental handicap but was convicted, although it was agreed that she would not have appreciated the risk that the shed would be destroyed even it she had considered the matter.

It should be noted that English law does not invariably interpret recklessness as objective. Some offences, especially those requiring proof of malice, require a standard of recklessness that is subjective. The leading English authority on subjective recklessness is *R. v. Cunningham* (1957), which involved a charge of unlawfully and maliciously causing a person to take a noxious thing so as thereby to endanger her life contrary to section 23 of the Offences Against the Person Act 1861.

The position in Ireland is different to *Caldwell*-type objectivity: for an accused to be found to be reckless as to a particular risk or result, he must have foreseen the risk but proceeded with his conduct regardless. The leading Irish case is *People (DPP) v. Murray* (1977). In this case, the two accused were husband and wife, and jointly held up a bank at gunpoint. They fled, but were pursued by an off-duty garda, who was out of uniform. The wife shot and killed him. Both were charged with capital murder, which was, so far as relevant, committed where a person murdered a garda acting in the course of his duty. Their defence was that the necessary *mens rea* was not present for all the elements of the offence: although there may have been an intention to kill or cause serious injury, they did not know that their pursuer was a garda and they therefore lacked the intention for an essential part of the offence.

The Supreme Court, in dealing with this argument, accepted the general principle that *mens rea* must be shown in respect of each component of an offence. In particular, it noted that the offence was meant to have a deterrent effect, which was lacking where a person was not aware that his intended victim was a garda. Equally, it pointed out that a much more severe penalty was attached to capital murder, and it was unfair and arbitrary to impose that higher penalty on the basis of a circumstance which the defendant knew nothing about.

However, it was argued for the prosecution that the necessary *mens rea* was present if the wife was aware or should have been aware that the pursuer might be a garda. The Supreme Court termed the first proposition *subjective* recklessness - i.e. actual awareness of a risk. The second was termed *objective* recklessness - i.e., a situation where a person should have been aware of a risk, but was not.

The Supreme Court, having differentiated between these two forms of recklessness, rejected the argument that objective recklessness could suffice. It was held that Irish criminal law had, at its core, the determination of moral blameworthiness, which could only be determined based on the subjective state of mind of the person charged. *Per* Walsh J. at page 386:

> "In this context objective recklessness is really constructive knowledge: and constructive knowledge has no place in our criminal system in establishing intent."

This result was widely accepted in the Irish legal system, on the grounds of fairness:

> "All modern common law systems reject a criminal law which imposes blame on the basis of what a reasonable man would have known, intended or suspected in the situation under analysis.". (Charleton, *Criminal Law - Cases and Materials* (Butterworths, 1992))

We will see that this preference for subjective tests over objective tests is a motif which repeats itself throughout Irish criminal law, in particular in the field of defences negativing *mens rea*.

Further reading. McAleese, "Just What is Recklessness?" [1981] D.U.L.J. 29; Newman, "Reforming the Mental Element of Murder" (1995) 5 I.C.L.J. 194

3.4 Criminal negligence

This particular class of *mens rea* is an anomaly twice over. It is limited to Irish law; and in Irish law, it is confined to the offence of manslaughter. Essentially, this class of *mens rea* is objective recklessness as defined in *People (DPP) v. Murray* (1977), that is, a very high class of negligence. Since *R. v. Caldwell* (1982), there seems to be less room for criminal negligence in English law, and it now seems to have been subsumed into recklessness. (See, *e.g.* Smith and Hogan, *Criminal Law: Cases and Materials* (5th ed., Butterworths, 1993), p. 439.) This class of *mens rea* will be dealt with under the topic of manslaughter.

3.5 Negligence

This class of *men rea* will be familiar from the area of tort: it is the doing of some act or the failure to do some act which a reasonable and prudent man would not do or would do, respectively. An example of a crime which has this form of *mens rea* is careless driving.

3.6 Strict liability subject to a defence of reasonable mistake; absolute liability

Strict liability exists where there is an absolute prohibition on the doing of a particular act, and where a person who does that act is subject to punishment regardless of intention or negligence. Liability is described as "strict" because the prosecution does not have to prove *mens rea* as to one or more of the elements of the *actus reus*. Whether a defence of reasonable mistake is available will depend on the terms of the particular statute; if it does not, then strict liability can be equated with absolute liability.

Most offences of strict liability are statutory offences, the only common law examples being public nuisance and criminal libel. They are generally regulatory offences dealing with matters such as pollution or health and safety which may be regarded by society as not truly criminal in nature but as being more akin to civil law.

Lord Scarman, in the leading case of *Gammon Ltd. v. A-G of Hong Kong* (1985), set out five propositions in relation to offences of strict liability:

1. There is a presumption of law that *mens rea* is required before a person can be held guilty of a criminal offence;

2. The presumption is particularly strong where the offence is "truly criminal" in character;

3. The presumption applies to statutory offences, and can be displaced only if this is clearly, or by necessary implication, the effect of the statute;

4. The only situation in which the presumption can be displaced is where the statute is concerned with an issue of social concern, and public safety is such an issue; and

5. Even where a statute is concerned with such an issue, the presumption of *mens rea* stands unless it can also be shown that the creation of strict liability will be effective to promote the objects of the statute by encouraging greater vigilance to prevent the commission of the prohibited act.

A well-known Irish example is the case of *McAdam v. Dublin United Tramways Co. Ltd.* (1929), in which the defendant company was charged with overloading a tram. The defendant claimed that it had done all that it possibly could to prevent its conductors from allowing overloading to take place. Could the defendant rely on this absence of fault or *mens rea*? No. *Per* Sullivan P., at page 333:

> "...the prohibitions contained in that regulation are absolute. The object of the regulation is to protect the public against the danger that may result from the overloading of an omnibus, and that object could be achieved only by absolutely prohibiting the carriage in any omnibus of more than a limited number of passengers, and by penalising the owner for any breach of such [a] prohibition, irrespective of his knowledge of such breach.
>
> The acts in this case are not in any real sense criminal, but in the public interest they are prohibited under a penalty. Having regard to that fact, and to the terms of the regulation and the object it had in view, I am of opinion that *mens rea* is not an essential ingredient in the offences charged against the defendants."

Another example of a crime of strict liability is *R. v. Prince* (1875-77). In that case, the accused was charged with abducting an unmarried girl under the age of sixteen out of the possession of her father. The girl was fourteen, but the accused honestly and reasonably believed her to be eighteen. This was held, however, to be irrelevant: the crime was created for the protection of young girls, and this statutory purpose would be frustrated if the absence of intention was accepted as a defence.

More recently, two modern cases are particularly good examples of the Irish approach to offences of strict liability. The first is *Maguire v.*

Shannon Regional Fisheries Board (1994). This concerned the Fisheries (Consolidation) Act 1959, which provides that any person who causes to fall into any waters any deleterious matter shall be guilty of an offence. The defendant operated a piggery near a river; a pipe fractured, resulting in the pollution of the river. The defendant was found to have taken all reasonable steps to prevent any accident of this sort, and to prevent pollution of the river from resulting once the accident had taken place (temporary dams, sandbags, *etc.*). The question presented was whether the offence was one of strict liability.

In deciding that it was, Lynch J. held as follows: (1) As a rule, *mens rea* is required for every offence. (2) However, this presumption could be rebutted where, as here, the offence created was regulatory rather than truly criminal. (3) In such situations, creating strict liability would promote the policy of the underlying legislation, while if *mens rea* was required, the policy of the legislation would be undermined, since it would be very difficult to establish that an offence had been committed. Consequently, the offence was one of strict liability. (4) Despite the absence of any fault on the part of the accused, he had caused the pollution by virtue of the running of his piggery, and the accused was therefore guilty of the offence.

The later case of *Shannon Regional Fisheries Board v. Cavan County Council* (1996) is on the same point. Here the Supreme Court had to deal with a situation where Cavan County Council had caused sewage to enter the water. Despite a statutory duty to provide sewage treatment, the County Council had not been provided with sufficient funds from central government to carry out that duty and were therefore unable to process the sewage, which they discharged in its untreated form. The County Council was charged under the Fisheries Acts. In the High Court, the decision in *Maguire v. Shannon Regional Fisheries Board* (1994) was followed, and the offence found to be one of strict liability. (Although Murphy J. did point out that the degree of fault which was found to be present would determine what penalty, if any, was appropriate.) This was accepted by the majority in the Supreme Court, which also found on the facts that the County Council was in fact acting with *mens rea* in that they were deliberately discharging untreated sewage.

However, the dissenting judgment of Keane J. is interesting. He outlines the historical development of offences of strict liability in "public welfare" or "regulatory" areas of the law, and goes on to question whether it is appropriate that this particular fisheries offence, which carries a maximum penalty of £25,000 or five years' imprisonment, or both, should be held to be one of strict liability. In particular, he questions whether to make such a serious crime into one of strict liability would be compatible with the constitutional guarantee of trial in due course of law. He accepts that not all crimes need have some moral culpability attached to them, but rejects the argument that there is no need for moral culpability in the present case as this sort of crime carries no real stigma.

Keane J. also points out that to allow a defence of taking all reasonable care would encourage greater vigilance on the part of potential offenders. To deny such a defence would in effect force the accused to act at his peril and would be a disincentive to maintaining standards. Since the expenditure of time and money on improving standards would not be acknowledged by the courts then some people in the position of the accused would not bother to take adequate precautions.

Keane J. refers to the position taken in Canadian law as set out in *City of Sault Ste. Marie* (1978), an approach also adopted enthusiastically by the New Zealand courts. This allows for a middle-ground whereby the doing of the prohibited *actus reus* will prove the offence without any necessity for the prosecution to prove *mens rea,* but where there is a defence of due diligence, or taking reasonable care, open to an accused.

Keane J. welcomes the Canadian position and holds at page 291 that:

> "the law should recognise that there is an intermediate range of offences, of which this is one, in which, while full proof of *mens rea* is not required and the proof of the prohibited act *prima facie* imports the commission of the offence, the accused may escape liability by proving that he took reasonable care."

He went on to argue that the county council did in fact take all reasonable care to prevent the discharge of sewage and should not, therefore, be found guilty of the crime.

3.7 *Mens rea* - the doctrine of transferred malice

Suppose A intends to shoot and kill B, but misses and hits and kills C. Has murder been committed? A did not intend to kill C, but the so-called doctrine of transferred malice will apply. This doctrine provides that where A has the *mens rea* required for a particular crime, and carries out the *actus reus* of that crime, then he will be found to have committed that crime, notwithstanding that the final result is in fact unintended, particularly with regard to the identity of the victim. An example is the case of *R. v. Latimer* (1886-87). In this case A hit B with his belt; the belt glanced off B and hit C, cutting her severely. This ricochet was held by the jury to be accidental and unforeseeable; nevertheless, the accused was found guilty of unlawfully wounding C.

However, the doctrine is limited. It applies only where the *actus reus* and the *mens rea* are of the same crime. If A shoots at a window, misses, and kills a person who unknown to him is standing close by, then he has not committed murder: the *actus reus* of murder and the *mens rea* of a crime against property do not add up to the crime of murder.

4. ACTION ELEMENT OF CRIMES

4.1 Introduction

The *actus reus* is the action element of a crime. It may be contrasted with the *mens rea*, the mental element. For example, a person cannot be convicted of murder unless he has the required mental state (intention to kill or cause serious personal injury) and has caused the death of his victim (the *actus reus*). A person who intends to kill or cause serious personal injury, yet does nothing but daydream about it, will not be guilty of any crime.

There must be an *actus reus* before any crime can be committed. With crimes of strict liability a defendant may be convicted on the basis of *actus reus* alone but the converse is never true: a person can never be convicted on the basis of *mens rea* alone. In *Deller* (1952), the accused was charged with obtaining a car by false pretences. He represented that he owned the vehicle he had traded in for the car but, in fact, he believed that a hire purchase company owned it. This turned out to be untrue as, due to an error in registering the hire purchase agreement, the accused was legally the owner of the vehicle. Deller was acquitted as, although he had the necessary *mens rea*, he was actually telling the truth when he claimed that the car was free from any encumbrances. There was no *actus reus* even though he had believed he was committing a crime.

4.2 *Actus reus* as a state of affairs

The *actus reus* may not always amount to an action. In certain circumstances it may be defined as a state of affairs not including an act at all. This is illustrated by the case of *Larsonneur* (1933) in which the accused was convicted of "being found" in a particular situation. An alien who had been refused leave to land, she was convicted under the Aliens Order 1920 of being found in the United Kingdom even though the police had brought her from Ireland against her will. A similar result to this decision was reached in *Winzar v. Chief Constable of Kent* (1983). Winzar was taken to hospital but was found to be intoxicated and asked to leave. Eventually the police were called and he was removed from the hospital to the public highway outside. Once there, he was charged by the police of being found drunk in the highway and was subsequently convicted.

These decisions have proved highly controversial and *Larsonneur* has been rejected by the Supreme Court of New Zealand in *Kilbride v. Lake* (1962). In that case a driver was charged with failing to display a current warrant of fitness on his motor car. It was accepted that the warrant had disappeared from his vehicle while he was absent from it. In finding the accused not guilty of the offence, Woodhouse J. remarked (at page 593):

> " ... it is a cardinal principle that ... a person cannot be made criminally responsible for an act or omission unless it was done or omitted in circumstances where there was some other course open to him. If this condition is absent, any act or omission must be involuntary or unconscious, or unrelated to the forbidden event in any causal sense regarded by the law as involving responsibility.".

Larsonneur and *Winzar* have been criticised as being contrary to the general principle that the action element of a crime must be voluntary. For example, a conviction for assault cannot be sustained if the accused's hand was forcibly grabbed by another and used to strike a third party. Voluntariness is an essential attribute of the *actus reus*. If the act is done without any control by the mind, such as a spasm or reflex action, then the accused may be able to rely on the defence of automatism.

4.3 *Actus reus* and *mens rea* must coincide

In looking at the *actus reus*, it is important to note that a crime is committed only when the *actus reus* and the *mens rea* exist at the same time. Suppose a husband decides to kill his wife. He changes his mind. Later that day his careless driving causes a crash in which his wife, a passenger in the car is killed. We have the *actus reus* of murder: he caused the death of his wife. We have the *mens rea* of murder: he intended to kill her. However, this is clearly not a case of murder, since the two did not coincide.

This can be seen from the case of *R. v. Scott* (1967), an Australian case in which the defendant escaped from jail after suffering a blow to the head. He claimed that he did not know what he was doing until two days after he left the jail, at which point he (sensibly) decided not to give himself up. Charged with escape from lawful custody, his defence was that he was incapable of forming the necessary *mens rea* at the time of the escape, although he later formed the intent to remain at large. This defence was accepted by the Supreme Court of Victoria, which held (*per* Gillard J.) that "[t]he two elements necessary to constitute the crime were never brought together. An unlawful action and an evil intention never concurred".

Having said that, where the *actus reus* is an ongoing act, then it is sufficient if the *mens rea* coincides with part of the *actus reus*: it need not coincide with the whole. An example is the case of *Fagan v. Metropolitan Police Commissioner* (1969). In that case the defendant accidentally drove his car onto the foot of a policeman, and then deliberately left it there. Charged with assault, his defence was that his conduct was complete before he formed any intention. However, this argument was rejected. His conduct was treated by the court as continuous, and the crime was committed when he decided to *leave* the car on the policeman's foot.

4.4 The *actus reus* may be an omission

Under most circumstances, the criminal law does not punish failure to act. Suppose A is on a beach, and sees B struggling in the sea. A stands by and watches B drown, despite the fact that A is a strong swimmer and could easily rescue B without any danger to himself. A is not guilty of a crime, however morally reprehensible his conduct is. As Hawkins J. put it in *R. v. Paine* (1880):

> "If I see a man, who is not under my charge, taking up a tumbler of poison, I should not become guilty of any crime by not stopping him. I am under no legal obligation to protect a stranger."

However, there are many situations where the law recognises a positive duty to act. The most obvious example is the duty of parents towards their children. If a parent deliberately fails to feed a child, intending to cause death or serious injury, then the crime of murder is committed if the child dies. In the case of *R. v. Bubb* (1851), the defendant was an aunt of a child, was *in loco parentis* to the child, and was charged with causing the child's death by deliberate neglect. It was held that the aunt, on those facts, had a duty to care for the child. In the recent unreported decision of *People (DPP) v. O'Brien* (1998), a similar duty between spouses was enunciated, Quirke J. stating that "there lies upon a man, who is cohabiting with his wife who is the mother of his children, a duty to have reasonable care for her health and welfare".

The common law has recognised several further categories where such a duty arises. One is where a duty has been voluntarily assumed. In *R. v. Stone & Dobinson* (1977), a man of low intelligence and his mistress kept his elderly sister as a lodger. She refused to eat and lived in her room in appalling conditions of her own making. The mistress attempted to wash her when she became bedridden and made inadequate efforts to summon medical help. When the sister died the defendants were convicted of manslaughter as it was held that they had accepted responsibility for the deceased and owed a duty to help her even though her death had been largely caused by her own eccentricity.

If a person creates a danger, there may be a duty to act to minimise the dangerous situation. In *R. v. Miller* (1983), a tramp set fire accidentally to a mattress by dropping a cigarette. He failed to take steps to put out the fire and was found to have been under a duty to do so and was convicted of arson.

A positive duty to act can also be created under contract or by virtue of one's status as a public official. In *R. v. Pittwood* (1902), a gatekeeper who failed to close the gate at a level-crossing, resulting in a death, was found guilty of manslaughter on the basis of his obligations under contract. *R. v. Dytham* (1979) was a case where a policeman failed to intervene in a brawl to come to the aid of the deceased. He was found guilty of misconduct of an officer of justice.

Certain statutory offences create a positive duty to act. An example is section 49 of the Road Traffic Act 1961, where a motorist who has been brought to a garda station and who fails to provide a specimen of breath when properly requested to do so, is guilty of an offence. A further example is section 13 of the Criminal Justice Act 1984, which places an obligation on a person who has been released on bail in criminal proceedings to appear before a court in accordance with his recognisance.

4.5 *Actus reus* and causation

For a defendant to be criminally liable, it must be shown that his conduct caused the prohibited outcome (for example, death in the case of homicide). This can be tested by asking whether the outcome would have happened but for what the defendant did. So, in *R. v. White* (1910) the defendant was charged with the murder of his mother, by putting cyanide into her drink. However, medical evidence established that she died of heart failure after drinking the drink, but before the poison could have had any effect. Consequently, the defendant could not be said to have caused her death.

However, it should be noted that the "eggshell skull rule" applies in the criminal law as well as the law of torts. This holds that an accused must take his victim as he finds him. If the victim has a particular weakness (such as a very thin skull) which makes him far more susceptible to injury than the average person, this cannot be used to reduce the liability of the accused. For example, if a victim dies from an assault that would not have killed the average person, the victim's vulnerability is legally irrelevant.

4.5.1 Break in the chain of causation?/Novus actus interveniens

Suppose that A is stabbed by B with a knife. A is rushed to hospital, where she is advised that a blood transfusion is necessary to save her life. She refuses the transfusion on religious grounds, and dies. Is A guilty of murder? These were the facts of *R. v. Blaue* (1975), and in that case it was held that B was guilty of murder. B was not entitled to argue that the religious beliefs of A were unreasonable: those who use violence on other people must take their victims as they find them. If the stab wound was still an operating cause of death, and a substantial cause, then death was still a consequence of the wound. Only if another cause was so overwhelming as to make the wound merely part of the history would it be possible to say that death had not been caused by the original action.

Compare *R. v. Jordan* (1956). That case also involved a stabbing, from which the victim was making a good recovery, with the wound almost healed. However, the victim died from pneumonia as a result of being given an antibiotic to which he was intolerant, in circumstances where it was grossly negligent for him to be given this treatment. The conviction of the accused for murder was quashed: the Court of Appeal accepted that the direct and immediate cause of death was the treatment the victim received.

However, *Jordan* was distinguished in *R. v. Smith* (1959). A soldier stabbed another soldier during a barrack-room fight. While being carried to a doctor the injured man was dropped twice. He was subsequently given incorrect medical treatment and died. The conviction for murder was upheld despite arguments that there had been no less than three breaks in the chain of causation. The court held that the test was whether the original wound was still an operating and substantial cause at the time of death, notwithstanding that some other cause also operated.

The same issue was later addressed in *R. v. Malcherek and Steel* (1981). The victim's injuries required treatment on a life support machine but a decision was made by doctors to switch the machine off when it became apparent that recovery was impossible. The accused argued that disconnecting the life support machine caused death and that this had broken the chain of causation. Again the "operating and substantial cause at the time of death" test was applied by the court and the accused's argument failed.

In *R. v. Cheshire* (1991), the victim of a shooting developed respiratory problems following surgery. His medical team failed to diagnose the cause of the problem and he died in hospital two months after the shooting. The court accepted that medical negligence was the immediate cause of death but held that the defendant's acts could be regarded as causing the death, even though they were not the sole or main cause, if they contributed significantly to it. The medical negligence would only relieve the defendant of responsibility for death if it was so independent of his acts and so potent in causing death that the defendant's actions could be regarded as insignificant.

5. HOMICIDE

5.1 Homicide

The term homicide is a label attached to crimes which result in death. There are a number of such crimes in Irish law: however, for the purposes of this discussion, the only ones which will be dealt with are murder, manslaughter, infanticide and suicide.

5.1.1 Year and a day rule

For either murder, manslaughter or infanticide to be committed, the victim formerly had to die within a year and a day from the infliction of the injury. This rule existed at common law, and seems to have been adopted at a time when medical science was rudimentary, and when it was impossible to tell if deaths after longer intervals were in fact caused by the injury inflicted. The rule has no such justification today, when medical science has advanced to a point where causation can be accurately determined. In fact, the rule was at odds with modern medicine, which may well keep a victim alive in a coma or with severe brain damage for a number of years before death occurs. Equally, after a syringe attack, a victim may be healthy for years before developing AIDS. Should a defendant responsible for the death of such a victim escape conviction for murder? These considerations led to the repeal of the rule by section 38 of the Criminal Justice Act 1999, and there is now no requirement that the victim die within any specified time.

5.1.2 Murder

Murder is a crime at common law. The elements of murder at common law are defined in a famous passage from Coke, *Institutes of the Law of England*:

> "Murder is when a man of sound memory, and of the age of discretion, unlawfully killeth with malice aforethought either expressed by the party or implied by law, so as the party wounded or hurt, etc. die of the wound or hurt, etc. within a year and a day after the same."

Murder is distinguished from manslaughter by the necessary intent. The intention required for murder is set out in section 4 of the Criminal

Justice Act 1964, which replaces "malice aforethought" under the common law:

> "(1) Where a person kills another unlawfully the killing shall not be murder unless the accused intended to kill, or cause serious injury to, some person, whether the person actually killed or not.
>
> (2) The accused person shall be presumed to have intended the natural and probable consequences of his conduct; but this presumption may be rebutted."

There is, therefore, no requirement of premeditation, spite, malice or ill-will. A mercy killing is still murder, as is participation in a suicide pact. (Even though suicide itself is no longer a crime. (Criminal Law (Suicide) Act 1993)

5.1.3 Attempted murder

Murder is a result crime, where the result of the defendant's conduct is death. Where the charge is attempted murder, and the result is not present, what mental element is required? The answer is that attempted murder is committed only where there is an intention to kill; an intention to cause serious injury is not enough.

5.1.4 Aggravated murder

We came across capital murder when dealing with *mens rea*, in the case of *People (DPP) v. Murray* (1977). The penalty for capital murder was, as is obvious from its name, death. However, section 1 of the Criminal Justice Act 1990 abolished the death penalty, and section 3 of that Act therefore creates what is now usually called aggravated murder, which is essentially the same crime as the former crime of capital murder. (Although the death penalty is abolished, sections 4 and 5 of the Act provide for minimum sentences and limitations on the power to commute or remit punishment or to grant temporary release in the case of aggravated murder.)

Section 3 applies to:

(a) the murder of a member of the Garda Síochána acting in the course of his duty;

(b) the murder of a prison officer acting in the course of his duty;

(c) murder in the course of specified offences under the Offences Against the State Act 1939, or in the course of the activities of an unlawful organisation under that Act;

(d) the murder of the head of a foreign state, or a member of the government of a foreign state, or a diplomat of a foreign state, when the murder is committed within the State, for a political motive.

Section 3(2)(a) deals with the *mens rea* required for aggravated murder:

> "a person shall not be convicted ... unless it is proved that he knew of the existence of each ingredient of the offence ... or was reckless as to whether or not that ingredient existed."

In summary, the offence of aggravated murder is the offence of murder, with the aggravating factor of the identity of the victim, or the subversive nature of the activities being carried out, together with the fact that the defendant knew or was reckless as to the existence of the aggravating factor.

5.1.5 Defences specific to murder

There is a complicated interaction between the crime of murder and the various defences. Each defence will be dealt with in more detail later, but it should be noted at this point that two defences are unavailable to a charge of murder (duress and necessity), while other defences are available only to a charge of murder, and operate to reduce the crime to manslaughter (provocation and excessive self defence).

5.1.6 The felony murder rule

Before the felony/misdemeanour distinction was abolished, a rule of law existed where any death which resulted from a felony was murder, regardless of whether there existed an intention to kill or cause serious injury. One famous example was the case of a man who shot at a chicken with the intention of stealing it, missed and killed a victim: he would be guilty of a murder, since stealing the chicken was a felony. This rule was however abolished by section 4 of the Criminal Justice Act 1964, which we have already dealt with.

5.1.7 Sentencing for murder

Murder attracts a mandatory sentence of imprisonment for life. Academic commentators (such as O'Malley, "Sentencing murderers: the case for relocating discretion" ((1995) I.C.L.J. 31) have raised doubts about the appropriateness of a mandatory sentence to the crime of murder. A life sentence is an indeterminate sentence which usually results in release after 11 or 12 years imprisonment. O'Malley points out that it is very difficult to plan a programme of rehabilitation for a prisoner whose release date is so uncertain. Mandatory life sentences have been abolished in several Australian states. In England, both the House of Lords Select Committee on Murder and Life Imprisonment, and the Penal Reform Trust Committee have recommended that the mandatory life sentence for murder should be replaced by determinate sentencing. The argument for discretion is probably most compelling when sentencing those who murdered under duress and the perpetrators of "mercy killings".

5.1.8 Suicide

(1) Legality of suicide

Suicide itself is no longer a crime, having been decriminalised by section 2(1) of the Criminal Law (Suicide) Act 1993, a piece of legislation which finally recognises the manifest absurdity of criminalising conduct which, by definition, leaves the offender beyond the jurisdiction of any court. This reform of the law is somewhat belated, coming more than thirty years after the Suicide Act 1961, which decriminalised suicide in England.

(2) Suicide pacts and assisted suicide

However, the decriminalising of suicide does not entirely remove the criminal law from the field of voluntary decisions to die: there remain difficulties when more than one person is involved. In the first place, it remains murder to kill another with the necessary intention, notwithstanding that the killing was done at the request and with the consent of that other. Consent is not a defence to murder. If, therefore, the doctor administers a fatal dose of morphine, with the intention of killing, that doctor is guilty of murder, notwithstanding that the fatal dose was administered at the request of the patient.

This rule of law has what might be regarded as curious results in the area of suicide pacts. Suppose A and B both decide to commit suicide, with each agreeing to inject the other with a fatal drug. Suppose further that they carry out their plan, but only B dies: A is found in time and an antidote administered. In this jurisdiction, it is quite clear that A is guilty of murder, notwithstanding the surrounding circumstances. By comparison, in England section 4(1) of the Homicide Act 1957 provides that:

> "It shall be manslaughter, and shall not be murder, for a person acting in pursuance of a suicide pact between him and another to kill the other or be a party to the other killing himself or being killed by a third party."

It is therefore clear that if A kills B at B's request, A is guilty of murder. The position is however different if A merely supplies B with the means by which B can kill himself. In these circumstances, it would not be appropriate to charge A with murder or manslaughter, since it cannot be said that his act caused the death of B. The act which causes the death of B is the act of B himself, not the act of A. There is an intervening decision on B's part, breaking the chain of causation.

Nor, in these circumstances, would A face any criminal liability under section 7 of the Criminal Law Act 1997, suicide no longer being a crime. (Section 7 is of course limited to the case of a person who aids, abets, counsels or procures the commission of *any crime*.)

A's criminal liability (if any) would, therefore, arise under section 2(2) of the Criminal Law (Suicide) Act 1993, which anticipates this situation by providing that:

> "A person who aids, abets, counsels or procures the suicide of another, or an attempt by another to commit suicide, shall be guilty of an offence and shall be liable on conviction on indictment to imprisonment for a term not exceeding fourteen years.".

Since the terminology used in this section is identical to that used in section 7 of the 1997 Act, authorities on what constitutes aiding, abetting counselling or procuring under section 7 would also be relevant in this context.

There are, however, authorities specifically relating to the case of suicide. So, in *Dunbar v. Plant* (1997) (a civil case) it was held that a woman aided and abetted the suicide of her fiancé where both she and her fiancé simultaneously attempted to hang themselves, she unsuccessfully. Similarly, in *Wallis* (1983), a defendant pleaded guilty to aiding and abetting the suicide of a flatmate in circumstances where the defendant bought the necessary tablets and alcohol, sat with the flatmate while she took the mixture, and refrained from calling an ambulance until the flatmate was dead.

The potential scope of the offence is shown by *Attorney General v. Able* (1984), where an injunction was sought restraining the publication of a pamphlet by the Voluntary Euthanasia Society entitled "A Guide to Self-Deliverance" which, as the title indicated, provided practical advice on killing oneself. Although the application was ultimately unsuccessful, it was accepted by Woolf J. (as he then was) that the supply of such a pamphlet could amount to an offence under the (essentially identical) English law where: the pamphlet was supplied to a person contemplating suicide; where the supplier acted with the intention of assisting or encouraging such a person to commit suicide; where such a person did in fact read it and as a result was assisted in or encouraged to commit or attempt suicide; and where such a person did in fact commit or attempt suicide.

In summary, therefore: if A kills B at the request of B, the appropriate charge is one of murder; while if A facilitates B in killing himself, the appropriate charge is one of aiding, abetting, counselling or procuring (as appropriate) B's suicide.

5.1.9 Manslaughter - definition, voluntary and involuntary manslaughter

Murder is the crime committed when the accused intends to kill or cause serious injury, and death results. Manslaughter, which is also an offence at common law, is the crime committed when death results, but the *mens rea* falls short of that required for murder. This is the case either where there is no intention to kill or cause serious injury, or where there is such an intention, but the culpability is lessened by the defence of provocation or excessive self-defence being available. This crime, therefore, has the peculiar feature that you cannot intend to commit manslaughter: rather, manslaughter is a residual category defined by reference to what it is not.

The categories of manslaughter are, therefore, as follows:

1. Where A kills B intending to kill or cause serious injury, but where the defence of provocation applies;

2. Where A kills B intending to kill or cause serious injury, honestly believing he was acting in self defence, but where the force used was excessive;

3. Where A kills B without intending to kill or cause serious injury, but by virtue of criminal negligence;

4. Where A kills B without intending to kill or cause serious injury, but as a result of an assault;

5. Where A kills B without intending to kill or cause serious injury, but as a result of a criminal and dangerous act. (Classification taken from Charleton, *Criminal Law - Cases and Materials* (Butterworths, 1992), p. 356.)

Categories 1 and 2 are usually described as cases of *voluntary manslaughter*, while categories 3, 4 and 5 are described as cases of *involuntary manslaughter*. This description is very misleading, since the distinction has nothing to do with voluntariness. Instead, the distinction relates to whether the accused intended to kill or cause serious injury. If he did, but can rely on provocation or excessive self-defence, then this is voluntary manslaughter; if he did not have this intention, this is involuntary manslaughter.

Categories 1 and 2 are dealt with under defences, in provocation and self-defence.

(1) Category 3 — Manslaughter by criminal negligence

This crime is committed where a person causes death by virtue of conduct which is criminally negligent: that is, so negligent that any reasonable person would have realised that the conduct created a high degree of risk of serious injury to others. This is an objective test and so differs from the subjective test applied to intention and recklessness: for manslaughter by criminal negligence, it is not necessary to show that the accused realised that he was creating such a risk. It is, therefore, an anomaly in Irish law: an accused can be convicted of manslaughter under this heading, without having any element of subjective fault. Given this anomalous status, it is important to remember that criminal negligence is a much higher standard than the standard of negligence in tort.

The leading case Irish case on manslaughter by criminal negligence is *People (AG) v. Dunleavy* (1948). Here, the accused was charged with manslaughter, having killed a cyclist while driving without lights on the wrong side of a busy city road. The jury was directed that it was to decide whether the conduct of the accused showed such a disregard for the lives and safety of others as to amount to a crime deserving punishment, but were not explicitly directed as to what degree of negligence was required. The Court of Criminal Appeal held that this direction was inadequate: the jury should have been directed as to the different degrees of negligence, and as to the very high degree of negligence which is required in the case of manslaughter. The jury should be told that the negligence required goes beyond a mere matter of compensation, showing a disregard for the life and safety of others, and that the negligence required must be:

> "of a very high degree and of such a character that any reasonable driver, endowed with ordinary road sense and in full possession of his faculties, would realise, if he thought at all, that by driving in the manner which occasioned the fatality he was, without lawful excuse, incurring, in a high degree, the risk of causing substantial personal injury to others". (*per* Davitt J. at pp. 101-102).

This definition is an extension of the definition which was previously laid down in the case of *R. v. Bateman* (1926). In that case, a doctor was charged with the manslaughter of a woman who had died while giving birth. Hewart C.J. stated at page 732 that the jury should be told that the negligence "went beyond a mere matter of compensation and showed such disregard for the life and safety of others as to amount to a crime against the State and conduct deserving punishment", but did not require that the jury be directed as to the very high degree of negligence required.

The standard laid down by *People (AG) v. Dunleavy* (1948) is a very high one, and in practical terms, very few defendants will be guilty of criminal negligence without having realised the risk which their conduct caused. However, this high standard is inappropriate in the context of negligence on the roads, where there is a need for an offence which will reflect the gravity of causing death due to careless driving, even where criminal negligence is not present.

Consequently, *People (AG) v. Dunleavy* was one reason for the enactment of section 53(1) and 53(2)(a) of the Road Traffic Act 1961, which create an offence of causing death by dangerous driving. The standard of carelessness which is required for dangerous driving is intermediate between "ordinary" negligence and criminal negligence: the test is objective, and dangerous driving occurs where a person drives in a manner which a reasonable man "would clearly recognise as involving a direct and serious risk of harm to the public" (*per* Ó'Briain J., quoted in Charleton, *Offences Against the Person* (Round Hall Press, 1992), p. 119).

The most recent Irish case in this area is *D.P.P. v. Cullagh* (1999). The accused was convicted of manslaughter at a fairground in Tipperary which he owned and operated. The victim was killed when the chairoplane she was being carried in became detached from the equipment. The standard of negligence required was described as "gross negligence – it had to be gross negligence and not the ordinary standard of civil negligence: *i.e.* mere inadvertence, which would attract liability in a civil action, was insufficient". The objective nature of the test was illustrated by the comments that "The particular factor which caused the tragedy would not have been apparent to Mr. Cullagh but Mr. Cullagh was making available for entertainment equipment which was of its nature to some degree hazardous and undoubtedly old".

R. v. Prentice, Adomako and Holloway (1993) is a recent English decision on the proper test of involuntary manslaughter by breach of professional duty of care. The accused, in three appeals heard simultaneously by the Court of Appeal, were junior doctors, an anaesthetist and an electrician. It was held that the ingredients of involuntary manslaughter by breach of duty were: (1) the existence of the duty; (2) breach of the duty causing death; (3) gross negligence which the jury considered justified a criminal conviction. Proof of any of the following states of mind in an accused could lead to a finding by a jury of gross negligence: (a) indifference to an obvious risk of injury to health; (b) actual foresight of the risk coupled with the determination nevertheless to run it; (c) an appreciation of the risk coupled with an intention to avoid it but with a high degree of negligence in the attempted avoidance; (d) inattention or failure to advert to a serious risk which went beyond "mere inadvertence" in respect of an obvious and important matter which the defendant's duty demanded he should address.

Certain cases discussed in the chapter on *actus reus* are relevant at this point. We have seen that if an omission is made with the intention of causing death or serious injury, then, if the accused is under a duty to perform the act by reason of contract, close relationship etc., the killing will be murder. If however, as illustrated by *R. v. Stone and Dobinson* (1977), the killing is due to criminal negligence on the part of a person having a positive duty to act, it will be manslaughter.

(2) Category 4 — Manslaughter as a result of an assault

> "It is manslaughter for the accused to kill the victim by an assault where the accused intends to hurt or cause the victim more than trivial harm." (Charleton, *Offences Against the Person* (Round Hall Press, 1992), page 83.)

This charge is appropriate where the accused did not intend to cause serious injury, but did intend to injure. In many cases, the accused will have been "unlucky", in that a seemingly minor crime will have had the unforeseen effect of the victim's death. An example is *R. v. Holzer* (1968). In that case, the accused got into a fight with the victim, and punched the victim in the face. The victim fell backwards and hit his head on the road. The victim later died. The accused testified that he did not intend to cause serious injury, but only to "cut his lip or bruise his lip or something". It was held that unless the physical injury intended was merely trivial or negligible, such as a scuff or a slap to the hand, then assault resulting in death would be manslaughter:

> "[A] person is guilty of manslaughter if he commits the offence of [assault] on the deceased and death results directly from that offence and the beating or other application of force was done with the intention of inflicting on the deceased some physical harm not merely of a trivial or negligible character, or, it would seem with the intention of inflicting pain, without more injury or harm to the body than is involved in the infliction of pain which is not merely trivial or negligible." (*Per* Stephen J. at p. 482).

Note that the word "assault" is used in this context in the modern sense, to include both assault and battery. This modern usage has now been followed in the Non-Fatal Offences Against the Person Act 1997, which uses the term assault for what would before, strictly speaking, have been battery.

(3) Category 5 — Manslaughter as a result of a criminal and dangerous act

> "For the accused to kill the victim by intentionally doing an unlawful Act which was also objectively dangerous, is manslaughter."(Charleton, *Offences Against the Person* (Round Hall Press, 1992), page 105.)

This category overlaps with manslaughter by criminal negligence and manslaughter by assault: an assault resulting in death may well be manslaughter under each of these three headings.

What forms of unlawful acts does this category apply to? It is not enough for an act to be a tort: it must amount to a criminal and objectively dangerous offence. Otherwise, every negligent killing would amount to manslaughter. This is illustrated by *People (AG) v. Maher* (1937), where the accused, while driving a car without having a licence, killed a man without any evidence of negligence. It was held that there was insufficient evidence to result in a conviction for manslaughter.

Another example of this category in operation is the case of *People (AG) v. Crosbie and Meehan* (1966). In this case, the victim was a docker, and died from a knife wound in the course of a fight in a crowded room. It was not clear how the wound was inflicted or with what intention: the defendant had brought the knife in self-defence (or so he claimed), and stated that while waving the knife around to frighten off attackers he must have accidentally hit the victim. This would not, therefore, amount to manslaughter by assault (although it might amount to manslaughter by criminal negligence). Could it amount to manslaughter by a criminal and dangerous act?

The Court of Criminal Appeal held that it could. If the knife was produced to frighten or intimidate, and not in self-defence, then the crime of assault was committed. Waving the knife around in a crowded room was an objectively dangerous act (even if the defendant did not realise it). If death resulted, therefore, that death would be manslaughter as a result of a criminal and dangerous act.

> "A person who produces a knife with the intention of intimidating or frightening another and not for self-defence commits an assault and the act done is therefore unlawful. When a killing results from an unlawful act ... the act causing death must be unlawful and dangerous to constitute the offence of manslaughter. The dangerous quality of the act must however be judged by objective standards and it is irrelevant that the person did not think that the act was dangerous." (*Per* Kenny J. at page 495.)

In *R. v. Pagett* (1983), the accused was convicted of manslaughter when he forcefully used a girl as a shield to protect himself from shots fired by the police. The court held that the accused had committed two unlawful and dangerous acts – the act of firing at the police and the act of using the girl as a shield when the police might fire in his direction in self-defence. Either act was deemed to constitute the actus reus of manslaughter.

In addition it is worth noting that this category of manslaughter does not apply where the act carried out is normally lawful, and becomes unlawful only because negligently carried out: *People (AG) v. Dunleavy* (1948). Otherwise, every death due to careless or inconsiderate driving (which are offences, albeit minor offences) would be manslaughter.

It is not required that the unlawful and dangerous act be aimed at the deceased. In *R. v. Mitchell* (1983), the accused attempted to skip a queue in a post office and hit a man who objected. The man fell against an old woman who suffered a broken femur necessitating an operation. While recovering from surgery, she died suddenly as a result of a blood clot of the left leg veins caused by the fracture to the femur. The accused was convicted of manslaughter.

5.1.10 Infanticide

Not all killings are equally culpable. It is well established that mothers, shortly after giving birth, face special circumstances both physical and psychological. Physical circumstances include the physical exhaustion of pregnancy and birth, and consequent hormonal changes, as the body readjusts. Psychological factors, meanwhile, include what is now known as post-natal depression, the stresses inherent in being responsible for a new life, new financial and relationship pressures, and in some cases the added strain attached to being a single mother. When a mother facing those circumstances kills her child, the law recognises that a murder conviction is not appropriate. The crime of infanticide is, therefore, created by the Infanticide Act 1949.

This offence is committed under section 1 if three conditions apply: the act or omission would otherwise have been murder; the victim is the child of the defendant and is under one year old and the balance of the defendant's mind was upset at the time by reason of not having fully recovered from giving birth to the child, or the effect of lactation after the birth of the child. The advantage of a verdict of infanticide is that the offender may be sentenced as if she had been found guilty of manslaughter.

Further reading: Charleton, *Offences Against the Person* (Round Hall Press, 1992), pp. 189-191.

6. SEXUAL OFFENCES

This is an area of the criminal law that has always been heavily influenced by prevailing attitudes and standards. Therefore, it is not surprising that there has been reform of many sexual offences in recent years as traditional attitudes to sexual offences were increasingly seen as outmoded.

We will deal with the following specific sexual offences: rape, sexual assault, incest, sexual offences against the mentally handicapped and sexual abuse of children. You should however be aware that these do not cover the full spectrum of sexual offences, but simply the most important in practice. For example, they do not include the Sexual Offences (Jurisdiction) Act 1996 which deals with the problem of "child sex tourism", that is where Irish citizens or residents engage in sex with children abroad.

6.1 Rape

Two distinct forms of rape exist in Irish law. The first is usually called "common law rape" since it was originally a common law offence, although it is now contained in section 2(1) of the Criminal Law (Rape) Act 1981 which provides:

> "A man commits rape if:
>
> (a) he has sexual intercourse with a woman who at the time of the intercourse *does not consent to it*, and
>
> (b) at the time *he knows that she does not consent* to the intercourse *or he is reckless* as to whether she does or does not consent to it.".

This section is a useful example of the division between the *actus reus* and *mens rea* of an offence, with (a) containing the former and (b) the latter.

6.1.1 Actus reus of common law rape

The *actus reus* of common law rape is sexual intercourse with a woman who does not consent to it. At common law there was a rule that a wife by her marriage gave irrevocable consent to intercourse, and therefore a husband could not be guilty of the rape of his wife. The 1981 Act appeared to recognise this rule by referring to "unlawful sexual intercourse", *i.e.* intercourse outside marriage. This rule was widely criticised as being both outmoded and demeaning to women, and was abolished in this jurisdiction by section 5 of the Criminal Law (Rape) Amendment Act 1990. The 1990 Act removed the word "unlawful" from the definition of rape, and provided that "any rule of law by virtue of which a husband cannot be guilty of the rape of his wife is hereby abolished". However, section 5(2) goes on to provide that any criminal proceedings for marital rape must have the consent of the D.P.P.

The statutory definition of rape in England also contained the phrase "unlawful sexual intercourse" and was also assumed to recognise the common law rule. However, in *R v. R* (1991), the House of Lords held that the word "unlawful" was simply redundant and that the statutory definition therefore applied to marital rape. The Court agreed with the Court of Appeal decision that the marital exemption in relation to rape was "a common law fiction which has become anachronistic and offensive" (at page 490). The position in both jurisdictions is therefore that rape within marriage is unlawful.

Sexual intercourse for common law rape means vaginal intercourse only, and some degree of penetration by the penis, however slight, is required (Section 1(2) Criminal Law (Rape) (Amendment) Act 1981); however, ejaculation is not required (*People (Attorney General) v. Dermody* (1951)). (Forced oral or anal intercourse and penetration by an object are now covered by section 4 rape.)

Penetration is a continuing act; failure by an accused to withdraw when he realises that the other is not consenting amounts to rape: *Kaitamaki v. R.* (1985). The argument cannot be made in those circumstances that *actus reus* and *mens rea* did not coincide.

6.1.2 Section 4 rape: difference between common law rape and section 4 rape

It was recognised that the common law definition of rape, now contained in section 2 of the Criminal Law (Rape) Act 1981, was inadequate, since it did not deal with anal or oral rape, or rape by an object, all of which are as degrading to the victim as common law rape. Section 4(1) of the Criminal Law (Rape) (Amendment) Act 1990 was therefore introduced, and it provides that:

> "In this Act 'rape under section 4' means a sexual assault that includes-
>
> (a) the penetration (however slight) of the anus or mouth by the penis, or

(b) penetration (however slight) of the vagina by any object held or manipulated by another person."

The *actus reus* of section 4 rape is, therefore, a *sexual assault* accompanied by certain acts of penetration. We have yet to look at the definition of sexual assault: however, for the moment, it is enough to know that it is an assault with "circumstances of indecency" and consent is a defence just as in common law rape. The *mens rea* for this offence is also essentially the same as for sexual assault or rape, which will be dealt with later.

What are the differences between common law rape and section 4 rape? Common law rape can only be committed by a man, while section 4 rape can be committed by either sex (rape with an object). Common law rape can only be committed against a woman, while section 4 rape can be committed against either sex (it includes anal or oral rape of a man).

6.2 Sexual assault

Until 1990, one of the offences of indecent assault was the appropriate charge for the majority of sexual attacks which did not amount to rape. The offences of indecent assault upon a male and upon a female existed at common law: although statute provided maximum penalties for each offence, there was no statutory definition of either.

There was dissatisfaction with this situation. The differentiation between indecent assault upon a male and upon a female was anachronistic. Until 1981 there were different maximum penalties depending on the sex of the victim. (This was remedied by the Criminal Law (Rape) Act 1981.) In addition, each offence covered a wide span of behaviour, from relatively minor offences to violent sexual attacks. Consequently, it was felt that the label of indecent assault and the maximum sentence available were inadequate for the more serious offences which were included in the definition of indecent assault.

The solution came in the Criminal Law (Rape) (Amendment) Act 1990. This combined the offences of indecent assault upon a male and upon a female into one offence, to be known as sexual assault, having a single maximum penalty of five years, regardless of the sex of the victim. In addition, the more serious cases of sexual attack are now dealt with in two ways. Those which involve penetration will now amount to section 4 rape, while other serious sexual attacks fall into a new category of aggravated sexual assault. This is a gender-neutral offence, and carries a maximum penalty of life imprisonment. (This penalty is the same as that for common law rape and section 4 rape, reflecting the fact that some attacks not involving penetration can be just as grave as those involving penetration.)

The following sections are relevant:

"s. 2(1) The offence of indecent assault upon any male person and the offence of sexual assault upon any female person shall be known as sexual assault.

(2) A person guilty of sexual assault shall be liable on conviction on indictment to imprisonment for a term not exceeding 5 years.

s. 3(1) In this Act 'aggravated sexual assault' means a sexual assault that involves serious violence or the threat of serious violence or is such as to cause injury, humiliation or degradation of a grave nature to the person assaulted.

(2) A person guilty of aggravated sexual assault shall be liable on conviction on indictment to imprisonment for life.".

However, the 1990 Act does not define indecent or sexual assault, but simply prescribes a new name and range of penalties for an existing offence at common law. It was argued after the passage of the 1990 Act that there was in fact no offence of indecent assault known to Irish law. If so, then the 1990 Act would have been ineffective as purporting to rename and give new penalties for an offence which did not exist. This argument was, however, rejected by O'Hanlon J. in *Doolan v. DPP* (1993) and by the Supreme Court in *People (DPP) v. EF* (1994), both of which held that an offence of indecent assault existed at common law, and that it was permissible to rename the offence and provide new penalties for it without re-enacting it. The 1990 Act creates, therefore, a mixed statutory and common law offence in much the same way as section 4 of the Criminal Justice Act 1964 does with regard to murder. So to define sexual assault, we have to see what constituted indecent assault at common law.

6.2.1 Indecent assault at common law

"An indecent assault has been defined as an assault (including a psychic assault) accompanied with circumstances of indecency." (Charleton, *Offences Against the Person* (Round Hall Press, 1992), p. 286.)

What is an assault? An assault is an act by which one person intentionally or recklessly causes another to apprehend immediate, unlawful personal violence or to sustain such violence. (For the definition of assault see the Non-Fatal Offences Against the Person Act 1997, discussed further in the chapter on Offences Against the Person, *infra*.) For an assault to take place, it is not necessary that there should be any element of hostility or aggression. Instead, "violence" simply means any unlawful touching of a victim without consent or lawful excuse: *Faulkner v. Talbot* (1981).

The difficulty lies in defining "circumstances of indecency". Some circumstances will be obviously indecent (an attempt to remove another's clothes) while others may or may not be indecent depending on the circumstances. In *R. v. Court* (1988), the accused was a shop assistant and struck a 12 year old girl in the shop several times on her buttocks, outside her shorts. Later asked why he did so, he replied "buttock fetish". Were there circumstances of indecency, given that the girl was unaware of his motive? The House of Lords upheld the conviction of the accused, laying down the following criteria:

1. The assault component of indecent assault includes not just physical violence, but conduct which causes another to fear immediate and unlawful physical violence;

2. Some circumstances are objectively incapable of being regarded as indecent, regardless of the motive of the accused: for example, to remove another's shoe is not capable of being regarded as indecent, even if the accused is a shoe fetishist;

3. Some circumstances are inherently indecent, regardless of the motive of the accused: for example, to remove a victim's clothes against her will amounts to indecent assault, regardless of whether the accused had a sexual intention, or simply intended to embarrass or humiliate the victim;

4. In other circumstances, the jury may consider all the surrounding factors in deciding if an assault is in fact indecent, including the relationship between the parties and the motive of the accused; (For example, for a parent to spank a child is not indecent.) and

5. It is not necessary to show that the victim was aware of the circumstances of indecency. So it was no defence that the victim was unaware of the accused's buttock fetish: clearly an indecent assault can take place on a sleeping or unconscious victim.

6.2.2 *Aggravated sexual assault*

Section 3(1) of the 1990 Act defines aggravated sexual assault to mean:

> "a sexual assault that involves *serious violence or the threat of serious violence* or is such as to cause *injury, humiliation or degradation of a grave nature* to the person assaulted". (Emphasis added.)

Where these factors are present the maximum penalty is life imprisonment, reflecting the gravity of the offence.

6.3 Consent

Failure to struggle or put up a fight does not amount to consent, despite misconceptions to the contrary. Absence of violence is not presence of consent. The Criminal Law (Rape) (Amendment) Act 1990 sought to put this beyond doubt by providing in section 9 that:

> "It is hereby declared that in relation to an offence that consists or includes the doing of an act to a person without the consent of that person any failure or omission by that person to offer resistance to the act does not of itself constitute consent to the act."

At first glance, consent seems a clear-cut issue: it is either present or not. But problems arise when consent results from fear or fraud. In the case of *R. v. Williams* (1923), for example, a singing teacher persuaded his 16-year-old pupil that intercourse was a necessary operation to improve her breathing control. Can it be said that there was consent in that case? It was held that there was not: fraudulently misrepresenting the nature of the act meant that the apparent consent was not real. Similarly, in *R. v. Dee* (1884) it was held that there was no real consent where a man induced a woman to have intercourse with him by pretending to be her husband. This position is also laid down by statute: section 4 Criminal Law Amendment Act 1885; section 20 Criminal Law Amendment Act 1935.

However, *R. v. Linekar* (1995) held that consent was present despite fraud. In that case, the defendant approached a prostitute and agreed to pay £25 for intercourse. He had no intention of paying, and subsequently made off without paying. Was the consent of the victim real? The Court of Appeal held it was: fraud as to a collateral matter did not undermine consent, although fraud as to the nature of the act or the identity of the actor would mean that apparent consent was not real.

In addition, there is no consent where the victim is *incapable* of giving consent. So, in *People (DPP) v. X* (1995), a man was convicted of rape for having intercourse with a woman while she slept.

6.4 *Mens rea* of sexual offences

For most sexual offences, an element of the offence is the absence of consent. The *mens rea* of the offence will, therefore, be that the defendant intended to commit the acts in question either *knowing* that the victim did not consent, or *being reckless* as to whether or not the victim consented. The first requires that the defendant is *conscious* of the lack of consent; the second, that the defendant was aware that the victim might not be consenting. This *mens rea* is explicitly set out by statute in the case of common law rape (Criminal Law (Rape) Act 1981, section 2(1)(b)), and has been held by the courts to apply also in the case of sexual assault (*R. v. Kimber* (1983)).

However, one difficulty arises. Suppose that a defendant *honestly believes* that a victim is consenting, *but his belief is unreasonable*. Should the defendant be found guilty of a crime? Two approaches to this situation are possible. An objective approach would find a defendant liable if he honestly believed that there was consent, but he had no reasonable grounds for his belief. A subjective approach would acquit the defendant, looking solely at his honest belief and not at whether it was reasonable of him to hold that belief.

In *DPP v. Morgan* (1975), this precise issue came before the House of Lords. In a bizarre set of facts, a husband invited three drinking partners back to his house to have sexual intercourse with his wife. He told them that she would put up a struggle, but that this would be simply an act and that she would in fact welcome having intercourse with them. The men went back to his house and each had sex with her while she was held down, fighting and screaming. The defence of each of the three men was that they had honestly, though obviously unreasonably, believed that the victim had consented to intercourse. The trial judge directed the jury that this could not amount to a defence unless the defendants had reasonable grounds for their belief. The defendants were convicted.

On appeal to the House of Lords, it was held (by a majority) that the defendants could not be convicted of rape if they had genuinely believed that the victim was consenting. *Per* Lord Hailsham L.C.:

> "Once one has accepted ... that the prohibited act in rape is non-consensual sexual intercourse, and that the guilty state of mind is an intention to commit it, it seems to me to follow ... that there is no room either for a 'defence' of honest belief or mistake ... Either the prosecution proves that the accused had the requisite intent, or it does not. In the former case it succeeds, and in the latter it fails. Since honest belief

clearly negatives intent, the reasonableness or otherwise of that belief can only be evidence for or against the view that the belief and therefore the intent was actually held ..." (At p. 361.)

Outrage followed this decision, which was described by the tabloids as "A Rapists' Charter". Pressure was exerted to change the *mens rea* of rape to an objective test, asking whether the accused had reasonable grounds for his belief. However, this was not done. The English Advisory Group on the Law of Rape accepted that *DPP v. Morgan* (1975) was correct in principle. Nevertheless, the Advisory Group did advise that legislation should clarify that:

1. An *honest belief* in consent would negative *mens rea*; and

2. This belief *did not need to be based on reasonable grounds*; but

3. The jury *may take into account whether reasonable grounds existed in deciding whether the belief was honest.*

English legislation adopted this approach in the Sexual Offences (Amendment) Act 1976, section 1(1) and this approach was also adopted in Ireland, in the Criminal Law (Rape) Act 1981, section 2(2) of which states:

> "It is hereby declared that if at a trial for a rape offence the jury has to consider whether a man believed that a woman was consenting to sexual intercourse, the presence or absence of reasonable grounds for such a belief is a matter to which the jury is to have regard, in conjunction with any other relevant matters, in considering whether he so believed."

This approach is a common sense compromise: the accused is entitled to claim a genuine belief in consent but the jury are entitled to consider whether such a belief would have been reasonable in deciding whether the accused did in fact have that belief. For the sake of comparison, consider the New Zealand approach, where the test is objective: an accused must believe in consent "on reasonable grounds" (section 128(3) Crimes Act 1961; Crimes (Amendment) Act 1985).

It is not necessary that the jury should be directed on the provisions of section 2(2) of the 1981 Act in every case where rape is charged: such a direction only becomes necessary where the defence raised is one of mistaken belief in consent. This was confirmed by the Supreme Court in *People (DPP) v. McDonagh* (1996). In that case, the defendants were charged with rape; their defence was that the complainant had consented to sexual intercourse in return for payment. They were convicted. On appeal, it was argued that the trial judge had erred in failing to explain to the jury the effect of section 2(2). This was a somewhat novel line of argument: section 2(2) had clearly been intended to facilitate prosecutions, and had been enacted in response to *R. v. Morgan* (1975). It was, therefore, ironic that the defendants were arguing in favour of an interpretation which would have the effect of facilitating defendants, by confusing juries with section 2(2) in cases where it was clearly of no relevance. It was held by Costello J., therefore, that section 2(2) was limited in its effect to cases where the defence mounted was one of mistaken belief in consent: it had no application in cases such as the present one, where the defence was the existence of actual consent.

6.4.1 Recklessness as to consent

Recklessness in this context has the same meaning as in *People (DPP) v. Murray* (1977), that is the accused must be consciously aware of the possibility that the victim is not consenting. Objective recklessness is not enough.

6.5 Incest

Incest is a crime governed by the Punishment of Incest Act 1908. The crime consists of sexual intercourse with a close blood relative. The majority of cases are violent or abusive, but this is not an element of the crime: consensual intercourse between close relatives will still amount to incest. Consent is not a defence. The majority of cases of incest deal with fathers abusing daughters, and for that reason, different considerations apply to incest by a male and incest by a female.

6.5.1 Incest by a male

"A male who has sexual intercourse with a woman who is to his knowledge his mother, sister, daughter or granddaughter commits incest." (O'Malley, *Sexual Offences: Law, Policy and Punishment* (Round Hall Sweet and Maxwell, 1996), page 114.)

Vaginal intercourse must be established: other forms of abuse or exploitation do not amount to incest. Brother and sister include half-brother and half-sister (*i.e.* where there is one parent in common) but not step-brother and step-sister, since the offence is one limited to blood-relations. Consequently, it follows that sexual abuse by adoptive parents does not amount to the crime of incest.

Until the enactment of the Criminal Law (Rape) (Amendment) Act 1990, there was a conclusive presumption that a boy under 14 years of age could not commit incest. However, this has now been abolished. On this point, see further the defence of infancy, *infra*.

6.5.2 Incest by a female

> "A female of or above the age of 17 years who with consent permits her father, grandfather, brother or son to have sexual intercourse with her commits incest provided she is aware of the relevant relationship between herself and the male." (O'Malley, *Sexual Offences: Law, Policy and Punishment* (Round Hall Sweet and Maxwell, 1996), page 118.)

The offence is the same as incest by a male, except that the female is not criminally liable until she reaches the age of 17, on the assumption that she is the victim of any incestual intercourse before that age.

6.5.3 Punishment of incest

Committed by a male, the maximum penalty is life imprisonment (section 1, Punishment of Incest Act 1908; section 12, Criminal Law Amendment Act 1935; section 5(1), Criminal Law (Incest Proceedings) Act 1995). Committed by a female, the maximum penalty is 7 years imprisonment (section 2, 1908 Act).

6.5.4 Reform

It is well-recognised that the crime of incest should be extended to adoptive relationships and step-children and that it should encompass sexual acts falling short of intercourse. See, for example, the discussion in Department of Justice, Equality and Law Reform, *The Law on Sexual Offences: A Discussion Paper* (Stationery Office, 1998).

6.6 Sexual offences against the mentally handicapped

Until 1993, the only offence of this type was contained in section 4 of the Criminal Law Amendment Act 1935 which made it an offence punishable by two years' imprisonment to have unlawful sexual intercourse with a woman who was "an idiot or an imbecile or feeble-minded". This was unsatisfactory, with (what is now regarded as) offensive terminology and offering no protection against other forms of sexual exploitation of the mentally handicapped. The Criminal Law (Sexual Offences) Act 1993 replaces section 4 of the 1935 Act. The 1993 Act creates in section 5 three distinct offences:

- Sexual intercourse with a mentally impaired person (10 years' imprisonment; 3 years' for attempt (first conviction); 5 years' for attempt (subsequent conviction);

- Buggery of a mentally impaired person (penalties as intercourse); and

- Commission of an act of gross indecency by a male with a male who is mentally impaired. (2 years' imprisonment).

The 1993 Act then defines "mentally impaired" as follows:

> "Suffering from a disorder of the mind, whether through mental handicap or mental illness, which is of such a nature or degree as to render a person incapable of living an independent life or of guarding against serious exploitation." (section 5).

There is a defence where a defendant is married to a mentally impaired person. A defence is also provided where an accused can show that at the time of the alleged commission of the offence he did not know and had no reason to suspect that the person in respect of whom he is charged was mentally impaired. However, consent is *not* a defence, even assuming that the victim has sufficient mental capacity to give consent.

It should be noted that the 1993 Act is designed for situations where a mentally impaired person is capable of giving consent: if a victim is so mentally disabled as to be incapable of consenting, then the accused will also be guilty of rape or sexual assault if he has the necessary *mens rea*. The necessary mental capacity to give consent is expressed by Glanville Williams to be as follows:

> "[T]he woman must both know the physical facts and know that the connection is sexual; failing either knowledge, she does not consent in law." (*Textbook of Criminal Law* (2nd ed., London, 1983), p. 571.)

6.7 Sexual abuse of children

There is no specific offence, as such, of sexual abuse of children. However, sexual activity with children may amount to an offence where the child is not old enough to consent to that activity. A person of either sex under 15 years of age cannot consent to activity amounting to a sexual assault by virtue of section 14 of the Criminal Law Amendment Act 1935.

Similarly, a girl under the age of 17 years cannot consent to sexual intercourse. Under sections 1 and 2 of the 1935 Act, unlawful carnal knowledge of a girl under 15 is an offence punishable by life imprisonment, while unlawful carnal knowledge of a girl aged between 15 and 17 is an offence punishable by five years' imprisonment. This prohibition applies regardless of the age of the offender: where two 16-year-olds have sex, then the male has committed an offence. Arguably, it would be more appropriate to criminalise sexual intercourse with under-age children on a gender-neutral basis, in a way which would reflect the fact that a graver offence is committed where a middle-aged man has sex with a 16-year-old girl than where two teenagers have sex.

In this context, carnal knowledge simply means vaginal intercourse; unlawful means that the parties must not be married. Otherwise, neither consent nor mistake on the part of the man as to age provides any defence. As regards consent, Maguire C.J., in *AG (Shaughnessy) v. Ryan* (1960), stated that the sections "were designed to protect young girls, not alone against lustful men, but against themselves" (at page 183). As regards mistake as to age see *R v. Prince* (1875), where even a reasonable mistake as to age was held not to amount to a defence.

6.7.1 Reform

The Law Reform Commission's Report on *Child Sexual Abuse* made a series of proposals on reform of the law relating to sexual abuse of children. In relation to statutory rape, it proposed the lowering of the age limit for the more serious offence in section 1 to thirteen but that the offence should remain punishable by a maximum of life imprisonment. It recommended that the maximum sentence for an offence under section 2 be seven years. A further recommendation was that it should not be an offence for a male to have intercourse with a girl aged over fifteen years of age unless he is either five years or more older than her or is a person in authority, *i.e.* any person having even temporary responsibility for her education, supervision or welfare. The existing strict liability in relation to statutory rape was criticised and the Law Reform Commission recommended that if the accused genuinely believed that the girl was over seventeen he should have a complete defence unless he was a person in authority or was five years or more older than the girl. If the defendant could demonstrate a reasonable belief that the girl was over thirteen but under fifteen, he should be liable to a maximum sentence of seven years' imprisonment.

The Law Reform Commission expressed concern about the offence of indecent (now sexual) assault on a person under fifteen years of age in section 14 of the Criminal Law Amendment Act 1935. The offence does not cover situations where an adult, without force or threat or touching, induces a child to undress before the adult or to touch him or her indecently. The Commission recommended a new definition of child sexual abuse or sexual exploitation to cover such scenarios. The Department of Justice Discussion Paper on *The Law on Sexual Offences* sought views on the above.

The Sex Offenders Act 2001, which has just been enacted, carries out further reforms, primarily by establishing a register of sex offenders, with particular reference to those who have committed offences against children. Such offenders are required to notify gardaí of their names and addresses. A risk assessment will be made of those on the register, and the gardaí are empowered to disclose the names of offenders where necessary to prevent an immediate risk of crime or to alert members of the public to a particular danger. Sex offenders coming into the jurisdiction from abroad are also required to register. A civil sex offenders order is also available against sex offenders whose behaviour in the community gives rise to reasonable concern that such an order is necessary to protect the public. The order is available to prohibit conduct which is not criminal but is nevertheless undesirable, *e.g.* loitering around school playgrounds. The act also creates a new offence where sex offenders seek or accept work involving unsupervised contact with children without first notifying the employer of their conviction.

6.8 Procedural aspects of sexual offences

6.8.1 Corroboration

Special procedural safeguards apply to cases of sexual offences. Some are protective of the alleged victim, while some were protective of the accused. An example of the latter is the old rule that a jury should be warned that it is dangerous to convict on the uncorroborated evidence of a complainant in a sexual offence, unless there existed independent corroborative evidence. Thus, in situations where it came down to one word against another, the accused enjoyed protection. Examples of corroborative evidence would include medical evidence of forcible intercourse, or proof that the accused was lying on a material issue because of a realisation of guilt.

This rule did not mean that the jury *could not* convict on uncorroborated evidence, merely that they should be warned that it was *dangerous to do so*. The rule was regarded as outdated, and as putting victims in sexual offences in a position where they were automatically regarded as untrustworthy. Section 7(1) of the Criminal Law (Rape) (Amendment) Act 1990 has now abolished this rule, and provides that it is at the discretion of the judge whether or not the case warrants such a warning being given.

6.8.2 Publicity

Another special factor of trials of sexual offences relates to publicity: whether trials are held in public and whether the anonymity of complainants and accuseds is guaranteed, section 7 of the Criminal Law (Rape) Act 1981 (as amended by section 17(2) Criminal Law (Rape) (Amendment) Act 1990) provides that matters tending to reveal the identity of a complainant shall not be published or broadcast except in limited circumstances relating to safeguards for the defence, or if anonymity imposes a substantial and unreasonable burden on the reporting of the trial, and it is in the public interest to remove the restriction. Section 8 of the 1981 Act guarantees the anonymity of an accused in a sexual case in a similar way, except until after he is convicted. Even then, as a result of section 7, the identity of the convicted person cannot be published if that would be likely to identify the complainant. There is a special regime for anonymity in incest cases: Criminal Law (Incest Proceedings) Act 1995.

As regards trials being held in public, there is a constitutional requirement in Article 34.1 that justice should be administered in public save in such special and limited cases as may be prescribed by law. Trials of sexual offences are one such case, and section 6 of the Criminal Law (Rape) Act 1981 (as amended by section 11 Criminal Law (Rape) (Amendment) Act 1990) provides that in the trial of certain sexual offences (cases involving rape and aggravated sexual assault), the judge shall exclude from the court the public, except for *bona fide* representatives of the media. The complainant is entitled to have a parent, relative or friend in court, as is the accused if the accused is under 18 years of age. Verdict and sentence must, however, be announced in open court.

The 1981 Act does not extend to sexual assault and other such crimes; however, under section 20 of the Criminal Justice Act 1951, the court may exclude the public if the offence is one of an "indecent or obscene nature". In other words, the court has a discretion to exclude.

6.8.3 Cross-examination of complainant

Another special feature relates to cross-examination of the complainant about her previous sexual history. At common law, this was considered to be relevant to the credibility of the complainant. However, cross-examination of the accused could be used as a tool to put the complainant herself on trial, or to mount an unwarranted intrusion on the complainant's private life. In addition, it was an example of outmoded ideas of morality to assume that sexual intercourse with others in the past meant that the complainant was more likely to have consented to the specific act forming the basis of the trial.

The legislative response was section 3 of the 1981 Act as amended by section 13 of the 1990 Act. This prohibits evidence being given or questions asked about the previous sexual experience of the complainant with any person except with the leave of the judge. The judge is to give leave to ask such questions only if satisfied that it would be unfair to the accused to refuse to allow the questions to be asked, that is, if the effect of allowing evidence to be given or questions to be asked might be to create a reasonable doubt in the mind of the jury as to the guilt of the accused.

6.8.4 Evidence by persons under 17 years

Another feature which is relevant, although not limited to cases involving sexual offences, is section 12 of the Criminal Evidence Act 1992. This provides for evidence to be given through television link by persons under 17 years in any criminal proceedings. Section 13 allows for the evidence of such a witness to be conducted through an intermediary provided the court is satisfied that this is appropriate due to the age or mental condition of the witness. Section 18 extends the above provisions to persons with a mental handicap who have reached the age of 17 years. Evidence via a television link was challenged as being unconstitutional in *Donnelly v. Ireland* (1998). The appellant argued that he had a constitutional right to confront his accuser in open court or, alternatively, that this was a vital element of his constitutional right to cross-examine witnesses. The Supreme Court held that there was no constitutional right to confront a witness in Irish law and noted that similar television link provisions had been upheld in the United States despite the express right to confront accusers in the United States Constitution.

6.8.5 Doctrine of recent complaint

The common law required that the victim of a rape case "raise hue and cry" by complaining about the rape as immediately as possible. This ancient rule has survived as the doctrine of recent complaint, whereby evidence of an early complaint by a victim of a sexual offence is important to establish consistency and credibility. It is an exception to the general rule that witnesses must not be asked if they have made a prior consistent statement. Complaint by the victim at the first opportunity does not, however, amount to corroboration. The complaint should be made at the earliest opportunity that reasonably afforded itself and must have been made voluntarily and not as a result of leading questions.

In *People (DPP) v. Brophy*, the complaint was held not to fall within the doctrine and was therefore inadmissible. The allegation was of sexual assault during a one-hour period which the complainant spent at the accused's house. He gave her a lift to a shopping centre afterwards and the complainant showed no distress and said "I'll see you tomorrow." She then met her mother but did not complain to her, only later in the afternoon complaining to her father and some companions. In *People (DPP) v. Kiernan* (1994), the complainant did not complain to her parents or boyfriend but did complain to him the following day. This was held not to be the first reasonable opportunity and the complaint was therefore inadmissible.

6.8.6 Legal representation for complainant

There has recently been a groundswell of opinion in favour of the view that complainants should have separate legal representation. This view was expressed by, for example, the Working Party on the Legal and Judicial Process, which took the view that this would provide support for complainants, render the trial process less traumatic for them, and would help bring about an increase in the reporting of rape.

However, there has been equally strong opposition from within the legal profession. In part, this is based on the view that such representation would unfairly prejudice the defendant. So, the Law Reform Commission took the view in its Consultation Paper on Rape (1987) that:

> "It might indeed be constitutionally suspect, since it tilts the balance of the criminal process significantly in favour of the prosecution in a defined range of offences by permitting a dual representation hostile to the interests of the accused, thereby depriving him of one of the long standing benefits of a criminal trial conducted "in due course of law" as that phrase was plainly understood at the time of the enactment of the Constitution." (At page 70.)

Similarly, Flood J., in *People (DPP) v. MC* (1995), indicated that section 5 of the Criminal Justice Act 1993 (giving a victim a right to give evidence of the impact of the offence on her) did not make the victim an independent party in the criminal trial, and took the view that "the constitutional validity of a statutory provision to that effect would be very doubtful".

Other opinion has been to the effect that separate legal representation would simply muddy the waters of the criminal trial, confusing the issue to the point where the jury might give up and return an unjustified acquittal.

Consequently, the recent trend has been towards other measures to improve the conditions of complainants (for example, the limitations on examination on prior sexual history, the grant of free legal aid for victims of rape or aggravated sexual assault to allow a complainant to consult a legal aid solicitor who may accompany the complainant into court (section 26(3) Civil Legal Aid Act 1995), the victim impact rights created by the Criminal Justice Act 1993, greater access to Gardaí and prosecution lawyers, automatic giving of copies of statements to complainants).

More recently, however, the Sex Offenders Act 2001 has introduced a limited form of separate legal representation for complainants in rape and other serious sexual assault cases. This representation will apply during applications to adduce evidence of or to cross-examine the complainant on her previous sexual history. It is felt that representation limited to such applications will not pose constitutional difficulties as such applications are made in the absence of the jury and the representation could therefore not impinge on the jury's view of the case.

Further reading: O'Malley, *Sexual Offences: Law, Policy and Punishment* (Round Hall Sweet and Maxwell, 1996); Charleton, *Offences Against the Person* (Round Hall Press, 1992), pp. 262-337; Department of Justice, Equality and Law Reform, *The Law on Sexual Offences: A*

Discussion Paper (Stationery Office, 1998); Charleton, "Criminal law – Protecting the Mentally Sub-Normal against Sexual Exploitation" (1984) 6 D.U.L.J. N.S. 165; Law Reform Commission Report, *Sexual Offences Against the Mentally Handicapped* (L.R.C. 1990); Law Reform Commission Consultation Paper, *Child Sexual Abuse* (L.R.C. 1989); Law Reform Commission Consultation Paper, *Rape* (L.R.C. 1987); Law Reform Commission Report, *Rape* (L.R.C. 1988), Ní Raifeartaigh, *Doctrine of Fresh Complaint in Sexual Cases* (1994) 12 I.L.T. 160.

7. OFFENCES AGAINST THE PERSON

7.1 Reform of the Law

Until 1997, the law of non-fatal offences against the person consisted of a variety of statutory and common law offences, the bulk of which were contained in the Offences Against the Person Act 1861. There was a wide range of specific offences: assault, assault occasioning actual bodily harm, unlawful wounding, wounding with specified intent, suffocation or strangulation, and so on. The definition of each offence was highly technical, and unduly complex. The law on this topic has now been comprehensively overhauled by the Non-Fatal Offences Against the Person Act 1997. This act largely follows the recommendations of the Law Reform Commission made in the *Report on Non-Fatal Offences Against the Person* (Dublin, 1994), and creates a hierarchy of offences ranging from assault, to syringe offences, to false imprisonment, to coercion and harassment. We will deal with each in turn.

7.2 Assault

This offence is created by section 2. Before the 1997 act there were two relevant offences: assault and battery. Assault was defined as an action causing the victim to fear that force would be immediately inflicted upon him. Battery was the infliction of force. The 1997 legislation refers to both situations as assault. Assault is now defined as follows:

> "A person shall be guilty of the offence of assault who, without lawful excuse [*e.g.* in the course of making a lawful arrest], intentionally or recklessly -
>
> (a) directly or indirectly applies force to or causes an impact on the body of another, or
> (b) causes another to believe on reasonable grounds that he or she is likely immediately to be subjected to any such force or impact,
>
> without the consent of the other."

Absence of consent is a part of the crime. Consent will be implied in circumstances such as contact sports, where each participant implicitly consents to the use of a certain level of force as part of the sport. As regards ordinary day to day conduct (tapping a person on the shoulder, for example) section 2(3) provides that no offence is committed if the force/impact is not intended or likely to cause injury, is generally acceptable in the ordinary conduct of daily life, and the defendant does not know or believe that it is in fact unacceptable to that particular person.

"Force" is defined in section 2(2) to include application of heat, light, electric current, noise or any other form of energy, or application of matter in any form. As regards force or impact generally, there is no minimum threshold (ordinary day to day conduct excluded): the slightest touching without consent amounts to an assault. The victim need not be aware of this touching, as where the victim is asleep.

Section 2 retains the effect of the pre-existing case law that, for an assault (as distinct from a battery) to occur, the victim must believe that he will be immediately subjected to force or impact. Threats to use force at some future date do not amount to assault, although they may amount to, for example, coercion or harassment as defined later in the 1997 Act. For the same reason, conduct which would otherwise amount to an assault may be negatived by circumstances which show that force is not about to be immediately used. In the renowned case of *Tuberville v. Savage* (1669), it was alleged that the plaintiff had placed his hand on his sword while saying "If it were not assize time, I would not take such language from you". This was held not to be an assault: placing of the hand on the sword would indicate immediate use of force, but the words indicated that the plaintiff was not about to use force, and so the defendant could not have believed that force was immediately to be used.

Equally, if I were to wave a knife at a person who was on the other side of a gorge, and to shout that I intended to kill him, no assault would be committed if the circumstances were such that the person was safely out of my range: the person would not be put in fear of the immediate application of force or subjection to an impact.

On the same point, an assault is not committed if the victim does not in fact apprehend immediate and likely force or impact. See example *infra,* under *Threats to kill or cause serious injury.*

Before the 1997 Act there was a debate in the case law as to whether words alone, unaccompanied by "menacing gestures" could amount to an assault. However, it is clear from the terms of section 2 ("causes another to believe on reasonable grounds") that words alone can amount to an assault, provided only that the words amount to reasonable grounds for the belief that the application of force or impact is immediately likely.

Under section 2, assault cannot be committed by omission except in special circumstances, for example *Fagan v. Metropolitan Police Commissioner* (1968). (See further the discussion in the chapter on *Actus Reus*.) This was also the position before the 1997 legislation was enacted.

Before 1997 the case law was uncertain as to whether assault was committed where a person indirectly applied force to another, for example by digging a pit for a victim to fall into, or by derailing a train. On balance, it seemed that it was: as in the case of *DPP v. K* (1990) in which a schoolboy was held to commit assault where he poured acid into a hot air dryer in a bathroom, injuring the next user. However, section 2 makes it clear that assault can now be committed by either the direct or indirect application of force.

7.3 Assault causing harm

The next offence created by the Act is contained in section 3, which provides that "A person who assaults another causing him or her harm shall be guilty of an offence". Harm is defined in section 1 as "harm to body or mind and includ[ing] pain and unconsciousness". This offence is, therefore, an aggravated form of assault, made up of the components of assault together with the infliction of harm. It is significant that harm is defined to include harm to body or mind: an assault which causes the victim no physical harm may nevertheless cause the victim psychological harm, and this would seem to fall within the terms of section 3.

7.4 Causing serious harm

Section 4 creates the offence of causing serious harm, in the following terms: "A person who intentionally or recklessly causes serious harm to another shall be guilty of an offence". Serious harm is defined in section 1 as meaning:

> "injury which creates a substantial risk of death or which causes serious disfigurement or substantial loss or impairment of the mobility of the body as a whole or of the function of any particular bodily member or organ."

It is very important to note that this does not follow the recommendations of the Law Reform Commission, which advocated the creation of an offence of assault causing serious harm. Instead, the 1997 Act simply adopts the concept of causing serious harm: it is not necessary that the conduct which causes the harm should also amount to an assault. (For example, suppose A knows he is HIV positive; he has unprotected intercourse with B without informing B of this status. B falls ill. In these circumstances there is no assault: nevertheless, if A has the requisite intention, then A's conduct may amount to the offence of causing serious harm to B.)

The offence is one of intentionally or recklessly causing serious harm, and the requirement of *mens rea* applies, therefore, both to the conduct in question and to foresight of serious harm. Again, the principles laid down in *People (DPP) v. Murray* (1977) apply: the defendant must intend serious harm, or be subjectively reckless as to whether it results.

7.4.1 Is consent a defence to causing serious harm?

Absence of consent is a constituent part of assault under section 2. Since assault causing harm is an aggravated form of assault, absence of consent is also a constituent part of assault causing harm contrary to section 3. However, section 4, causing serious harm, contains no reference to consent being a defence. Is consent a defence notwithstanding this omission? Before the 1997 Act consent could only be a defence to the causing of bodily harm under the Offences Against the Person Act 1861 in limited circumstances: consent was not a general defence. The report of the Law Reform Commission on Non-Fatal Offences Against the Person recommended that there should be a statutory scheme for determining when consent would be a defence to the infliction of serious harm: however, this recommendation was not followed in the 1997 Act. Consequently, one must look to the case law to see when consent will be a defence.

The issue of consent as a defence to serious harm will arise in three main contexts. The first is that of sport, where players consent to physical contact within the rules of the sport. This will seldom result in serious harm, except in the case of boxing. The second is that of dangerous exhibitions: stunts and the like. The third is that of sadomasochistic sexual activities. When will consent be a defence in each context? The leading authority is the case of *R. v. Brown* (1993). In this case, the defendants had consensually and in private inflicted various sadomasochistic tortures on each other. They were unwise enough to video these activities; the video tape fell into the hands of the police, and they were charged with occasioning actual bodily harm on each other. The question presented was whether lack of consent was an essential part of the offence.

It was held by the House of Lords that, in the circumstances, consent was irrelevant. As a general rule, a person could not consent to bodily harm: in the words of an earlier case (*Attorney General's Reference, Number 6 of 1980* (1981)): "it is not in the public interest that people should try to cause or should cause each other actual bodily harm for no good reason". The House of Lords accepted the decisions in earlier cases that consent was a defence in cases of "properly conducted games and sports, lawful chastisement or correction, reasonable surgical interference, dangerous exhibitions, etc. These apparent exceptions can be justified as involving the exercise of a legal right, in the case of chastisement or correction, or as needed in the public interest, in the other cases.". (*Attorney General's Reference, Number 6 of 1980* (1981))

It therefore appears that consent is a defence only where the conduct in question is "in the public interest": needless to say, the House of Lords did not accept that the "gratification of sadomasochistic desires" was in the public interest. In general, therefore, it seems that the court will look to the public utility of the act in determining whether consent can amount to a defence. In particular, it should be noted that *R. v. Brown* (1993) accepted the legality of boxing, notwithstanding that the participants in boxing certainly do intend to inflict on each other actual or serious bodily harm.

7.5 Threats to kill or cause serious harm

Section 5 of the 1997 Act deals with threats other than in the context of assaults and provides that:

> "A person who, without lawful excuse, makes to another a threat, by any means intending the other to believe it will be carried out, to kill or cause serious harm to that other or a third person shall be guilty of an offence."

This section is entirely distinct from assault, even though the same conduct might at the same time amount to both assault and an offence under section 5. For example, if A stands in front of B with an upraised knife and shouts "I'm going to kill you" then this would most probably amount to both assault and an offence under section 5. However, if A phones B and says "I'm going to kill you", but B knows that he is in another country, then this will not amount to assault: the necessary element of immediacy is lacking. It will, however, amount to an offence under section 5.

This section is also distinct from assault in one particularly important way. The crime of assault is established only where a victim actually believes that he is likely to be subjected to immediate force or impact. It is not established where a victim does not so believe. Suppose A threatens B with a replica firearm. If B knows that the firearm is a replica, then B will not believe that this is likely. The crime of assault has not been established. On the other hand, an offence under section 5 will be established: A has made a threat, intending B to believe that it will be carried out, to kill or cause serious injury to B. Under section 5, the subjective state of mind of the victim is irrelevant.

7.6 Syringe attacks and related offences

Section 6 creates a number of distinct offences relating to syringes, blood and contaminated blood. Before looking at each, terms must be defined. Section 1 defines these as follows:

> "'contaminated blood' means blood which is contaminated with any disease, virus, agent or organism which if passed into the bloodstream of another could infect the other with a life threatening or potentially life threatening disease;";

> "'contaminated fluid' means fluid or substance which is contaminated with any disease, virus, agent or organism which if passed into the bloodstream of another could infect the other with a life threatening or potentially life threatening disease;";

> "'contaminated syringe' means a syringe which has in it or on it contaminated blood or contaminated fluid;"; and

> "'syringe' includes any part of a syringe or a needle or any sharp instrument capable of piercing skin and passing onto or into a person blood or any fluid or substance resembling blood.".

The offences are then created as follows. First is the offence created by section 6(1) in two components. The first component is injuring another by piercing the skin of that other with a syringe, or threatening to so injure the other with a syringe. The second component is that the defendant intends the victim to believe, or it is likely that the victim will be caused to believe, that he may become infected with disease as a result.

Second is the offence created by section 6(2), which is again in two parts. The first is spraying, pouring or putting onto another, blood or any substance resembling blood, or threatening to do so. The second is the same as in section 6(1): that the defendant intends the victim to believe, or it is likely that the victim will be caused to believe, that he may become infected with disease as a result.

Third is the offence created by section 6(3):

> "A person who in committing or attempting to commit an offence under section 6(1) or section 6(2)-
>
> (a) injures a third person with a syringe by piercing his or her skin, or
> (b) sprays, pours or puts onto a third person blood or any fluid or sub-stance resembling blood,
>
> resulting in the third person believing that he or she may become infected with disease as a result of the injury or action caused shall be guilty of an offence."

This is a secondary offence, which comes into play only once a person is committing or attempting to commit an offence under section 6(1) or section 6(2), and covers the situations where A threatens or attacks B, but manages to also injure C. In these circumstances, A is guilty of an offence.

Finally, there are the offences created by section 6(5). These offences are distinguished from the preceding offences in that they involve actual (not merely threatened) attacks with contaminated blood or syringes, and therefore a real risk of actually causing disease. Under section 6(5)(a) it is an offence to intentionally injure another by pierc-ing the skin of that other with a contaminated syringe. Under section 6(5)(b) it is an offence to intentionally spray, etc., another with con-taminated blood. Under section 6(5)(c) it is an offence, similar to that created by section 6(3), to injure a third person while committing or attempting to commit an offence under section 6(5)(a) or (b). For each of these penalties, the maximum penalty is life imprisonment.

7.6.1 Possession of syringes

Section 7 creates an offence of possession of a syringe, etc., with inten-tion to cause or to threaten injury or to intimidate another. Section 8 creates two distinct offences of placing or abandoning syringes in places where they are likely to injure another: the offences depend on whether there is an intention to injure and whether the syringe is contaminated.

7.7 Coercion

The 1997 Act creates a general offence of coercion in section 9. Before 1997 there had been only one specific offence of coercion, which was limited in its scope to threats of violence. Section 9 is wider, and covers various forms of harassment and intimidation intended to coerce:

> "A person who, with a view to compel another to abstain from doing or to do any act which that other has a lawful right to do or to abstain from doing, wrongfully and without lawful authority -
>
> (a) uses violence to or intimidates that other person or a member of the family of the other, or
> (b) injures or damages the property of that other, or
> (c) persistently follows that other about from place to place, or
> (d) watches or besets the premises or other place where that other resides, works or carries on business, or happens to be, or the approach to such premises or place, or
> (e) follows that other with one or more persons in a disorderly manner in or through any public place,
>
> shall be guilty of an offence."

The offence has two constituent parts: the intention to compel, and the use of unacceptable means to do so. However, it seems that the offence will not be committed by, for example, a creditor who resorts to following a debtor around to secure payment: in that case, it cannot be said that the debtor has a lawful right to abstain from payment.

7.8 Harassment

This is a distinct offence from coercion, and was intended by the Law Reform Commission to cover acts of harassment which interfere with a person's right to a peaceful and private life even if those acts do not give rise to a fear of violence. The offence is created by section 10, as follows:

> "(1) Any person who, without lawful authority or reasonable excuse, by any means including by use of the telephone, harasses another by persistently following, watching, pestering, besetting or communicating with him or her, shall be guilty of an offence.

(2) For the purposes of this section a person harasses another where -

(a) he or she, by his or her acts intentionally or recklessly, seriously interferes with the other's peace or privacy or causes alarm, distress or harm to the other, and

(b) his or her acts are such that a reasonable person would realise that the acts would seriously interfere with the other's peace and privacy or cause alarm, distress or harm to the other.".

This section is intended to deal with situations such as stalking, where one person behaves in an unacceptable way, causing distress to another. However, the *mens rea* for the offence is inadequate to cover every such situation. The person who acts in a way that a reasonable person would realise would "seriously interfere with ... peace and privacy or cause alarm, distress or harm" but who subjectively believes that his behaviour is acceptable, will not be convicted. For example, an individual besotted with a person who stalks his victim while believing that he is merely pursuing her romantically or that his behaviour is actually welcome to the victim. Similarly, an unsavoury character who acts in a manner he knows will distress another but which would not be seen as particularly distressing by a reasonable person, will not be caught by the section. This could apply to a situation where the defendant knows that the victim has an extreme aversion to something which the reasonable person would not be affected by, and uses this knowledge to inflict harm.

It should be noted that the offence of harassment is regarded as less serious than coercion. It is not intended to cover situations where there is a good reason for what might otherwise amount to harassment. It was stated by the Law Reform Commission that:

> "The question may also arise as to whether a creditor who repeatedly seeks to have a bill paid should be guilty of an offence. The answer would seem to be that, while clearly the point can be reached where persistence becomes harassment, the legitimacy or justifiability of the intrusion is a factor to which weight should be attached in determining whether the conduct was worthy of criminal sanction. For this reason we recommend that it should be necessary to prove that the conduct was without lawful authority or reasonable excuse. We appreciate that this introduces an element of uncertainty, but without a proviso on these lines the offence would seem overbroad.". (Law Reform Commission, *Report on Non-Fatal Offences Against the Person* (Dublin, 1994), page 258.)

If a person is convicted of harassment, the court is given the power to order that he not communicate with the victim or approach closer than a specified distance to the victim's home or workplace, for such period as the court determines (section 10(3)). It is an offence to fail to comply with such an order (section 10(4)). Interestingly, the court is also given the power to make such an order even if the defendant is not convicted, provided that it considers it to be "in the interests of justice to do so" (section 10(5)). This would seem to include cases where the prosecutor meets the civil standard of proof but not the criminal standard, or cases where the defendant has carried out the conduct charged but without the necessary *mens rea*, or where the defendant is dealt with under the Probation Act.

7.9 Demands for payment of debts

Section 11 of the 1997 Act deals with the special case of demands for the payment of a debt. These may amount to coercion (if the debt is not in fact due) or harassment (depending on their nature) but will also be subject to this section which provides:

"A person who makes any demand for payment of a debt shall be guilty of an offence if -

(a) the demands by reason of their frequency are calculated to subject the debtor or a member of the family of the debtor to alarm, distress or humiliation, or

(b) the person falsely represents that criminal proceedings lie for non-payment of the debt, or

(c) the person falsely represents that he or she is authorised in some official capacity to enforce payment, or

(d) the person utters a document falsely represented to have an official character."

7.10 Poisoning

Section 12 creates the offence of poisoning:

"A person shall be guilty of an offence if, knowing that the other does not consent to what is being done, he or she intentionally or recklessly administers to or causes to be taken by another a substance which he or she knows to be capable of interfering substantially with the other's bodily functions."

The section goes on to specify that "a substance capable of inducing unconsciousness or sleep is capable of interfering substantially with bodily functions" (section 12(2)).

7.11 Endangerment

Section 13 creates a general offence of endangerment:

> "A person shall be guilty of an offence who intentionally or recklessly engages in conduct which creates a substantial risk of death or serious harm to another."

Note that serious harm is defined in section 1 as:

> "injury which creates a substantial risk of death or which causes serious disfigurement or substantial loss or impairment of the mobility of the body as a whole or of the function of any particular bodily member or organ."

Section 14 creates a more specific offence of endangering traffic:

> "A person shall be guilty of an offence who -
>
> (a) intentionally places or throws any dangerous obstruction upon a railway, road, street, waterway or public place or interferes with any machinery, signal, equipment or other device for the direction, control or regulation of traffic thereon, or interferes with or throws anything at or on any conveyance used or to be used thereon, and
>
> (b) is aware that injury to the person or damage to property may be caused thereby, or is reckless in that regard."

The maximum penalty is the same as for the general offence of endangerment, even though the *mens rea* is lesser: under section 14, a person need only be reckless as to the possibility of injury or damage to property, while under section 13 a person must be reckless as to the possibility of *serious* injury.

7.12 False imprisonment

Before 1997 there were two distinct offences related to restraints on personal liberty: kidnapping and false imprisonment. The offence of kidnapping was a common law offence, and was committed where a person was taken by force or fraud against his will. The offence of false imprisonment was also a common law offence, and was committed where the accused "unlawfully impose[d], for any time, a total restraint on the personal liberty of another". Both were declared to be felonies punishable by life imprisonment by section 11 of the Criminal Law Act 1976.

The 1997 Act amalgamates the two offences, reflecting what was happening in practice, with prosecutors relying on the charge of false imprisonment because of the ambiguity of the offence of kidnapping. (Charleton, *Offences Against the Person* (Round Hall Press, 1992), p. 244.) Section 15 therefore provides:

> "(1) A person shall be guilty of the offence of false imprisonment who intentionally or recklessly -
>
> (a) takes or detains, or
> (b) causes to be taken or detained, or
> (c) otherwise restricts the personal liberty of,
>
> another without that other's consent.
>
> (2) For the purposes of this section, a person acts without the consent of another if the person obtains the other's consent by force or threat of force, or by deception causing the other to believe that he or she is under legal compulsion to consent."

The provision regarding consent is important: consent is vitiated by force, but is only vitiated by fraud if this causes the victim to believe that there is a legal obligation to consent. It is pointed out by the Law Reform Commission that:

> "In other cases of deception, the victim is free to withdraw consent at any time without fear of force being used, so that his or her liberty cannot be said to be totally restrained."(*Report on Non-Fatal Offences Against the Person* (Dublin, 1994), page 319.)

As regards the restraint on personal liberty, it is clear that section 15 retains the common law position that a person can be falsely imprisoned without being aware of the fact: *Dullaghan v. Hillen and King* (1957). So a person can be falsely imprisoned although asleep, or mentally handicapped so as to be unable to appreciate the fact.

How severe must the restraint on personal liberty be to amount to false imprisonment? At common law, the imprisonment must be total: that is, a person must be confined within fixed bounds, so as to prevent movement in all directions. (However, those fixed bounds could be quite large: a room, a house, a country estate.) It did not take place where a person was walled in on three sides, but free to walk away through the third. However, a person was not required to take an unreasonable risk (for example, of personal injury) or to undergo some major humiliation to avoid an obstacle created by the defendant.

Section 15 at first glance appears to be wider in scope, in that it refers to "restricting personal liberty", which might be read to include situations where a person's freedom of movement was constrained in some directions, but not in others. However, the Law Reform Commission did not recommend such a radical change in the law, and it therefore seems that imprisonment must still be total: a mere obstruction in a person's path will not amount to false imprisonment. For the same reason, there is no false imprisonment where a person is under close surveillance which does not actually confine them. In *Kane v. Governor of Mountjoy Prison* (1988), the applicant was kept under extremely close Garda surveillance while a warrant for his extradition was pending. He alleged that he had in effect been detained by this surveillance. This argument was rejected by the Supreme Court: the surveillance had not interfered with his ability to go where he chose, which was the essence of detention.

7.13 Child abduction

The 1997 Act creates two distinct offences of child abduction. The first, contained in section 16, relates to the abduction of a child by a parent or guardian, who takes the child out of the State either in defiance of a court order or without court approval or the consent of each guardian of the child. It does not apply where the person is a parent, but is not a guardian. It is a defence that the person was unable to communicate with the other persons from whom consent is required but believed that they would consent; it is also a defence that the person did not intend to deprive others of their rights in relation to the child. The sensitivity of this offence is reflected in the fact that proceedings cannot be instituted without the consent of the D.P.P.

The second relates to abduction of children by other persons. Section 17 makes it an offence for a person other than one to whom section 16 applies (parents, guardians and persons having custody) to intentionally take or detain or cause to be taken or detained a child under the age of 16 so as to remove or keep the child from the lawful custody of another person having control of the child. This offence does not require that the child be taken out of the jurisdiction. Belief that the child is 16 or over is a defence. The consent of the child is irrelevant for both this offence and the offence under section 16: the offences are designed to protect parents as well as children, who will not be in a position to give an informed consent, particularly where the child is quite young.

7.14 Assault with intent to cause bodily harm or commit an indictable offence

This offence is created by section 18 of the Criminal Justice (Public Order) Act 1994, and is quite straightforward:

> "Any person who assaults any person with intent to cause bodily harm or to commit an indictable offence shall be guilty of an offence."

7.15 Blackmail, extortion, demanding money with menaces

Section 17(1) of the Criminal Justice (Public Order) Act 1994 creates the offence which can loosely be described as blackmail:

> "It shall be an offence for any person who, with a view to gain for himself or with intent to cause loss to another, makes any unwarranted demand with menaces."

Unwarranted demand is defined as follows by section 17(2)(a):

> "a demand with menaces shall be unwarranted unless the person making it does so in the belief -
>
> (i) that he has reasonable grounds for making the demand, and
> (ii) that the use of the menaces is a proper means of reinforcing the demand."

This is a two-stage test: for a defendant to escape liability he must believe that the demand is reasonable and that the menaces are reasonable. Threatening to publish nude photographs of a person could not be believed to be a proper way of reinforcing an otherwise legitimate demand for payment of a debt, for example.

In addition, section 17(2)(b) specifies that the nature of the act demanded is immaterial, as is whether the menaces relate to action to be taken by the person making the demand. In other words, it does not matter what is demanded, nor whether the defendant's threat relates to something to be done by him or by others.

The components of the offence are therefore threefold:

(i) an unwarranted demand;

(ii) with menaces; and

(iii) with a view to gain for the defendant, or to cause loss to another.

"Menaces" are not defined in the 1994 Act and therefore we must look to the case law on the previous offences of blackmail under sections 29-31 of the Larceny Act 1916. These cases originally defined menaces as threats of injury to the person or to property, but later cases gave menaces a wider meaning, with Lord Wright stating that:

> "the word menace is to be liberally construed, and not as limited to threats of violence but as including threats of any action detrimental to or unpleasant to the person addressed." (*Thorne v. Motor Trade Association* (1937))

In that case, the defendant was a trade association who demanded that a member pay a fine for breach of the rules of the association (selling at below an agreed price); failure to pay the fine would result in the member being boycotted by other members. It was held that this did not constitute the offence of demanding money with menaces without reasonable or probable cause (under the 1916 Act) since it did not go beyond the promotion of lawful business interests. However, the definition of menaces will encompass, for example, the threat of publication of details of a person's sexual life. So, in *R. v. Tomlinson* (1895) the victim was caught with a woman who was not his wife, and the defendant threatened to tell the world. This was held to come within the meaning of menaces, notwithstanding that neither the conduct of the victim nor the activity of the defendant in revealing this conduct would itself be illegal.

Further reading: Law Reform Commission, *The Law Relating to Dishonesty* (L.R.C. 43-1992), pp. 115-120, 297-307.

8. OFFENCES AGAINST PROPERTY

8.1 The statutory framework

The law governing offences against property is largely contained in the Larceny Acts 1916 to 1990. These create the offences of simple larceny, various forms of aggravated larceny, obtaining by false pretences, robbery, burglary, handling stolen property, and so on. However, it must be noted that the law in relation to property offences will be substantially changed in the near future by the Criminal Justice (Theft and Fraud Offences) Bill 2000, which proposes to completely reform this area. Accordingly, this chapter will consider first the law as it now stands and will then go on to consider the changes which the Bill will make.

8.2 Simple larceny and elements common to other offences

Simple larceny is governed by section 2 of the 1916 Act:

> "Stealing for which no special punishment is provided [under any other provision] shall be simple larceny"

It should be noted that section 2 does not create the offence of simple larceny, but merely specifies the punishment for larceny contrary to common law: *State (Simmonds) v. Governor of Portlaoise Prison* (1968); *State (Foley) v. Carroll* (1980).

What is "stealing"? This word is key to the entire scheme of the legislation, and is defined in section 1 as follows:

> "A person steals who, without the consent of the owner, fraudulently and without a claim of right made in good faith, takes and carries away anything capable of being stolen with intent, at the time of such taking, permanently to deprive the owner thereof."

Section 1 goes on to define "takes" as including the obtaining of possession (not ownership):

(a) by any trick;

(b) by intimidation;

(c) under a mistake on the part of the owner, with knowledge on the part of the taker that possession has been so obtained; or

(d) by finding, where at the time of the finding the finder believes that the owner can be discovered by taking reasonable steps.

These two definitions are crucial for understanding the statutory scheme, and must be broken down into their individual parts:

(i) "Without the consent of the owner". A taking is not stealing if the owner consents to it. However, an apparent consent will not be valid if obtained by a trick, intimidation, or if it is the result of a mistake on the part of the owner. However, larceny by a trick must be distinguished from obtaining by false pretences. If the owner parts with possession only, the relevant offence is larceny by a trick. If the owner parts with both possession and ownership, the relevant offence is obtaining by false pretences.

It will be clear when consent results from intimidation. When might consent result from a mistake? The textbook example is where a shopper pays for goods with a five pound note and is given change from a ten pound note. In these circumstances, the shopkeeper consents to the shopper taking the excess change, but his consent is invalid if the shopper knows of the mistake.

(ii) "Fraudulently and without a claim of right made in good faith". This element relates to the *mens rea* of the crime. The taking must be dishonest or immoral. The test is subjective - "made in good faith" - and the jury must assess whether the defendant acted in a way which he subjectively believed to be honest. In *People (DPP) v. O'Loughlin* (1979), the defendant was a farmer who took some machinery from a neighbour's yard. His defence was that he believed he was entitled to do so since the neighbour had refused to repay money which he owed to the defendant. The trial judge refused to allow this defence to go before the jury, since the farmer had no legal right to engage in this sort of "self-help" remedy. On appeal, the farmer's conviction was quashed by the Court of Criminal Appeal. *Per* O'Higgins C.J.:

> "the question which should have been considered was not whether the claim put forward was one known to the law but whether it was one in which the accused believed honestly and whether, with that honest belief, what he did could be excused.".

In short, the issue is not whether the defendant had a right to do what he did, but whether he honestly believed he had such a right. If so, the defendant will not be guilty of stealing. Similar is the case of *People*

(AG) v. Grey (1944), where the defendant took batteries belonging to his employer in what he believed to be a lawful substitution for his contractual entitlement to free fuel.

(iii) "Takes and carries away". Section 1 defines "carries away" further, to include "any removal of anything from the place which it occupies". It is not enough to lay one's hands on the goods with a view to taking them. However, it will be enough to move the goods even slightly from their original location. In *R. v. Taylor* (1911), the accused put his hand in the victim's pocket and attempted to remove his purse, but failed to do so when it became stuck on the victim's belt. It was held that even this slight degree of movement was enough to constitute a taking and carrying away for the purposes of larceny.

When does a "taking" occur? In *R. v. Ashwell* (1885), the English Court for Crown Cases Reserved took the view that a taking occurred only where the person doing the taking was aware of what he had got. In that case, the accused had been loaned a sovereign rather than a shilling by accident. He did not notice at the time, subsequently discovered the mistake and held on to the money. Whether he was guilty of larceny clearly depended on when the taking took place. Common sense would suggest that it took place when the money was handed over, in which case the intention did not coincide with the taking. However, the court held that a taking took place only when the accused became aware of what he had: he

> "did not take it till he knew what he had got; and when he knew what he had got, that same instant he stole it." (*Per* Lord Coleridge C.J.).

However, this view has been rejected in Ireland in *R. v. Hehir* (1895). The facts were essentially the same (a ten pound note mistaken by both for a one pound note). However, the Irish Court for Crown Cases Reserved took a different and more pragmatic view, holding that possession passed to the defendant once the note reached him. Although he had to be aware of its existence, he did not have to be aware of its qualities. If my friend gives me what we both believe to be a raspberry, I have taken it and possess it notwithstanding that I subsequently discover that it is in fact a strawberry.

(iv) "Anything capable of being stolen". At common law not everything was capable of being stolen. Anything which was intangible (for example, electricity), immovable (for example, real property) or not capable of being the property of any person (for example, abandoned articles, wild animals, dead bodies) could not form the basis of a charge of larceny. This element of the statutory definition recognises this common law rule. Note that the fraudulent abstraction of electricity is specifically dealt with by section 10 of the 1916 Act. Note also that some things which are not capable of being the property of any person can become the property of a person when reduced into possession. For example, a landowner cannot have any property in the wild animals on his land. But once he kills or captures those animals, they become his property and therefore capable of being stolen. A similar result takes place where a person finds and keeps an abandoned article.

(v) "With intent, at the time of such taking, permanently to deprive the owner thereof". This is one of the single most important elements of the definition, and has two distinct effects. The first is that there must be an intention *permanently to deprive the owner* of the article taken. The joyrider who goes for a spin in a car which he intends to return is not guilty of larceny. So, in *R. v. Phillips and Strong* (1801), the accused were not guilty of larceny having ridden off on two horses which they left at some distance, on the finding that they did not intend to make any further use of the horses. However, it is not necessary that the defendant should himself hold on to or benefit from the article stolen: it is enough that they intend that it should not return to the victim. An article is stolen even where the defendant intends to destroy it rather than retain it.

The second effect of this definition is that *the intention is gauged at the time of such taking.* In other words, an honest taking followed by a subsequent intention to deprive the owner of the article will not amount to larceny. In *R. v. Leigh* (1800), the defendant rescued goods from a burning shop. She subsequently decided to hold on to the goods. Her intention at the time of the taking was, therefore, not the intention required for larceny. Since the *actus reus* - the taking - and the *mens rea* - the intention to deprive - did not coincide, the defendant was held not to be guilty of larceny. Larceny is not, therefore, a continuing act in the sense laid down in *Fagan v. Metropolitan Police Commissioner* (1968).

This definition ties in with the earlier definition of taking under a mistake on the part of the owner. We saw that this constitutes a "taking" only if the taker has knowledge of the mistake. In addition, for larceny to take place, the taker must have this knowledge at the time of the taking. Suppose I pay for goods with a five pound note and receive change for a ten pound note. If I notice this mistake at the time but stay silent, I commit larceny. If, however, I notice the mistake on my way home and decide to keep the excess, then larceny is not committed: the intention to permanently deprive did not coincide with the taking: *R. v. Hehir* (1895).

However, one technical exception to this point should be noted. If the initial possession is lawful, a subsequent intention does not make it a felony. But if the initial possession is wrongful - a trespass to the owner's property - then a subsequent intention will relate back to the original taking to comprise the crime of larceny. In *Ruse v. Read* (1949), the defendant took a bicycle at a time when he was too drunk to be able to form the *mens rea* for larceny. On sobering up, he formed the intention of permanently depriving the owner. It was held that he was guilty of larceny, even though he did not have the necessary intention at the time of the taking, since the initial taking was a trespass to the property of the owner.

Similarly, in *R. v. Riley* (1853), the defendant took (as he thought) his flock of 29 lambs from another's field. He subsequently discovered that he had also taken one lamb belonging to the owner of the field, but decided to go ahead and sell it. Again, the defendant was found guilty of larceny. His initial taking was wrongful (that is, a trespass to the owners property even though innocent) and it was therefore enough that the necessary intention was formed later.

It therefore seems that the joyrider who later decides to hold on to the car which he initially "borrowed" is guilty of larceny. This result has, however, been criticised by commentators:

> "[T]hat would be to extend artificially the act of taking which in reality occupies only an instant. The joyrider takes the car when he acquires possession by entering it; it could hardly be said that the taking is still in progress two and a half hours (and a police car chase) later." (McCutcheon, *The Larceny Act 1916* (Dublin, 1992), p.11.)

8.3 Larceny by a trick

This is not a distinct form of aggravated larceny, along the lines of larceny in a dwelling house, or larceny from the person. Instead, it is a particular method of committing the basic crime of larceny. (For that reason, it can form part of a distinct form of aggravated larceny: you could, for example, commit larceny in a dwelling house by a trick.)

Section 1(2)(i) of the 1916 Act provides that "takes" includes the obtaining of possession by any trick. The requirement in section 1(1) that the taking be without the owner's consent still applies. But in the case of larceny by a trick, there will be an apparent consent, which is undermined by the fact that it is obtained by a trick.

One crucial distinction drawn by the courts relates to the nature of the consent which is obtained. If the apparent consent relates to the passing of *property* (that is, ownership) in the goods, then the appropriate charge is one of obtaining property by false pretences contrary to section 32 of the 1916 Act. However, if the apparent consent relates to the passing of *possession* only, then the appropriate charge is one of larceny by a trick.

This distinction can be seen in an example. If A induces B to *sell* him a car by representing that B owes him money equivalent to the value of the car, then B intends property in the car to pass, and the appropriate charge is obtaining by false pretences. Suppose, however, that A induces B to *rent* a car to him by representing that B owes him money equal to the amount of rental. If A now sells the car, the appropriate charge is larceny: B intended to part with possession of the car, but not with property in it.

8.4 Larceny by intimidation

Just like larceny by a trick, this is a particular *means* of committing larceny rather than a distinct form of larceny. Section 2(1)(b) provides that the term "takes" includes cases where possession is obtained by intimidation; and clearly in those cases any apparent consent is undermined by virtue of that intimidation. An example is the case of *R. v. McGrath* (1869), where the victim was present at a mock auction. The defendant alleged that she bid for a particular item, and told her that she would not be allowed leave until she paid for it. She did so. The defendant was held on those facts to be guilty of larceny by intimidation. Most forms of intimidation will involve the use or threatened use of force, and will therefore overlap with the crimes of assault and robbery.

8.5 Larceny by mistake

This again is not itself a distinct form of larceny, but merely a particular way of committing it. Section 1 provides that "takes" includes the obtaining of possession "under a mistake on the part of the owner with knowledge on the part of the taker that possession has been so obtained". This gives statutory effect to the decision in *R. v. Middleton* (1873), where the defendant sought to withdraw money from his post-office account but was, by mistake, given a larger sum. Noticing the mistake at the time, he pocketed the sum and left. The defendant was found guilty of larceny. However, the knowledge must, as we have already noted, coincide with the time of the taking: if the defendant in *R. v. Middleton* (1873), had only subsequently discovered the mistake and then decided to keep the excess, then larceny would not have been committed.

8.6 Larceny by finding

Again, this is not a distinct form of larceny. It takes place where a finder is, at the time of finding either aware of the identity of the true owner or believes that the true owner could be found by reasonable steps. The state of mind at the time of the finding is crucial: as with all forms of larceny, a *subsequent* intention to permanently deprive will not render an initially innocent taking criminal.

8.7 Larceny by a bailee or part-owner

At common law, a bailee or part-owner of an item could not be guilty of larceny of that item, inasmuch as he had lawful possession of the item. Section 1 of the 1916 Act does away with this position:

> "Provided that a person may be guilty of stealing any such thing notwithstanding that he has lawful possession thereof, if, being a bailee or part owner thereof, he fraudulently converts the same to his own use or the use of any other person."

This is one of the few occasions where a person can be convicted of larceny on the basis of an intention formed after possession has been obtained. Fraudulent conversion does not equate to a "taking" - a person may fraudulently convert goods without moving them, as in *Roger v. Arnott* (1960), where the accused was found to have fraudulently converted goods held by him on bailment by offering them for sale contrary to the terms of the bailment. A fraudulent conversion, therefore, takes place wherever a bailee conducts himself in such a way as to show his intention to deprive the owner of his rights in relation to the goods. This offence should not be confused with fraudulent conversion contrary to section 32 of the 1916 Act.

8.8 Larceny from the person

This offence is created by section 14 of the 1916 Act which criminalises "any person who steals ... from the person of another". There are two elements to this offence: stealing within the meaning of section 1, and doing so from the person of another. For a theft to be "from the person of another" there must be a complete removal of the articles from the person. So, in *People (AG) v. Mills* (1955), it was held by the Court of Criminal Appeal that the offence of larceny from the person was established where a purse was removed entirely from a handbag, but would not be established if the thief had not succeeded in removing the purse. (Contrast *R. v. Taylor* (1911), where an attempt to remove a man's purse which stuck on his belt constituted simple larceny but not larceny from the person.) This offence overlaps with assault.

8.9 Larceny in a dwelling house

Section 13 of the 1916 Act creates the offence of larceny in a dwelling house: any person who "steals in any dwelling house ... shall - (a) if the value of the property stolen amounts to five pounds; or (b) if he by any menace or threat puts any person being in such dwelling house in bodily fear" be guilty of an offence. This offence overlaps with assault, burglary and robbery.

8.10 Larceny and embezzlement by clerks or servants

These offences are created by section 17 of the 1916 Act:

> "Every person who -
>
> (1) Being a clerk or servant employed in the capacity of a clerk or servant -
>> (a) steals any chattel, money or valuable security belonging to or in the possession or power of his master or employer; or
>> (b) fraudulently embezzles the whole or any part of any chattel, money or valuable security delivered to or received or taken into possession by him for or in the name or on the account of his master or employer;
>
> [commits an offence]".

The penalty for this offence is higher than the penalty for simple larceny to reflect the greater breach of trust involved in dishonesty by an employee, as well as to deter those who have greater opportunity for theft, access to property, and so on. The section creates two distinct offences: larceny by a servant and embezzlement by a servant. The case of larceny by a servant is generally straightforward, being simple larceny plus aggravating factors.

However, consider the situation where a servant receives money to be passed on to his employer, but instead decides to hold on to it. Would that servant be guilty of larceny? No. We must ask from whom the money could have been stolen. It was not stolen from the person paying it, who consented to the money being taken by the servant. (Although in some cases there could be an issue as to whether larceny by a trick, larceny by mistake, or obtaining by false pretences had been committed.) It was not stolen from the master, since the money at all times was in the possession of the servant. (And there could, therefore, be no "taking".) The servant could not therefore, be guilty of larceny. This point was established at common law by the case of *R. v. Bazely* (1799), a case where a bank clerk accepted a lodgement from a customer and pocketed it.

The legislative response was what is now section 17(1)(b) of the 1916 Act governing embezzlement. This in essence criminalises an employee's appropriation to himself of any item received by him on behalf of his employer. We can see the difference between larceny by an employee and embezzlement by an employee if we consider the case of a person working in a bank. If he receives money from a customer but pockets it, then the money was never in the possession of his employer, and the appropriate charge is embezzlement. If he receives the same money, lodges it into the cash drawer, and at the end of the day retrieves it from the cash drawer and walks off, then the money passed into the possession of the employer at the point when he placed it in the cash drawer, and the appropriate charge is larceny.

In practice, it can be difficult to tell which charge is appropriate, if the circumstances are such that it is unclear whether the property passed into the possession of the employer or the employee. In *R. v. Murray* (1830), for example, the defendant was given money by another employee, with instructions as to how to use it. He pocketed the money. It was held that he was guilty of larceny rather than embezzlement, since the money had remained in the (constructive) possession of the employer throughout. Compare *R. v. Masters* (1848), where the defendant was given money by another employee, who had been given the money by a third party to give to the employer. In that case, a charge of embezzlement was held to be appropriate. Because of this ambiguous boundary between the two offences, section 44(2) allows for the substitution of verdicts depending on which offence the jury finds to be appropriate. The distinction between the two offences is therefore of little importance at a practical level.

Note that embezzlement must be "fraudulent". This has been held to import the defence of a claim of right made in good faith from larceny into embezzlement: an employee will not be guilty of embezzlement where the conduct complained of is done in pursuance of a claim of right made in good faith. *People (AG) v. Grey* (1944), which has already been dealt with, is on point: although that case related not to embezzlement but to fraudulent conversion, it was held generally that the meaning of "fraudulent" required either dishonesty or some other moral wrong, and did not encompass situations where an accused honestly believed he had a legal right to do what he did.

8.10.1 What is a clerk or servant?

For an offence under section 17 to be committed, the defendant must be a "clerk or servant": that is, an employee. If the defendant, although working for another, was an officer, agent or independent contractor, then the appropriate charge is one of fraudulent conversion contrary to section 20.

How do we tell if a person is a clerk or servant? In modern terminology, the question is whether the defendant is employed by the victim under a contract of service rather than a contract for services. In making this determination, the trend in modern cases is to use a mixed test, which considers a number of factors including: the label which the parties put on the relationship, the extent to which the "employer" controls how the "employee" performs his duties, the extent to which the "employee" can be said to be in business on his own behalf, and whether the "employee" is on a fixed remuneration, or has the possibility of making a greater or lesser profit.

An example is the case of *Ready Mixed Concrete Ltd v. Minister for Pensions* (1968) in which truck drivers who owned their own trucks but had to wear company clothes, bear company logos on their trucks, and work the routes specified by the company were held to be self-employed, largely on the basis that by owning their own trucks they were in business on their own behalf, despite their lack of control over their daily activities.

8.11 Situations where conduct constitutes a number of offences

Suppose a pickpocket runs off with a purse from a woman's handbag. His conduct constitutes simple larceny together with the aggravating factor which makes up larceny from the person. He can, therefore, be charged with two different offences: simple larceny and larceny from the person. Does he have any right to be charged with the more particular offence? In *State (Foley) v. Carroll* (1980), this issue was presented. The applicant was convicted of simple larceny on facts (theft of plastic sheeting from his place of work) which would also have constituted larceny by a servant. He contended that, in those circumstances, he could not be convicted of simple larceny under section 2 of the 1916 Act since section 2 referred to "stealing for which no special punishment is provided". Section 17, he contended, provided for special punishment for larceny by employees, and therefore a charge under section 2 could not be brought.

This argument was rejected by the High Court. First, it was held that section 17 and section 2 were entirely distinct offences, and a charge under section 2 could be brought even though the same conduct might amount to an offence under section 17. Second, it would lead to absurd results if a person had to be charged with the most specific offence available on the facts:

> "If such were the case then a person charged with simple larceny could avoid conviction by establishing that the offence was aggravated by being accompanied by force, or carried out by use of a threat or whilst armed with an offensive weapon." (*Per* Finlay P. at p. 154.)

This principle applies generally throughout the criminal law: if conduct amounts to a number of different offences, the accused has no right to be charged with any particular offence. It is entirely legitimate for a less serious offence to be charged, and this will often happen if, for example, there is a possibility that there will be a difficulty with the proofs for the more serious offence.

8.12 Obtaining by false pretences

This offence is created by section 32 of the 1916 Act:

> "Every person who by any false pretence -
>
> (1) with intent to defraud, obtains from any other person any chattel, money, or valuable security, or causes or procures any money to be paid, or any chattel or valuable security to be delivered to himself

or to any other person for the use or benefit or on account of himself or any other person ...

[shall be guilty of an offence]".

The offence can be broken down into three parts: a false representation, an intention to defraud, and a consequent parting with property on the part of the owner. Each of these elements has important subtleties.

8.12.1 False pretence

The representation which is made must be one of fact rather than opinion. A mere "sales puff" is not a sufficient representation. In *R v. Bryan* (1857), for example, the defendant had stated to a pawnbroker that spoons made by him were of the very best quality, and were equivalent in quality to those made by a prominent manufacturer. They were not. It was held that a representation of this sort could not amount to a false pretence. *Per* Pollock C.B.:

> "I think it may fairly be laid down that any exaggeration or depreciation in the ordinary course of dealings between buyer and seller during the progress of a bargain is not the subject of a criminal prosecution."

However, if the representation as to the quality of goods relates to a specific fact, then this will suffice. In *R. v. Ardley* (1871), the accused represented to a shopkeeper that a gold chain was 15-carat gold, when in fact he knew it to be only 6-carat gold. On these facts, the accused was convicted, since his representation was not a vague statement of quality but a statement as to a particular fact which could be expected to be within his knowledge.

The false pretence must also relate to present fact rather than future fact or future conduct. This rule, it seems, has its origins in the fear that otherwise any person who committed a breach of contract might be thus exposed to criminal prosecution. This point was made in the main case in the area: *R. v. Dent* (1955). In that case, the accused was a pest destructor, who agreed with farmers to carry out work on their farms. He obtained payment in advance, and simply failed to carry out the work. The alleged false pretences were that he *bona fide* intended to perform the contracts, and that he would be able and willing to do so. However, these representations were held not to fall within the meaning of false pretences. The prosecution argued that they related to present fact: the intention of the accused at the time of entering into the contracts, even though this intention itself related to future conduct. This was rejected by the English Court of Criminal Appeal. *Per* Devlin J.:

"a statement of intention about future conduct, whether or not it be a statement of existing fact, is not such a statement as will amount to a false pretence in criminal law." (At p. 595.)

Having said that, the court went on to note two important qualifications. The first is that a promise as to future conduct may include a false representation of existing fact, and the latter may amount to the necessary false pretence. The court referred to *R. v. Jennison* (1862) as an example. In that case a man obtained money from a woman by stating that he was an unmarried man and that he intended to marry her. He was convicted not on the basis of his expressed intention to marry (which related to future conduct) but on the basis of his statement that he was unmarried (which was an untrue statement of present fact).

Consequently, if a person represents that he is in business as a pest destructor, and that he intends to carry out a contract, then the latter representation cannot form the basis of a charge, but the former might, if the person in fact does not carry out that business.

The second qualification noted was that some statements of present fact shade into representations of future conduct:

"It is clear from the authorities that the law does not seek to divide the future meticulously from the present. If a man says: 'If you give me the goods now, I will hand over £10,' while as a matter of chronology payment follows after delivery, as a matter of business it is all one transaction." (*Per* Devlin J. at p. 597.)

In some cases, therefore, the statement might in form relate to future conduct but in substance relate to present fact. A statement that I will publish a directory next month carries with it the implicit representation that preparations for it are well advanced: if they are not, then a prosecution may properly be brought.

It should also be noted that, more generally, the representation which is alleged to constitute a false pretence need not be express but may be implied or tacit. The classic example is the case of *R. v. Barnard* (1837), where the accused went into an Oxford shop wearing a cap and gown: this was held to amount to a false representation that he was a member of the University, notwithstanding that he said nothing to that effect.

To similar effect is *People (AG) v. Finkel and Levine* (1951). In that case, the defendants sold dollars to another, which turned out to be counterfeit. The false pretence alleged was that the dollars were genuine. The defendants had not made any statement to that effect. The defendants were convicted. One of the grounds of appeal was that, absent any such statement, neither could be said to have made any false pretence. This was, however, rejected by the Court of Criminal Appeal:

> "It is quite true that there is no evidence of any statement being made ... that the dollar bills were genuine. There is, however, evidence that both accused [told the victim] the price of the dollars [was above the normal exchange rate]. [Since exchange controls were in place, the transaction itself was on the black market.] The jury were quite entitled to conclude that no-one in their senses would either agree to pay or expect to receive full face value and more for counterfeit money, and it seems to the Court that there was quite sufficient evidence from which the jury could conclude that the accused by their conduct, if not in so many words, represented that the bills were genuine ... A person who, without making verbal representation, presents a counterfeit coin or bank note and requests and obtains change quite clearly represents the note to be genuine and is guilty of obtaining the change by false pretences ..." (*Per* Maguire C.J., at p. 128.)

8.12.2 Intention to defraud

This requirement again echoes the requirement for larceny that the accused not act with a claim of right made in good faith. In short, an accused will not be deemed to have an intention to defraud simply because he knows his representation to be false. Of course, if the accused knows his representation to be false, then this *prima facie* establishes intent (*People (AG) v. Thompson* (1960) per Walsh J.):

> "Generally speaking it may be said that where money is obtained by false pretences there is a *prima facie* case of an intent to defraud."

However, there may well be circumstances where this *prima facie* intent can be rebutted by the defendant, and "[t]he ultimate question is whether the accused intended to defraud and not merely whether he knew that the representation was false." (McCutcheon, *The Larceny Act 1916* (Dublin, 1992), p. 109). A relatively clear-cut case is that of *R v. Williams* (1836). The accused in that case was a servant who obtained goods from another by a false pretence, intending that his master should hold onto the goods to secure payment of a debt which the master was owed. It was held that this was not an intention to defraud, being analogous to a "claim of right, made in good faith".

More difficult are the "cheque" cases: cases in which the defendant pays for goods by way of a cheque drawn on an empty account, but where the defendant claims to have believed that the account would be in funds by the time that the cheque was presented. *People (AG) v. Thompson* (1960) is an example. In that case, the accused opened a bank account (with £10) in a false name, and was given a cheque book. Later that day, he bought a car with a post-dated cheque for £135. He then re-sold the car, himself taking a cheque, which he lodged to the account in the false name. However, the second cheque was stopped and the account was not therefore in funds to meet the first cheque. The false pretence alleged was that the accused represented that he had authority to draw a cheque for £135, which clearly he did not.

The defence put forward was that the transaction had been "an honest attempt to do honest business and it went wrong": the defendant submitted that when he purchased the car he had no doubt that he would be able to sell it on in time to cover the cheque with which he had paid for it. In particular, the defendant pointed out that he had lodged the second cheque to his account rather than simply cashing it and making away with the proceeds.

The defendant was convicted and, on appeal to the Court of Criminal Appeal, his conviction quashed. The trial judge had directed the jury in terms that suggested that, if the defendant knew that he did not have authority to draw a cheque for £135, then this was sufficient to establish an intent to defraud. It was held that this direction was incorrect. The drawing of the cheque did carry with it a false pretence — that the accused had authority to draw a cheque for that sum. However, if, at the time of the drawing of the cheque, the accused honestly believed that it would be met, then the necessary intent to defraud was not present.

The case of *People (DPP) v. Shanahan* (1978) involved very similar facts (purchase of tractors by post-dated cheque; inadequate funds in account; another cheque lodged to account which would, if honoured, have covered the post-dated cheque). It was held by the Court of Criminal Appeal that in cases of this sort the onus remains on the prosecution at all times to establish that at the time of the issuing of the cheque the accused was aware that it was not likely to be met. However, in this case the accused was aware of the absence of funds and subsequently actively tried to conceal the reason why the cheque was not met, and on that basis there was a *prima facie* case of fraudulent intent which could be put to the jury.

8.12.3 Consequent parting with property on the part of the owner

Obtaining by false pretences means just that: it does not mean retaining by false pretences. In *People (AG) v. Singer* (1961), the accused had been given money, and as a result of representations made by him, was directed to retain that money for re-investment. It was held by the Court of Criminal Appeal that the offence of obtaining by false pretences could not be stretched to include a case of retention. (*Per* Ó Dálaigh J. at pages 230-231.)

For the offence of obtaining by false pretences to be established, there must be proof of causation: the owner must part with property as a result of the false pretence alleged. It would be a good defence to show, for example, that the owner did not believe the representation but parted with the property regardless. Suppose I sell a piece of antique furniture and state that it is a Chippendale. Suppose further that the buyer does not believe this, but buys anyway, feeling that the piece is a good purchase regardless. In those circumstances, the offence has not been committed. There is a false pretence, there is an obtaining of money, but there is no causation of the latter by the former.

So, in *R. v. Sullivan* (1945). the defendant was charged with obtaining money by false pretences, by advertising that he was a dartboard maker and would provide dartboards, when he was not and had no intention of supplying dartboards. However, none of his victims had been asked in so many words why they parted with their money. The defendant claimed that without their evidence as to the effect of his advertisement, he could not properly be convicted.

This contention was rejected by the English Court of Criminal Appeal. It was accepted that the prosecution must show that the victims parted with their property as a result of the false pretence and not for any other reason. It would be desirable if this could be done by having the victims testify that "I believed that statement and that is why I parted with my money". Nevertheless, in this case the victims did not need to do so. They were all strangers to the defendant; they saw the advertisement; shortly afterwards they sent their money to the defendant. What other reason could there be for their parting with their property, other than the representation made by the defendant?

Of course, in cases which are not so straightforward, it will be necessary to have the victims testify as to the effect which the representation had on them, if only to negative the possibility that they might have parted with the property for some other reason.

Finally, it must be noted that for the offence of obtaining by false pretences to be established, the prosecution must show that the owner of the property intended to pass both possession of and title to the property in question. If I pretend to be a cloakroom attendant, take in a coat and make off with it, this is not an offence under section 32: the owner did not intend to part with title to the coat, merely possession.

The appropriate offence would be larceny by a trick. The reverse result is reached if I pretend to be the true owner of goods held by someone else: this is not larceny by a trick, since the person parting with the goods intends to part with title to them, and so the appropriate offence is obtaining by false pretences. Section 44 of the 1916 Act, therefore, enables a verdict of obtaining by false pretences to be returned if a person is charged with larceny, and *vice versa*. The fact that the prosecution might have chosen the wrong charge is, therefore, no longer critically important.

8.13 Handling stolen property

This offence has been comprehensively overhauled by the Larceny Act 1990 after the recommendations made by the Law Reform Commission in its *Report on Receiving Stolen Property* (L.R.C. 23 - 1987). The offence was formerly contained in section 33 of the Larceny Act 1916, but section 3 of the 1990 Act substitutes the following section in place of section 33:

"(1) A person who handles stolen property knowing or believing it to be stolen property shall be guilty of an offence ...

(2) For the purposes of this Act-

(a) a person handles stolen property if (otherwise than in the course of the stealing), knowing or believing it to be stolen property, he dishonestly -
    (i)   receives the property, or
    (ii) undertakes or assists in its retention, removal, disposal or realisation by or for the benefit of another person, or
    (iii) arranges to do [(i) or (ii)];

(b) where a person -
    (i)   receives stolen property, or
    (ii) undertakes or assists in its retention, removal, disposal or realisation by or for the benefit of another person, or
    (iii) arranges to do [(i) or (ii)],
    in such circumstances that it is reasonable to conclude that he knew or believed the property to be stolen property, he shall be taken to have so known or believed unless the court or the jury, as the case may be, is satisfied having regard to all the evidence that there is a reasonable doubt as to whether he so knew or believed; and

(c) believing property to be stolen property includes thinking that such property was probably stolen property.".

This new section was introduced to deal with difficulties which had manifested themselves with regard to the old section 33. In particular, under the previous law, an offence was not committed unless the defendant *knew* that the goods in question were stolen: suspicion or belief were not enough. Equally problematic was the fact that the accused had to take possession of stolen property; other degrees of involvement were not specifically criminalised. Similarly, it appeared that the offence did not include receiving the proceeds of the theft (*AG v. Farnan* (1933)). The new section deals with these difficulties by expanding both the *actus reus* and the *mens rea* of the crime.

8.13.1 Mens rea

The Law Reform Commission had recommended (*Receiving Stolen Property* (L.R.C. 23 - 1987)) that the mental element of the offence should be extended so that a person would be guilty who knowingly or recklessly dealt with stolen property. However, this approach was rejected in the 1990 Act which opted for "knowing or believing" property to be stolen (section 3(1)). "Believing" is then further defined to include "thinking that such property was probably stolen property" (section 3(2)(c)). Finally, section 3(2)(b) introduces an objective element to the test of *mens rea* by providing that a person shall be presumed to know or believe that property is stolen if the circumstances are such that it is reasonable to so conclude, unless the evidence raises a reasonable doubt. In short, a jury may infer knowledge/belief from the surrounding circumstances, and to that extent section 3(2)(b) merely formalises what was already the position.

8.14 Stolen property

Before the offence can be committed, the property in question must be stolen. Stolen property is given an extremely wide definition by section 7, and includes property which has been stolen, embezzled, fraudulently converted, or obtained by false pretences. In addition, the definition of stolen property now includes any property which directly or indirectly, in whole or in part, represents:

• the stolen property in the hands of the thief, being the proceeds of a disposal of the stolen property, or of the disposal of the proceeds; or

• the stolen property in the hands of a handler, being the proceeds of a disposal of the stolen property, or of the disposal of the proceeds.

In summary, stolen property includes the proceeds of the disposal of stolen property, regardless of whether converted by a thief or by a handler. The taint of the original theft attaches to the proceeds. This taint is only lost when an item is acquired innocently, at which point it is no longer in the hands of either a thief or a handler. An example of this definition in action is the following:

> "A steals a car which he sells to B, who knows of its origin, for £1000. B sells the car to C for £1500. A purchases a video recorder from D with £100 of the money he obtained from B. Here B is guilty of handling the car, the original stolen property. C is guilty of handling the car if he is aware of its provenance. The £1000 paid by B to A is 'stolen' as it represents stolen property in the hands of the thief. Thus, the £100 he paid to D is also stolen, it being part of the 'property so representing the stolen property.' D's liability will depend on whether he possessed the requisite mens rea in respect of the money." (McCutcheon, *Irish Current Law Statutes Annotated*, 90/9-15).

Under section 7, property ceases to be stolen once it passes into the hands of its owner or other lawful possession, or the owner has lost any right to restitution in respect of the property, which will be the case if, for example, a *bona fide* purchaser for value without notice acquires property under a voidable contract. The significance of this is that once property ceases to be stolen, it can no longer form the subject matter of a handling charge; if the police recover stolen goods but allow another to proceed with handling them for the purposes of entrapment, that other cannot be guilty of handling.

8.14.1 Stolen by someone else

Section 33(2) contains the important words "otherwise than in the course of the stealing", the effect of which is that a thief does not commit the offence of handling stolen goods simply by virtue of his having stolen them. This is a re-enactment of the pre-1990 law on this point, and has the effect that the prosecution must establish beyond a reasonable doubt not merely that the goods were stolen, but that they were stolen by someone else. An example is the case of *People (AG) v. Carney and Mulcahy* (1955). In that case, the two defendants were charged with larceny and receiving stolen goods. They were acquitted on the charge of larceny, but convicted of receiving. They appealed on, *inter alia*, the ground that it had not been demonstrated that they themselves had not stolen the goods. This was rejected by the Supreme Court, which accepted that it is an essential element of the crime that the goods in question should have been stolen by someone else, and that the prosecution must prove this element beyond reasonable doubt; however, the jury had been clear that the two charges were mutually exclusive, and that if the defendants had stolen the goods they could not also be found guilty of receiving.

This judgment has since been applied in *People (AG) v. Byrne* (1966), which held that it was inconsistent for the jury to find the accused guilty of both larceny and receiving of the same goods; in those circumstances, both verdicts must be quashed.

8.14.2 Definition of handling

What conduct will amount to handling? The wide scope of the *actus reus* is demonstrated by the fact that 34 different permutations of receiving, undertaking, and assisting are possible (McCutcheon, *Irish Current Law Statutes Annotated*, 90/9-07). Receiving is a term carried over from the 1916 Act and is therefore well defined by case law. For receiving to take place, the property in question must be in the possession of the accused at some point. Temporary possession is sufficient. Possession need not be actual — constructive possession will also suffice. It follows that a person who does not himself possess stolen property is nevertheless in receipt of that property if it is in the hands of a person over whom he has control, as was the case in *People (AG) v. Lawless* (1968).

The next category of handling is undertaking or assisting in retention, removal, disposal or realisation of stolen property, by or for the benefit of another person. This may be committed in two ways, first by undertaking to do something for the benefit of another, second, by assisting another to retain, remove, etc. The significance of this point is demonstrated by *R. v. Bloxham* (1983), which demonstrates a gap in the law.

In that case, the accused had innocently purchased a stolen car, and, having discovered that it was stolen, sold it. He was charged with handling stolen property within the meaning of the very similar definition in English law, in that he had dishonestly undertaken or assisted in the disposal of the car by or for the benefit of the purchaser. It was held by the House of Lords that, on those facts, the defendant could not be guilty of handling stolen goods. His initial purchase of the car was innocent, and could not, therefore, amount to receiving stolen goods. Could his subsequent sale amount to undertaking or assisting in its retention, removal, disposal or realisation by or for the benefit of another person? No. He was not assisting the purchaser to retain, etc. the car, nor could the sale of the car be said to be for the benefit of the purchaser rather than the vendor.

8.14.3 Doctrine of recent possession

If a person is in possession of goods shortly after those goods were stolen, what inferences can be drawn from that fact? This is the so-called doctrine of recent possession, which was considered by the Court of Criminal Appeal in *People (AG) v. Oglesby* (1966). The accused was found in possession of a tape recorder which had been stolen some ten days before. He informed the Guards that he had bought it "from a man in a pub". The trial judge directed the jury on the burden of proof, and went on to add that if they rejected his explanation they were entitled to convict.

On appeal, it was held by the Court of Criminal Appeal that the directions were unsatisfactory and that the so-called doctrine of recent possession was merely a convenient shorthand label for inferences which may be drawn as a matter of common sense; the "doctrine" did not have the effect of shifting onto the accused the burden of proof once recent possession had been established. At all times the burden of proof remained on the prosecution to prove beyond reasonable doubt that the accused knew the goods to have been stolen. The jury could not, therefore, be directed that they were entitled to convict if they disbelieved the story of the accused; the ultimate question is always whether the prosecution has proved each element of its case beyond reasonable doubt.

8.15 Robbery

The offence of robbery is created by section 23 of the 1916 Act, as replaced by section 5 of the Criminal Law (Jurisdiction) Act 1976:

> "A person is guilty of robbery if he steals, and immediately before or at the time of doing so, and in order to do so, he uses force on any person or puts or seeks to put any person in fear of being then and there subjected to force."

This offence is essentially larceny coupled with a modified form of assault, and therefore certain elements of both offences must be established. So, for example, if the defendant did not steal within the meaning of section 1 of the 1916 Act then he cannot be guilty of robbery.

This includes, *inter alia*, the requirement of a taking; if the victim is threatened and relinquishes goods, but the defendant does not take them, then there is no robbery (*R v. Farrell* (1787)). (In that case the defendant was apprehended before he could take the goods.)

Equally, under section 1 of the 1916 Act, stealing does not take place where a person acts "with a claim of right made in good faith". Such a person, therefore, could not be convicted of robbery, although he might be convicted of assault or any other appropriate offence against the person.

The term used in section 23 (as replaced) is "force" which replaces the term "violence" under the old law. This appears to be intended to do away with some of the technicalities which attached to the definition of "violence" and it is now clear that, for example, wrenching a shopping basket from a victim's hand can amount to force, although one might have difficulty describing it as violence *(R. v. Clouden* (1987)).

The main case on this point is *R. v. Dawson and James* (1977). Here, the defendants pickpocketed a sailor, by nudging him until he lost his balance, when one of them reached into his pocket and took his wallet. Was there sufficient evidence of robbery to be put before the jury? The Court of Appeal held that there was; the word "force" had been chosen to eliminate the technicalities inherent in the previous term "violence". The word is a common one, and one which the jury can apply based on common sense. As a matter of law, the conduct of the defendants could amount to force. There is therefore an element of overlap between robbery and larceny from the person.

The element of force required is, significantly, not quite the same as that required for assault. For assault, what is required is either the actual use of force or causing another to apprehend the immediate use of force. For robbery, what is required is either the actual use of force, or causing or *seeking* to cause another to apprehend the immediate use of force. The distinction can be illustrated by an example. If A threatens B with the immediate use of force, but B does not believe the threat, then assault is not committed; B must actually experience fear. But if A threatens B with the immediate use of force in order to steal, and does steal, then robbery is committed even where B does not believe the threat, since A *sought* to put B in fear of being subjected to force.

Against whom must the force be used? Under the old law, it was necessary to show that the force was used against a person in possession of or in the presence of the goods, which led to difficulties where

force was used against other persons. Now, there is no such requirement, so long as the force is used immediately before or at the time of
stealing and in order to steal. This would include the making of threats
against a hostage to induce the owner to surrender goods or the use of
force against a passer-by who attempts to prevent a larceny (McCutcheon, *The Larceny Act 1916* (Dublin, 1992), p. 73).

When must the force be used? Section 23 provides that for robbery
to be committed force must be used "immediately before or at the time
[of stealing]". This marks a change from the old law which included
the use of force immediately after the stealing. It is unclear just when
the time of the stealing ceases, but the current state of the law on this
point appears to be summarised by the views of the Law Reform Commission that:

> "the exact relevant words of the statute may be considered to embrace
> the threat or use of force during the time when it may be said that the
> defendant is doing the act of stealing. Thus, a person who hauls a mail-
> bag over a post office counter no doubt has already done sufficient to
> be judged guilty of larceny but it would be an abuse of ordinary lan-
> guage to say that he does not continue to engage in the act of larceny
> when he drags it from the counter towards the door. Where the cut-off
> point should be may be a proper subject of debate; but the point is that
> debate is not foreclosed merely by showing that the force occurred at
> some point after the earliest at which the defendant could successfully
> be charged with larceny." (*Receiving Stolen Property* (L.R.C. 23-
> 1987), p. 123).

The *mens rea* of the offence is not defined in the section, but the general rule laid down in *People (DPP) v. Murray* (1977) should still apply
to require the prosecution to establish *mens rea* as regards each component of the offence.

8.16 Fraudulent conversion

This offence is created by section 20(1) of the Larceny Act 1916:

> "Every person who -
>
> (i) being entrusted either solely or jointly with any other person with
>   any power of attorney for the sale or transfer of any property fraud-
>   ulently sells, transfers or otherwise converts the property or any
>   part thereof to his own use or benefit, or the use or benefit of any
>   person other than the person by whom he was so entrusted, or

(ii) being a director, member or officer of any body corporate or public company, fraudulently takes or applies for his own use or benefit or for any use or purposes other than the use or purposes of such body corporate or public company, any of the property of such body corporate or public company, or"

...

"(iv)(a)being entrusted either solely or jointly with any other person with any property in order that he may retain in safe custody or apply, pay, or deliver, for any purpose or to any person, the property or any part thereof or any proceeds thereof, or

(b) having either solely or jointly with any other person received any property for or on account of any other person,

fraudulently converts to his own use or benefit, or the use or benefit of any other person, the property or any part thereof or any proceeds thereof [shall be guilty of an offence]".

Section 20 does not extend to fraudulent conversion by trustees, which is dealt with by section 21:

"Every person who, being a trustee ... of any property for the use or benefit either wholly or partially of some other person, or for any public or charitable purpose, with intent to defraud converts or appropriates the same or any part thereof to or for his own use or benefit, or the use or benefit of any person other than the person as aforesaid, or for any purpose other than such public or charitable purpose as aforesaid, or otherwise disposes of or destroys such property or any part thereof [shall be guilty of an offence]."

Note that "trustee" is given a very restrictive meaning elsewhere in the Act (section 46(1)) and is limited to trustees of express trusts created by writing; persons holding property on an implied, resulting or constructive trust will be appropriately dealt with under section 20 rather than section 21.

These two offences deal with misappropriation by persons who hold property in a fiduciary capacity, such as a trustee on behalf of the beneficiaries of the trust. At common law, there was no criminal sanction for misappropriation of funds by persons in such a position. Nor are other offences under the 1916 Act adequate to deal with such misappropriation. It will not amount to larceny, since the defendant will have obtained possession lawfully. Equally, the offence of obtaining by false pretences is inapplicable where there is a genuine entrusting of the property to the defendant, which subsequently goes wrong.

Sections 20 and 21 therefore create offences appropriate to persons holding in a fiduciary capacity. Section 20(1)(i), section 20(1)(ii) and section 21 deal with specific situations (fraudulent conversion by those with a power of attorney, directors and trustees), while section 20(1)(iv) creates a catch-all offence where a person:

(a) is entrusted with property to apply to a specific purpose; or

(b) has received property for or on account of another person,

and converts that property to his or another's own use.

This catch-all offence is the most important for our purposes, and may be committed in two ways, depending on how the property comes into the possession of the defendant. In both cases, it is necessary to show that the accused acted fraudulently. This again requires some element of dishonesty, and, for example, a claim of right made in good faith will defeat a charge of fraudulent conversion.

It is also necessary to show either that the defendant was entrusted with property to apply to a particular purpose, or that he received property for or on account of another person. This has posed some difficulties. In the case of *People (AG) v. Heald* (1954), the accused was the manager of a convalescent home run by an order of nuns. She received lump sums from two patients, representing that this would entitle them to be patients in the home for the remainder of their lives. In fact, there was no such policy. She was convicted of fraudulent conversion contrary to section 20(1)(iv)(b). On appeal, it was held that she could not be convicted of fraudulent conversion unless she had, in fact, authority to receive the money on behalf of the nuns. Since she had no such authority, she could not be said to have received it for or on account of another person, and could not be convicted under section 20(1)(iv)(b); the appropriate charge was one of obtaining by false pretences.

However, the effect of *People (AG) v. Heald* (1954) was severely narrowed in *People (AG) v. Cowan* (1958). In that case, a solicitor tricked a client into signing a bank draft, making it possible for the solicitor to lodge the bank draft to his own account. The Supreme Court limited the decision in *People (AG) v. Heald* (1954) to its own facts, holding that it was not necessary for a defendant to have authority to receive money on behalf of another before he can be said to have received money for or on account of that other. Instead, a person receives property "for or on account of another person when he receives it in such circumstances as to give rise to a duty or obligation to account for it to such other person." (*Per* O'Daly J. at page 58.)

In any event, it is possible to avoid the complexities of this discussion: the conduct in *People (AG) v. Heald* (1954) would presumably have amounted to an offence under section 20(1)(iv)(a) (entrustment of money to be applied to a particular purpose), and it will often be more appropriate to charge an offence contrary to that provision rather than under section 20(1)(iv)(b).

It is also necessary to show that the accused obtained *property* rather than *possession* in the items in question, and that there was a genuine entrustment of the property which subsequently went wrong. If the accused acquires possession as an employee, for example, then there will be no fraudulent conversion since the ownership of the goods remained with the employer. The appropriate charge would be simple larceny or larceny by a servant, or embezzlement if there is no wrongful taking. Equally, if ownership was obtained by false pretences, then there is no genuine entrustment, and the appropriate charge is obtaining by false pretences. The two offences, obtaining by false pretences, and fraudulent conversion, are mutually exclusive (*People (AG) v. Singer* (1961)).

It is desirable that the accused should be charged with specific acts of misappropriation of the property; however, circumstantial evidence of misappropriation will suffice. In particular, if the accused is under a duty to account for property and fails to do so when required, then that is material from which the jury may draw the conclusion that the property has been fraudulently converted. For example, in *People (AG) v. Murphy* (1947), a solicitor was convicted of fraudulent conversion on failing to account for money paid to him as the deposit on the purchase of a house.

8.17 Burglary

This offence is created by section 23A of the Larceny Act 1916 as inserted by section 6 of the Criminal Law (Jurisdiction) Act 1976:

"(1) A person is guilty of burglary if -

(a) he enters any building or any part of a building as a trespasser and with intent to commit [designated offences]; or
(b) having entered any building or part of a building as a trespasser he steals or attempts to steal anything in the building or that part of it, or inflicts or attempts to inflict on any person therein any grievous bodily harm."

The designated offences are: stealing anything in the building, inflicting grievous bodily harm on any person therein, rape of any person therein, or doing unlawful damage to the building or anything therein.

"Building" includes inhabited vehicles or vessels. Maximum penalty: 14 years imprisonment.

Burglary can, therefore be committed in two distinct ways, either by:

1. Entry as trespasser with intention to:

   (a) steal,

   (b) inflict grievous bodily harm,

   (c) rape,

   (d) do unlawful damage; or by:

2. Entry as trespasser, and consequent

   (a) (attempted) stealing, or

   (b) (attempted) infliction of grievous bodily harm.

It will be noted that this gives rise to an anomaly: entry with intention to rape or do unlawful damage amounts to burglary, while entry and a later decision to rape or do unlawful damage will not. It pays the trespasser to put off making up his mind.

For burglary to be committed, the defendant must enter as a trespasser. This replaces the old requirement of "breaking and entering" and the defendant may simply wander in through an open door. Trespass takes place where a person enters without either the consent of the occupier or a right of entry conferred by law. However, a requirement of *mens rea* applies in the context of burglary, and in this context:

> "a person entering a building is not guilty of trespass if he enters without knowledge that he is trespassing or at least without acting recklessly as to whether or not he is unlawfully entering." (*R v. Collins* (1973) at p. 104, *per* Edmund Davies L.J.)

Trespass also takes place where a person exceeds his right of entry or enters for a purpose other than that for which permission was given. In *R v. Jones and Smith* (1976), the two accused entered the home of the father of one of them, intending to steal from it. The father had given the son unreserved permission to enter the house at any time, and it was therefore argued that the accused had not been trespassing. This was rejected by the Court of Appeal: a person is a trespasser if he enters for a purpose other than the one for which the permission was granted. (See also *DPP v. McMahon* (1987).)

What amounts to entering? Has a person entered where part only of his body has passed the threshold? At common law entry was governed by highly technical rules, and an entry could be effected either by an instrument or by the accused putting any part of his body, however slight, over the threshold. The amendment of the law seems to have been intended to do away with these refinements, and in England the test has been stated to be whether an entry is "effective". So, in *R. v. Brown* (1985), the accused was charged with burglary, having broken a shop window, leaned in and rummaged around the shop front display. Could this amount to entering? It was held by the Court of Appeal that it could. There was no requirement that a person wholly enter the building. Instead, whether an entry had taken place was a matter for the jury to decide, and they should be directed to consider whether an effective entry had taken place.

What is a building? The leading case is *B & S v. Leathley* (1979), which accepted that a freezer container which was resting on old railway sleepers was a building, since it was "a structure of considerable size intended to be permanent or to endure for a considerable time". However, in *Norfolk Constabulary v. Seekings and Gould* (1986), truck trailers supplied with electricity and used as temporary storage space were held not to be buildings.

Burglary can also take place where a person enters part of a building as a trespasser, which is an important qualification. Consider the case of a person who is invited to apartment 1 and then breaks into the adjoining apartment 2. Clearly he did not enter the apartment block as a trespasser; nevertheless, he enters apartment 2, which is a part of the building, as a trespasser and so may be guilty of burglary. This may be extended further: in *R. v. Wilkington* (1979), the accused was present in a department store and entered the area inside a three sided counter area, in which there was a till. It was held that the area inside this counter area was capable of being a "part of a building", and since it was part of the store from which the public were excluded it was open to the jury to find that he had entered that part of the building as a trespasser.

The offence can be committed by entry with the intention of committing a specified offence. What form of intention is necessary? Is it enough that a person enters with a conditional intent, such as an intention to steal if there is anything worth stealing? In *R. v. Wilkington* (1979) the accused went behind the counter area and opened a till to see if there was anything in it worth stealing, if there had been, he would have taken it. This form of conditional intent was held to be sufficient for the crime of burglary, it was irrelevant that, unknown to the accused, there was nothing worth taking.

8.17.1 Aggravated burglary

This offence is created by section 23B of the Larceny Act 1916, as inserted by section 7 of the Criminal Law (Jurisdiction) Act 1976:

> "A person is guilty of aggravated burglary if he commits any burglary and at the time has with him any firearm or imitation firearm, any weapon of offence or any explosive.".

The terms firearm, etc., are given an extended definition in section 7, with the definition of "weapon of offence" being particularly important: "any article made or adapted for use for causing injury to or incapacitating a person, or intended by the person having it with him for such use". This therefore includes items:

(a) made for causing injury, etc.;

(b) adapted for causing injury, etc.; and

(c) intended for causing injury, etc.

Guns would fall within (a); broken bottles within (b); and items such as screwdrivers or hammers within (c) if they were intended to cause injury, etc. The reference to incapacitation would mean that items used to disable but not injure, such as ropes or chloroform soaked pads, could amount to weapons of offence.

The accused must have the item in question with him at the time of the burglary, and the time of the burglary will depend on whether what is alleged, is entry with a specified intention, or entry followed by the commission of a specified offence. If entry with a specified intention, then the item must be with the accused at the time of entry; if entry followed by commission of a specified offence, then the item must be with the accused at the time of the commission of the specified offence.

8.18 Forgery

The offence of forgery is largely governed by the Forgery Act 1913. Basic definitions are contained in section 1 of the Act:

> "(1) ... forgery is the making of a false document in order that it may be used as genuine...
>
> (2) A document is false ... if the whole or any material part thereof purports to be made by or on behalf or on account of a person who did not make it or authorise its making; or if, though made by or on behalf or

on account of the person by whom or by whose authority it purports to
have been made, the time or place of making, where either is material,
or, in the case of a document identified by number or mark, the number
or any distinguishing mark identifying the document is falsely stated
therein; and in particular a document is false:-

(a) if any material alteration, whether by addition, insertion, oblitera-
    tion, erasure, removal, or otherwise, has been made therein;
(b) if the whole or some material part of it purports to be made by or on
    behalf of a fictitious or deceased person;
(c) if, though made in the name of an existing person, it is made by
    him or by his authority with the intention that it should pass as hav-
    ing been made by some person, real or fictitious, other than the per-
    son who made or authorised it.".

Sections 4 and 6 create the two offences with which we are concerned:
forgery and uttering a forged document. While various specific
offences are created by the 1913 Act depending on the class of document forged (public documents, bank notes, etc.), the catch-all offence
is that created by section 4(1):

"Forgery of any document ... if committed with intent to defraud, shall
be [an offence]."

The necessary *mens rea* is an intent to *defraud*. This is a significant
departure from the specific offences of forgery of public documents,
where the necessary *mens rea* is an intent to *defraud* or *deceive*. What
is the distinction between the two? In *Re London and Globe Finance
Corporation* (1903), the following definitions were given:

"To deceive is, I apprehend, to induce a man to believe that a thing is
true which is false, and which the person practising the deceit knows or
believes to be false. To defraud is to deprive by deceit: it is by deceit to
induce a man to act to his injury. More tersely it may be put, that to
deceive is by falsehood to induce a state of mind; to defraud is by
deceit to induce a course of action." (*Per* Buckley J. at p. 732-733)

It is, therefore, necessary to show an intention to defraud. What exactly
is this? In *Welham v. DPP* (1961), the accused obtained money from
finance companies by submitting forged documents. His defence was
that he did not intend to defraud the companies, but merely to circum-
vent governmental restrictions on borrowing, preventing the companies
from making straight loans. The House of Lords held that, on those
facts, there was an intention to defraud. It was not necessary that any
person should suffer financial or economic loss as a result of the forgery, nor that they should be deprived of something of value. If anyone

may be prejudiced in any way by the fraud, that is enough. It was therefore sufficient that he intended to induce the companies to act in a way in which they would not have done had he not acted deceitfully.

As with most other offences of dishonesty, an intention to defraud may be negatived by, for example, a claim of right made in good faith.

Section 6 of the 1913 Act creates the other general offence, that of uttering a forged document:

> "(1) Every person who utters any forged document ... shall be guilty [of an offence]
>
> (2) A person utters a forged document, seal or die who, knowing the same to be forged, and with either of the intents necessary to constitute the offence of forging the said document ... uses, offers, publishes, delivers, disposes of, tenders in payment or in exchange, exposes for sale or exchange, exchanges, tenders in evidence, or puts off the said forged document ..."

This offence requires some use of the forgery; it is not an offence merely to possess a forged document. However, the breadth of the offence is such that virtually any use by the defendant of the forged item with the necessary *mens rea* will suffice. Note that the *mens rea* is two-fold: first, the defendant must know the document to be forged; and second, the accused must act with an intention to deceive or defraud (in the case of forged public documents, etc.) or an intention to defraud (in the case of other forgeries).

8.19 Arson and criminal damage

The offences of arson and criminal damage were formerly dealt with under the Malicious Damage Act 1861, a notoriously badly drafted piece of legislation, in that it created a number of extremely specific offences with highly technical differences between them. The Law Reform Commission therefore recommended (*Report on Malicious Damage* (L.R.C. 26-1988)) that these should be replaced by generic offences of criminal damage, capable of being carried out by means of arson. These recommendations were implemented by the Criminal Damage Act 1991.

This Act creates three distinct offences: damaging property *simpliciter*, damaging property with an intention to endanger life or reckless as to whether life is endangered, and damaging property with intent to defraud. Each of these offences may be committed by damaging property by fire, in which case they shall be charged as arson. If committed by arson each offence carries a higher penalty, reflecting the danger to third parties which arson represents:

> "Fire is capable of inflicting enormous injury and damage. It respects no legal boundaries. Anyone who starts a fire with the intention of damaging or destroying property is engaging in an act that may be considered distinctively different (at least in its potential implications) from damaging or destroying a house (or other property) by other means." (Law Reform Commission, *Report on Malicious Damage* (L.R.C. 26-1988), p. 27). (Although the Law Reform Commission went on to recommend that arson should not carry a higher penalty than other means of damaging property, this recommendation was not followed.)

8.19.1 Elements common to each offence

"Property" is defined in section 1 as including both property of a tangible nature and data.

"Damage" is defined in section 1 so as to include destroying, defacing, dismantling, rendering inoperable and preventing the operation of tangible property. In relation to data, damage is defined as including adding to, altering, corrupting, erasing or moving that data, or doing any act contributing to such addition, alteration, etc. This element of the definition is significant: the activities of computer hackers will almost invariably fall within the offence of damaging property; where they do not, section 5 of the Act creates the offence of unauthorised accessing of data.

"Lawful excuse" is dealt with in section 6, and shall include situations where the defendant:

> "believed that the person ... he believed to be entitled to consent to or authorise the damage to ... the property in question had consented, or would have consented ... if he ... had known of the damage ... and its circumstances", or

> "[caused the damage] in order to protect himself or another or property belonging to himself or another or a right or interest in property which was or which he believed to be vested in himself or another and ... he believed -

> (i) that he or that other or the property, right or interest was in immediate need of protection, and

> (ii) that the means of protection adopted ... were or would be reasonable having regard to all the circumstances."

8.19.2 Damaging property

Section 2(1):

"A person who without lawful excuse damages any property belonging to another intending to damage any such property or being reckless as to whether any such property would be damaged shall be guilty of an offence."

(1) Damaging property with intent to endanger life

Section 2(2):

"A person who without lawful excuse damages any property, whether belonging to himself or another -

(a) intending to damage any property or being reckless as to whether any property would be damaged, and

(b) intending by the damage to endanger the life of another or being reckless as to whether the life of another would be thereby endangered,

shall be guilty of an offence."

Note the overlap between this offence and endangerment contrary to section 13 of the Non-Fatal Offences Against the Person Act 1997.

(2) Damaging property with intent to defraud

Section 2(3):

"A person who damages any property, whether belonging to himself or another, with intent to defraud shall be guilty of an offence."

This offence is intended to deal with, for example, the problem of insurance fraud, and therefore applies even where a person damages his own property.

(3) Compensation orders

Section 9 of the Act provides that:

"On conviction of any person of an offence under section 2 of damaging property belonging to another, the court, instead of or in addition to dealing with him in any other way, may, on application or otherwise, make an order (in this act referred to as a "compensation order") requiring him to pay compensation in respect of that damage to any person (in this section referred to as the "injured party") who, by reason thereof, has suffered loss (other than consequential loss)."

This jurisdiction parallels the right of action of a victim against the offender; the amount of the compensation order may not exceed the amount which would be payable if the victim were to take an action in tort.

8.20 Criminal Justice (Theft and Fraud Offences) Bill 2000

As was already mentioned, this Bill will, when enacted, substantially change the law in relation to property offences. It will completely repeal several pieces of legislation, most notably the Forgery Act 1913, the Larceny Act 1916, and the Larceny Act 1990. The intention underlying the Bill is to simplify and consolidate the law in this area; it will, therefore, sweep away the multitude of specific offences created by the 1916 Act (such as larceny, larceny from the person, larceny by a clerk or servant, larceny in a dwellinghouse, and so on) and replace these with a smaller range of more general offences. The following is a brief summary of its provisions.

Section 4 introduces a new offence of theft, defined as dishonestly appropriating property without the consent of its owner and with the intention of depriving its owner of it. The concept of appropriation is distinct from the current requirement of "carrying away", as it does not require that the property be moved. In addition, "depriving" is defined to include temporarily depriving as well as permanently depriving. Consequently, the joyrider will be guilty of theft under the new law, despite lacking an intention to permanently deprive the owner of the vehicle.

Sections 6 and 7 introduce two new offences of making gain or causing loss by deception and obtaining services by deception. These are wide-ranging offences, which cover substantially more conduct than the equivalent offences under the old law. Section 6 provides that:

"A person who dishonestly, with the intention of making a gain for himself or herself or another, or of causing loss to another, induces another to do or refrain from doing an act is guilty of an offence."

This section overlaps with the old offence of obtaining by false pretences under section 32 of the Larceny Act 1916, but is significantly wider. For example, section 32 only applies where a defendant obtains property by false pretences; under section 6 it is sufficient that the defendant caused loss to a victim, even if the defendant did not himself obtain any property or other benefit.

Section 7 makes it an offence for a person, by any deception, to dishonestly obtain services (including a loan) with the intention of making a gain, either personally or for another, or causing loss to any person. As with section 6, this will cover much conduct which would not have been an offence under the 1916 Act.

Section 8 provides for an offence of making off without payment and section 9 introduces an offence of unlawful use of a computer. This will be made out where a person dishonestly, whether within the State or outside the State, operates, or causes to be operated, a computer within the State with the intention of making a gain for himself or another or causing a loss to another. This exceptionally wide-ranging offence will cover any situation where a computer is used as a tool in a crime of dishonesty.

The offences of burglary and aggravated burglary are contained in sections 12 and 13, and are essentially identical to the existing offences of burglary and aggravated burglary. Similarly, section 14 provides for the offence of robbery, which is also identical to the offence as it stood under the 1916 Act.

Section 15 goes on to deal with possession of certain items which might be used in crimes against property, and makes it an offence to possess items intended to be used for such a purpose.

Part 3 of the Bill deals with the difficult area of handling stolen property and other proceeds of crime, and substantially reworks the law on this point. It provides for offences of handling stolen property, possessing stolen property, withholding information relating to stolen property, and money laundering.

Parts 4 and 5 deal with forgery and counterfeiting, and update these offences. Part 4 is concerned with forgery and provides that it is an offence to make a false instrument intending it to be genuine, resulting in prejudice to the person accepting it. Using and copying false instruments will also be offences as will having custody or control of certain false instruments. Part 5 deals with the offence of counterfeiting in relation to currency.

Further reading: Criminal Justice (Theft and Fraud Offences) Bill 2000; and Explanatory Memorandum.

9. OFFENCES AGAINST THE ADMINISTRATION OF JUSTICE

9.1 Perjury

Perjury is an offence at common law, "committed by any person lawfully sworn as a witness or as an interpreter in a judicial proceeding who wilfully makes a statement, material in that [sic.] proceedings, which he knows to be false or does not believe to be true" (Law Reform Commission, *Report on Oaths and Affirmations* (L.R.C. 34-1990), p.21)

Judicial proceedings include proceedings which are complementary to the main proceedings of the court, statutory tribunals at which evidence must be given on oath, and proceedings before persons authorised by law to hear, receive and examine evidence on oath. (So, proceedings before coroners, the Employment Appeals Tribunal, and so forth would be included.) Evidence given on affirmation is also included: section 1 of the Oaths Act 1888.

The elements are, therefore:

(a) judicial proceedings;

(b) evidence on oath/affirmation;

(c) which is material evidence;

(d) which is known or believed to be false.

The false evidence given must be material; it is not perjury for a vain witness to lie about her age, unless of course her age is relevant to the proceedings.

9.2 Contempt of Court

Contempt of court can be classified as either civil or criminal contempt. The distinction between the two is explained in *State (Keegan) v. De Burca* (1973). In that case, the defendant had refused to answer a question of the court, and had been sentenced to imprisonment until she purged her contempt; that is, until she agreed to comply with the direction of the court to answer the question. The effect was to impose imprisonment for an indefinite period. This would have been the appropriate result if the contempt had been civil; but she contended that the contempt was criminal, and so she should have been sentenced to a definite period of imprisonment, or a fine. In differentiating between the two forms of contempt, Ó Dálaigh C.J. stated:

> "Criminal contempt consists in behaviour calculated to prejudice the due course of justice, such as contempt *in facie curiae* [*in the face of the court*], words written or spoken or acts calculated to prejudice the due course of justice or disobedience to a writ of *habeas corpus* by the person to whom it is directed - to give but some examples of this class of contempt. Civil contempt usually arises where there is a disobedience to an order of the court by a party to the proceedings and in which the court generally has no interest to interfere unless moved by the party for whose benefit the order was made. Criminal contempt is a common law misdemeanour and, as such, is punishable by both imprisonment and fine at discretion, that is to say, without statutory limit, its object is punitive: see the judgment of this Court in *In Re Haughey* (1971). Civil contempt, on the other hand, is not punitive in its effect but coercive in its purpose of compelling the party committed to comply with the order of the court, and the period of committal would be until such time as the order is complied with or until it is waived by the party for whose benefit the order was made. In the case of civil contempt only the court can order release but the period of committal cannot be commuted or remitted as a sentence for a term definite in a criminal matter can be commuted or remitted pursuant to Article 13.6 of the Constitution." (At p. 227.).

It was then held by the Supreme Court that the refusal to answer a question constituted criminal contempt for which a determinate sentence should have been imposed.

Criminal contempt can be loosely divided into four categories: contempt in the face of the court (conduct within the courtroom such as assaulting the judge); scandalising the court (conduct calculated to reduce public confidence in the administration of justice); breach of the *sub judice* rule; and acts, other than publication, which interfere with the course of justice (such as attempts to intimidate witnesses or counsel: *In re Kelly v. Deighan* (1984)). Further examples of criminal contempt would be: disruptions of court proceedings (as in *Morris v. The Crown Office* (1970) in which students protesting in favour of the Welsh language took over a court in session); attempts to intimidate witnesses or counsel (*Brown v. Putnam* (1975)); jurors making their decision on the toss of a coin (*Langdell v. Sutton* (1737)); jurors arriving at court drunk (*Re Reynolds* (1952)); or the publication of material in breach of the *sub judice* rule (as in *R v. Thomson Newspapers Limited, ex parte AG* (1968) where the accused was described as a brothel-keeper, procurer and property racketeer).

One particularly important form of contempt is the *sub judice* rule under which it is a contempt of court to publish material intending to interfere with the administration of justice. The test here is whether a particular publication has a real tendency (other than a *de minimis* tendency) to interfere with the due administration of justice in the particular proceedings. It is not necessary to show that the publication did in fact impair the proceedings; the risk of interference is enough. The main function of the *sub judice* rule is to prevent material being published which might prejudice a jury. However, the rule also applies, in some cases, to matters decided by a judge sitting alone. For example, the Supreme Court, in *Eamonn Kelly v. Paul O'Neill and Conor Brady* (1999), recently held that the rule applies to publications about defendants after conviction but before sentence.

9.2.1 Mens rea

Breach of the *sub judice* rule is an offence of strict liability. It is unclear whether *mens rea* is required for contempt in the face of the court. Similarly, there is academic debate as to whether *mens rea* is required for the offence of scandalising. It is an offence of strict liability in England, Australia, New Zealand and Canada, although South African law requires *mens rea*. In Ireland, no clear authority on this point exists. The most recent authority is *In re Kennedy and McCann* (1976) where O'Higgins C.J. remarked (at page 387) "The offence of contempt by scandalising the court is committed when, as here, a false publication is made which intentionally or recklessly imputes base or improper motives and conduct to the judge or judges in question". Although this appears to require *mens rea*, the Law Reform Commission, in its *Consultation Paper on Contempt* (at p. 63), suggested that one interpretation of the case may be that O'Higgins C.J. was referring not to an intent to interfere with the administration of justice but to impute improper motives to the judiciary. As regards acts, other than publication, which interfere with the course of justice, the *mens rea* question is also unclear.

9.2.2 Procedure

Contempt of court is usually dealt with summarily by the judge having seisin of the matter. In *The State (DPP) v. Walsh* (1981), the defendants submitted that the court lacked jurisdiction to try them upon charges of scandalising the court, in the absence of a jury. They argued that a summary jurisdiction existed in respect of contempt in the face of the court but that this did not extend to situations of scandalising. It was held that there was an inherent jurisdiction to dispose summarily of offences of scandalising the court.

Further reading: Walley, "Criminal Contempt of Court" *Bar Review* Vol. 5, Issue 6 (April, 2000) 295; Law Reform Commission, *Consultation Paper on Contempt of Court* (L.R.C. 1991); Law Reform Commission, *Report on Contempt of Court* (L.R.C. 1992).

9.3 Offences of a public nature

9.3.1 Public order offences

The law relating to public order offences was reformed by the Criminal Justice (Public Order) Act 1994. This act abolished the common law offences of riot, rout, unlawful assembly and affray, and replaced these with offences on a statutory footing. The Act also created more minor public order offences, including being intoxicated in a public place; disorderly conduct in a public place; threatening, abusive or insulting behaviour in a public place; distribution or display in a public place of material which is threatening, abusive or obscene; wilful obstruction of the free passage of any person or vehicle in a public place; entering a building with intent to commit an offence and trespass on a building. In addition, it created certain "crowd control" powers to be exercised by the gardaí, controlling access to public events and enabling the seizure of alcohol, bottles, etc., found on persons going to public events. We will look at the three primary offences under this Act.

9.3.2 Riot

The first of these is *riot*, contrary to section 14 of the Act:

"Where -

(a) 12 or more persons who are present together at any place [*public or private*] ... use or threaten to use unlawful violence for a common purpose, and

(b) the conduct of those persons, taken together, is such as would cause a person of reasonable firmness present at that place to fear for his or another person's safety,

then, each of the persons using unlawful violence for the common purpose shall be guilty of the offence of riot.".

Section 14 goes on to provide that: the threats or uses of violence need not take place simultaneously or at the same place; the common purpose may be inferred from conduct; and no person of reasonable firmness need actually be present, or likely to be present.

9.3.3 *Violent disorder*

Next is the offence of *violent disorder* contrary to section 15. This is essentially a scaled-down version of the offence of riot, and is committed where (a) a minimum of three persons present at any public or private place use or threaten to use violence; and (b) the conduct of those persons, taken together, is such as would cause a person of reasonable firmness, present at that place to fear for his or another person's safety; and (c) the particular defendant himself used or threatened to use violence. In this, it differs from riot; the offence of riot is only committed by persons who use, rather than threaten, violence. In addition, there is a safeguard that is not present for the offence of riot:

"A person shall not be convicted of the offence of violent disorder unless the person intends to use or threaten to use violence or is aware that his conduct may be violent or threaten violence." (section 15(3)).

9.3.4 *Affray*

Finally, we have the offence of affray, contrary to section 16:

"Where -

(a) two or more persons at any place [*public or private*] ... use or threaten to use violence towards each other, and
(b) the violence so used or threatened by one of those persons is unlawful, and
(c) the conduct of those persons, taken together, is such as would cause a person of reasonable firmness present at that place to fear for his or another person's safety,

then, each such person who uses or threatens to use unlawful violence shall be guilty of the offence of affray.".

No person of reasonable firmness need be present. The offence is not committed where threats are made by words alone.

Each of these offences has in common the element of causing or potentially causing fear in others, and the offences are graduated from the large-scale public disorder to the small scale late night fight outside a night-club.

9.3.5 Incitement to hatred

The Prohibition of Incitement to Hatred Act 1989 implemented Ireland's obligations under the UN Convention on Civil and Political Rights, which requires, *inter alia*, that advocacy of national, racial and religious hatred constituting incitement to discrimination, hostility or violence should be prohibited by law.

It does so by creating three main offences, each of which is phrased in terms of stirring up hatred. "Hatred" itself is defined in section 1 as meaning:

> "hatred against a group of persons in the State or elsewhere on account of their race, colour, nationality, religion, ethnic or national origins, membership of the travelling community or sexual orientation."

This definition focuses on the group and its distinguishing characteristics; it is not an offence to stir up hatred against an individual, *per se*, although it may be if the effect of doing so is also to stir up hatred against the group of which he is a member.

The first offence is that of *actions likely to stir up hatred* contrary to section 2 of the Act:

> "It shall be an offence for a person -
>
> (a) to publish or distribute written material,
> (b) to use words, behave or display written material -
>   (i) in any place other than inside a private residence, or
>   (ii) inside a private residence so that the words, behaviour or material are heard or seen by persons outside the residence, or
> (c) to distribute, show or play a recording of visual images or sounds,
>
> if the written material, words, behaviour, visual images or sounds, as the case may be, are threatening, abusive or insulting and are intended or, having regard to all the circumstances, are likely to stir up hatred."

This offence draws a distinction between public and private conduct: a person is free to stir up hatred within his or someone else's private residence, so long as they do not do so by way of video or audio cassette.

However, a private residence will be treated as being a public place where a public meeting is held there.

Section 3 then creates an offence of *broadcasts likely to stir up hatred*:

> "If an item involving threatening, abusive or insulting images or sounds is broadcast, each of the persons [specified later] is guilty of an offence if he intends thereby to stir up hatred or, having regard to all the circumstances, hatred is likely to be stirred up thereby."

Those persons are then defined as the persons providing the broadcasting service, and persons producing the item concerned, and any person whose words or behaviour in the item are threatening, abusive or insulting. Detailed defences are then provided: for example, it is a defence to show that the offending clip could not practicably be removed, that the defendant was not aware that the offending clip would be broadcast, or that the offending clip would be broadcast in a context likely to stir up hatred, and so forth.

Finally, section 4 creates an offence of *preparation and possession of material likely to stir up hatred*:

> "It shall be an offence for a person -
>
> (a) to prepare or be in possession of any written material with a view to its being distributed, displayed, broadcast or otherwise published, in the State or elsewhere, whether by himself or another, or
> (b) to make or be in possession of a recording of sounds or visual images with a view to its being distributed, shown, played, broadcast or otherwise published, in the State or elsewhere, whether by himself or another,
>
> if the material or recording is threatening, abusive or insulting and is intended or, having regard to all the circumstances, including such distribution ... as the person has, or it may reasonably be inferred that he has, in view, is likely to stir up hatred."

This offence would address a situation where, for example, neo-nazi groups were using Ireland as a base for preparing materials to be used abroad.

Defences are available to the above offences where the person charged did not intend to stir up hatred and was not aware of the content of the material in question, and had no reason to suspect that it was threatening, abusive or insulting, or was not aware that his words, behaviour or the material concerned might be threatening, abusive or insulting.

Further reading: Keogh, "The Prohibition of Incitement to Hatred Act 1989 – A Paper Tiger?" 6 *Bar Review* 178 (December 2000)

9.4 Offences against the State

There are a wide variety of offences designed to deal with the special problems caused by paramilitary activity. Among the offences created by the Offences Against the State Act 1939 are: membership of an unlawful organisation; recruiting for an unlawful organisation; usurpation of the functions of government; obstruction of government, obstruction of the President; interference with military or other employees of the State; printing, etc., certain documents; possession of treasonable, seditious or incriminating documents; unauthorised military exercises; formation of secret societies in army or police; administering unlawful oaths; and holding certain public meetings.

We will deal with three of the offences created by the Offences Against the State Act 1939 and the five new offences contained in the Offences Against the State (Amendment) Act 1998. The offence of treason will not be examined. While this is the ultimate offence against the State, governed by Article 39 of the Constitution and the Treason Act 1939, it is of no practical importance. It should be borne in mind that most paramilitary offences are dealt with under the ordinary law of homicide, offences against the person, and so on, although they will be dealt with before the Special Criminal Court.

First and most significant, in practical terms, is the offence of membership of an unlawful organisation. Section 18 of the Offences Against the State Act 1939 provides that an organisation which:

"(a) engages in, promotes, encourages, or advocates the commission of treason, or any activity of a treasonable nature, or

(b) advocates, encourages, or attempts the procuring by force, violence or other unconstitutional means of an alteration of the Constitution, or

(c) raises or maintains or attempts to raise or maintain a military or armed force in contravention of the Constitution or without constitutional authority, or

(d) engages in, promotes, encourages, or advocates the commission of any criminal offence or the obstruction of or interference with the administration of justice or the enforcement of the law, or

(e) engages in, promotes, encourages, or advocates the attainment of any particular object, lawful or unlawful, by violent, criminal or other unlawful means, or

(f) promotes, encourages or advocates the non-payment of moneys payable to the Central Fund or any other public fund or the non-payment of local taxation."

shall be an unlawful organisation. This is self-executing; it is not necessary for the government to declare a particular organisation to be unlawful before the powers relating to unlawful organisations come into effect with regard to that organisation. However, under section 19 the government may, if of the opinion that a particular organisation is unlawful, make a suppression order with regard to that organisation, and the effect of such an order is to provide conclusive evidence that a particular organisation is an unlawful organisation. Proceedings may, however, be brought to have the organisation declared legal under section 20 of the Offences Against the State Act 1939.

The Offences Against the State Act 1939, having defined unlawful organisations, goes on in section 21 to provide that membership of such an organisation is an offence. It shall be a defence that a member did not know the true nature of the organisation, or that, once he became aware of its true nature, he ceased to be a member and disassociated himself from it.

There are special provisions in place governing proof of membership. Section 24 of the Offences Against the State Act 1939 provides that possession of an incriminating document (a document issued by or emanating from an unlawful organisation, or aiding or abetting such an organisation, or calculated to promote the formation of an unlawful organisation) shall be evidence of membership until the contrary is proved: *O'Leary v. Attorney General* (1995) 2 I.L.R.M. 259. Similarly, section 3(2) of the Offences Against the State (Amendment) Act 1972 provides that the belief of a chief superintendent or higher officer that an accused is or was a member of an unlawful organisation shall be evidence to that effect, while section 3(1) provides that any conduct of an accused person leading to a reasonable inference of membership of such an organisation shall be evidence to that effect, including failure to deny published reports of membership.

Section 17 of the 1939 Act prohibits the administration of unlawful oaths. Section 17(1) provides that the oaths prohibited are:

"(a) to commit or to plan, contrive, promote, assist or conceal the commission of any crime or any breach of the peace, or

(b) to join or become a member of or associated with any organisation having for its object or one of its objects the commission of any crime, or breach of the peace, or

(c) to abstain from disclosing or giving information of the existence or formation or proposed or intended formation of any such organisation, association, or other body as aforesaid or from informing or giving evidence against any member of or person concerned in the formation of any such organisation, association, or other body, or

(d) to abstain from disclosing or giving information of the commission or intended or proposed commission of any crime, breach of the peace, or from informing or giving evidence against the person who committed such an act."

The offence applies to any person who administers such an oath, causes it to be administered, takes part in, consents to or is present at the administration of such an oath. Section 17(2) provides a defence to a charge of taking an oath if the accused can show that he was "compelled by force or duress" to take the oath. In addition, a defendant must come within the terms of section 17(2)(b):

"that within four days after the taking of such oath ... if not prevented by actual force or incapacitated by illness or other sufficient cause, or where so prevented or incapacitated then within four days after the cessor of such hindrance ... he declared to an officer of the Garda Síochána the fact of his having taken such oath ... and all the circumstances connected therewith and the names and descriptions of all persons concerned ...so far as such circumstances, names and descriptions were known to him."

Section 27 of the 1939 Act prohibits public meetings by unlawful organisations. This includes meetings "held by or on behalf of or by arrangement or in concert with an unlawful organisation" and prohibits meetings purporting to be held "for the purpose of supporting, aiding, abetting, or encouraging an unlawful organisation or of advocating the support of an unlawful organisation". A public meeting is defined to include a procession and includes meetings held in buildings or on enclosed land to which the public are admitted, whether with or without payment. Section 27(2) provides that a garda, not below the rank of chief superintendent, may prohibit the holding of a meeting by giving a notice to the organisers or publishing it "in a manner reasonably calculated to come to the knowledge of the persons so concerned". Section 27(3) states that any person can apply to the High Court requesting the court to annul such notice.

The Offences Against the State (Amendment) Act 1998 was introduced in the wake of the Omagh bombing and created new offences of: directing an unlawful organisation; possession of articles connected with certain offences; unlawful collection of information likely to be used in the commission by members of any unlawful organisation of serious offences; withholding information which might be of material assistance in preventing the commission of a serious offence; and training persons in the making or use of firearms. We have previously examined its significance for the right to silence.

Section 6 prohibits the directing of an unlawful organisation. This applies to a person who directs the activities of such an organisation at any level of the organisation's structure.

Section 7 prohibits the possession of articles connected with certain offences relating to firearms and explosive substances. It applies to persons having such articles "in his or her possession or under his or her control in circumstances giving rise to a reasonable suspicion that the article is in his or her possession or under his or her control for a purpose connected with the commission, preparation or instigation of" a firearms or explosives offence. It is a defence if the person proves that the article was not in his possession or under his control for any of the specified purposes.

Section 8 makes it an offence for a person to "collect, record or possess information which is of such a nature that it is likely to be useful in the commission by members of any unlawful organisation of serious offences generally or any particular kind of serious offence". The term "serious offence" is defined in section 8(4) and includes actions or omissions done outside the State which would be serious offences if done in the State.

The withholding of information which might be of material assistance in preventing the commission by any other person of a serious offence is prohibited by section 9. Note that this is one of the few occasions where a person may be found criminally liable for omitting to do something.

Section 12 prohibits the training of persons in the making or use of firearms and the receiving of such instruction. It is a defence if it is proved that the training was either done with lawful authority or that the accused had reasonable excuse for giving or receiving such instruction or training.

Further reading: Editorial, "Offences Against the State (Amendment) Act 1998 – Two views" (1998/99) 4 *Bar Review* 5.

10. DEFENCES

10.1 Introduction

Defences can be divided into three categories. The first is defences which are specific to murder and which result in a conviction for a lesser offence than murder if successful. The second category is defences which are available to every offence except for murder. The third and largest category is defences which are generally available.

10.2 Defences specific to murder

Two defences are specific to murder: provocation and excessive self-defence. This is not to say that these matters cannot be raised in other proceedings; and if they are, then they will be mitigating factors in sentencing. However, only in the case of murder are these two defences available to enable a conviction to be brought in for a lesser offence than that which is charged. This is because of the particularly grave status of murder, creating a judicial reluctance to label as murderers those who act under the pressure of the moment, even though that would not amount to a defence in another, less serious, context. In addition, allowing these defences in the case of murder does not allow the accused to escape all liability for his actions; these defences merely reduce murder to manslaughter.

10.2.1 Provocation

This defence is well summarised in Charleton, *Offences Against the Person* (Round Hall Press, 1992), page 131:

> "Where the accused, in killing the victim, acts under the influence of provocation his crime will amount only to manslaughter, and not murder, notwithstanding that the accused intended to kill or cause serious injury. The test in Irish law is subjective. The provocation under which the accused was acting must be such that having regard to the particular accused's character, temperament and circumstances, it causes him to temporarily lose control of himself to the extent that he ceased to be master of himself when he killed the victim. The accused must use no more force than is reasonable having regard to the effect which the provocation had on him."

(1) Subjective test

What do we mean by a subjective test in this area? The law early on adopted a test limiting the availability of provocation to situations in which a reasonable man would have lost his self-control. This makes sense; there is clearly some element of danger in allowing a particularly temperamental person to plead his hot-headedness as a defence in circumstances where a person of ordinary self control would not have reacted to the particular provocation. However, a sequence of English cases took this objective approach to absurd lengths.

The high point of this approach was the case of *R. v. Bedder* (1954). In that case, the defendant was an eighteen-year-old boy who was sexually impotent. He attempted to have intercourse with a prostitute; when he failed, she taunted him. A struggle followed, in which she slapped and punched him and kicked him in the crotch. He drew a knife and stabbed her twice. Clearly, the boy's impotence had been the reason for his extreme reaction; the taunt of impotence would not have been effective otherwise. However, the House of Lords held that the boy's impotence could not be taken into account in assessing the effect of the provocation on the boy. The reasonable man was not impotent, and would not have lost his self-control as a result of the taunt; and therefore the boy could not raise the defence of provocation.

The absurdity of this position was recognised in England in *R. v. Camplin* (1978). This case involved a fifteen-year-old boy, who killed the deceased after (he alleged) the deceased had forcibly buggered him and then jeered at him. The trial judge refused to direct the jury to consider the effect of the provocation on a fifteen-year-old boy in the same position as the accused. On appeal, the House of Lords departed from *R v. Bedder* (1954), and held (at page 721), that, on a proper application of the test:

> "The jury had to consider whether a young man of about the same age as the accused but placed in the same position as that which befell the accused could, had he been a reasonable young man, have reacted as did the accused and could have done what the accused did."

This is a mixed subjective/objective test. It is subjective insofar as the jury are to consider the effect of the provocation on a person in the defendant's circumstances; but it is objective in that the jury are not to consider the effect of the provocation on the defendant himself, but on a reasonable person in his circumstances. The jury may not, therefore, take into account the fact that the accused had a quick temper or was particularly excitable or pugnacious; they should consider how a hypothetical reasonable 15-year-old would react if in all other respects placed in the shoes of the defendant.

At around the same time as *R. v. Camplin*, the Irish decision of *People (DPP) v. MacEoin* (1978) was reached, in which the Court of Criminal Appeal took a very different view of the law of provocation. We have already seen that Irish law favours subjective tests in, for example, the area of recklessness. This approach also holds true in the area of provocation. In *People (DPP) v. MacEoin*, the accused and the deceased lived together in a flat. Both men were heavy drinkers, and on the day of the killing both had been drinking heavily. In the course of their drinking, the deceased began to behave aggressively towards the defendant, and eventually attacked the defendant with a hammer. The defendant wrestled it from him, and (as he put it) "simmered over and completely lost control", killing the deceased with several blows to the head.

The primary issue before the court was whether a person could rely on the defence of provocation where they intended to kill or cause serious injury. However, the court also dealt with the correct test to be applied in cases of provocation, and held that the objective test for provocation should be abandoned. Those factors which were excluded in *R. v. Camplin*, such as the particularly hot temper of the defendant, are to be taken into account; the test in Ireland is not whether a hypothetical reasonable man in the defendant's shoes would have been provoked, but whether the defendant himself was provoked:

> "A hot-tempered man may react violently to an insult which a phlegmatic one would ignore." (At p.32, *per* Kenny J.)

(2) What is provocation?

Given that the test is subjective, just what extent of loss of self-control will amount to a defence? The test applied in *People (DPP) v. MacEoin* is as follows:

> "Provocation is some act or series of acts, done by the dead man to the accused which actually caused in the accused, a sudden and temporary loss of self-control, rendering the accused so subject to passion as to make him or her for the moment not master of his mind."

This test focuses on loss of self-control; and where a person has time to think and plan revenge, then there is sufficient mental control that the defence of provocation will not apply:

> "Circumstances which induce a desire for revenge are inconsistent with
> provocation, since the conscious formulation of a desire for revenge
> means that a person has had time to think, to reflect, and that would
> negative a sudden temporary loss of self-control, which is of the
> essence of provocation." (*R v. Duffy* (1949) *per* Devlin J.)

However, the fact that a delay has taken place does not conclusively
indicate that there is no sudden loss of self-control, but is merely a factor making it less likely that a sudden loss of self-control has taken
place. Similarly, it is not necessary that the acts of provocation should
take place all at the same time: it is possible for cumulative acts of
provocation to take place over an extended period. Both of these points
are illustrated by *R. v. R.* (1981). This was an Australian case in which
the defendant was married to the deceased. He had, over a period of
time, committed incest with all the daughters of the family. On the day
of the killing he told the defendant what he had done; later that day,
one of the daughters told her of another attempted rape by him. That
night, a row took place; later, as the husband lay asleep in bed, the
defendant went out, took an axe, and killed him. On appeal, it was held
that the defence of provocation should have been left to the jury; the
evidence could support a cold-blooded decision to kill, but it could
equally be compatible with a delayed loss of self-control, particularly
against the backdrop of what had gone before.

(3) Proportionality of force used

People (DPP) v. MacEoin appears to state that the force used should be
reasonable having regard to the provocation to which the defendant
was subject:

> "If the prosecution can prove beyond reasonable doubt that the force
> used was unreasonable and excessive having regard to the provocation,
> the defence of provocation fails." (At p. 35.)

This is a remarkable requirement; having decided that the accused was
provoked so as to lose self-control, the court goes on to require that he
should exercise self-control in regard to the choice of weapon to be
used. It is, of course, true that the extent of force used is evidence of
whether the accused was truly provoked; it will be hard for a defendant
to argue provocation in most cases where he responds to a minor insult
by stabbing, while he may more easily argue provocation where he
responds with a blow to the stomach. The more extreme response
would tend to argue against provocation and in favour of premeditated
intention waiting on an excuse.

It therefore appears from *People (DPP) v. MacEoin* that there must be a balance between the provocation generated and the amount of force used. However, this view has since been rejected by the Irish courts, in two 1997 cases which reassess this aspect of the defence. The first is *People (DPP) v. Mullane* (1997). In this case, the accused admitted killing his girlfriend who had taunted him about his lack of sexual prowess; the only question left to the jury was whether the defence of provocation was available. The trial judge put the applicable test of provocation to the jury, and went on to read out two paragraphs from the judgment in *People (DPP) v. MacEoin* to the jury. The accused was found guilty. On appeal, it was argued that the judge had erred in simply quoting the passages from *People (DPP) v. MacEoin*, since this might have given the jury the impression that an objective test applied in relation to the amount of force used, when the whole of the test was a subjective one.

The matter again came before the Court of Criminal Appeal in *People (DPP) v. Noonan* (1998), where the trial judge had, in his directions to the jury, put a form of objective test for provocation before the jury, based on a combination of Irish and English case law. Although no objection was taken to this direction to the jury at the time, the court held that this was due to an oversight, and that in the interests of justice this point would be addressed. The court went on to hold that the jury may well have been left in confusion as to whether provocation was to be assessed on an objective or subjective basis, and on that ground the appeal was successful.

It appears from these two cases, therefore, that the Court of Criminal Appeal has explained away the passage in *People (DPP) v. MacEoin* (1978) which seems to require an objective test in respect of the amount of force used, and has reaffirmed the principle of a purely subjective test for all aspects of provocation. (See also Byrne and Binchy, *Annual Review of Irish Law 1997*, pp. 286-287.)

This conclusion is confirmed by the decision of the Court of Criminal Appeal in *People (DPP) v. Bambrick* (1999) which restates the law in relation to provocation. He was a person who had had a very deprived and unhappy childhood and adolescence including physical and sexual abuse. He had a low intelligence level, and was virtually an alcoholic. On the night of the killing the appellant was drunk. The appellant and the victim came into each other's company and began to drink together. The appellant maintained that the victim then made suggestive, sexual remarks to him. The appellant claimed also that the victim made a physical, sexual advance towards him. The appellant claimed that this advance brought back memories of childhood abuse which he had suffered, and that as a result he lost all control of himself. At this point the appellant then pulled a wooden stake from the ground and killed the victim with it. The appellant put a defence of provocation.

In dealing with this defence, the trial judge directed the jury that to determine whether the defence of provocation is available it was necessary for them to decide on the appellant's state of mind. The trial judge directed the jury that if it was "likely" that the accused came into the category of being sensitive to a trigger mechanism which would cause him to lose all control, then he should be acquitted of murder. The trial judge also directed the jury that when a defence of provocation is raised the jury should determine whether they would regard it as being reasonable that the provocation could "probably" have triggered off the uncontrollable reaction which the accused alleged.

The Court of Criminal Appeal found that this direction to the jury was incorrect. In the first place the court found that the trial judge had misdirected the jury on the question of intention. In particular, the trial judge had erred in linking provocation with intention. The impression given to the jury was that the defence of provocation was not available where the accused intended to kill or cause serious injury. However this was not the law. Secondly, the trial judge had misdirected the jury with regard to the test to be used in determining if provocation had taken place. The test is not whether it was "likely" or "probable" that the provocation triggered off the alleged reaction, but rather whether it was reasonably possible that it could have done so, in which event a reasonable doubt would have been established. Finally, the Court of Criminal Appeal reiterated that the test in relation to provocation was a subjective one, and that that it was not necessary to show that the accused lacked an intention to kill or cause serious injury.

This decision is, therefore, important in that it makes it clear that the defence of provocation is entirely distinct from an absence of intention to kill or cause serious injury. Two other recent decisions in the area of provocation are *People (DPP) v. Kelly* (1999) and *People (DPP) v. Heaney* (2000). Both cases reiterate that the test for provocation is a *subjective* one, perhaps outlining the difficulty which trial judges have in explaining this point to juries.

(5) Provocation and battered women

The application of a defence of provocation to battered women who kill their aggressors has proved controversial. The defence of provocation is based on the concept of a sudden loss of control and the law therefore requires the accused to have acted in the heat of the moment. The longer the delay between the provoking act and the accused's actions, the more likely a court is to view it as vengeance rather than provocation.

Battered women tend not to react immediately to provocation as they have learned that this is likely to give rise to increased violence from their spouses. (O'Donovan, "Defences for battered women who kill" (1991) 18 J Law and Soc 219). They more usually suffer a "slow burn" of anger which eventually erupts and results in the killing of the abuser, often while he is asleep or drunk. The event which triggers the killing may appear relatively trivial but, when viewed in the context of a long history of domestic violence, can be seen as the last straw in a cycle of abuse.

The concept of "cumulative" provocation, whereby a court will look at the most recent provoking act not in isolation but in the context of long-term abuse, would seem to have been accepted in Ireland: *The People (DPP) v. O'Donoghue* (1992), where the accused had obtained a barring order against her husband after a history of abuse. Having allowed him to return home, he again verbally abused her, whereupon she snapped and killed him with a hammer. She was convicted of manslaughter and given a suspended sentence.

However, there is still a requirement of a sudden loss of self-control under English law, although the position in Ireland is less clear. In *R. v. Thornton (No.2)* (1996) and *R v. Ahluwalia* (1993), the defendants were battered women who waited for some time before reacting to provocation from their husbands. It was held that such a "cooling-off" period was inconsistent with a defence of provocation. However, in the latter case a less rigid approach was adopted whereby delay does not automatically rule out the defence but will be evidentially highly important as to whether provocation is made out. It could be argued that, in the light of *MacEoin*, Irish law does not require a battered woman to react in the heat of the moment. *MacEoin* illustrates a subjective approach to provocation, taking into consideration all the characteristics of the accused. In the case of a battered woman, evidence that a long history of abuse reduces the likelihood of such women killing in the heat of the moment, might well be allowed.

(6) Self-induced provocation

An accused cannot rely on the defence of provocation where he has deliberately engineered a situation in which he can claim to have been enraged. This is so even if he was, in fact, sufficiently provoked at the time of the killing. Charleton draws an analogy with the defence of intoxication:

> "The situation is analogous to a person who drinks in order to get himself into a homicidal state; in that situation drunkenness is not a defence even though at the moment of the killing the accused may be so intoxicated as to be incapable of acting with intent." (Charleton, *Offences Against the Person* (Round Hall Press, 1992), p. 149)

This principle extends to situations where the accused, although not engineering a situation in which he can claim that a killing was justified, nevertheless creates a situation where the conduct alleged to constitute provocation is a predictable outcome of his behaviour. In *R. v. Edwards* (1973), for example, the accused was a blackmailer. The victim, furious at the blackmail attempt, lunged at the defendant with a knife. The accused took the knife and killed the victim. Was the defence of provocation available? The Privy Council held that the accused could not rely on the "normal reactions" of a blackmailed person in those circumstances, but the jury should have been asked to decide whether the conduct of the victim went beyond those normal reactions. *Per* Lord Pearson:

> "No authority has been cited with regard to what may be called 'self-induced provocation'. On principle it seems reasonable to say that (1) a blackmailer cannot rely on the predictable results of his own blackmailing conduct as constituting provocation sufficient to reduce his killing of the victim from murder to manslaughter, and the predictable results may include a considerable degree of hostile reaction by the person sought to be blackmailed, for instance vituperative words or even some hostile reaction such as blows with a fist; (2) but if the hostile reaction by the person sought to be blackmailed goes to extreme lengths it might constitute sufficient provocation even for the blackmailer. (3) There would in many cases be a question of degree to be decided by the jury." (At p. 658.)

(7) Provocation by a third party

At common law provocation must come from the deceased. This would appear to be at odds with the underlying rationale of the defence as provocation was not developed to reflect condemnation of the conduct of the deceased but the sudden loss of self-control of the accused.

Further reading: McAuley, "Anticipating the Past: The Defence of Provocation in Irish Law" (1987) 50 M.L.R. 133; McAleese, "The Reasonable Man Provoked?" (1978) D.U.L.J. 53.

10.2.2 Excessive self-defence

Self-defence is a defence generally in the criminal law. Where a person uses force which is necessary to ward off an attack, and uses no more force than is necessary, then no crime is committed. (This defence has now been put on a statutory footing by section 18 of the Non-Fatal Offences Against the Person Act 1997.) However, what happens where a person acts in self-defence, but uses force which is more than is reasonably necessary?

In relation to most crimes, excessive self-defence is no defence, although it will of course be an important mitigating factor in passing sentence. This is also the position in England and Northern Ireland in relation to murder, as reiterated in *R v. Clegg* (1995). In that case, the defendant was a British soldier in Northern Ireland who was on duty at a vehicle checkpoint. A car drove through the checkpoint and then accelerated down the road. The defendant fired at the car as it went by, killing a passenger. He claimed that he fired at the car because he believed that the life of another soldier, on the other side of the road, was in danger. This defence was accepted with regard to three of the shots which he fired, but not the fourth, which was fired when the car had already passed and was fifty feet further down the road. This fourth shot had caused the death of the passenger, and he was convicted of murder with regard to this death. On appeal to the House of Lords, it was submitted that there should be a qualified defence available in those circumstances, which would reduce the offence from murder to manslaughter. This was rejected; it was well established that excessive self-defence was not available to reduce murder to manslaughter, and the House of Lords declined to change the law on this point. In England, therefore, self-defence is an all or nothing affair; an accused is either guilty of murder or entirely innocent. There is no halfway house. This is also the position in Australia.

The position in Ireland in relation to murder is different. The Supreme Court dealt with this issue in *People (AG) v. Dwyer* (1972), where the defendant had been involved in a fight outside a chip shop. He believed (he claimed) that the victim was armed with some item and that he feared for his life; as a result, he took a knife and stabbed and killed the victim. This was clearly not an objectively proportional response to any danger, and as such a plea of self-defence was not available. But could the defendant's subjective belief that the force was necessary reduce the crime to manslaughter? The Supreme Court held that it could. Two judgments were given which adopted different reasons for this result. Walsh J. held that the effect of section 4 of the Criminal Justice Act 1964 (replacing "malice aforethought" with the modern *mens rea* for murder) was to make the mental element for murder entirely subjective. It followed that, if the defendant honestly believed that the force used was necessary, then he could not be guilty of murder:

> "Our statutory provision makes it clear that the intention is personal and that it is not to be measured solely by objective standards. In my opinion, therefore, when the evidence in a case discloses a question of self-defence and where it is sought by the prosecution to show that the accused used excessive force, that it to say more than would be regarded as objectively reasonable, the prosecution must establish that the accused knew that he was using more force than was reasonably necessary. Therefore, it follows that if the accused honestly believed that the force that he did use was necessary, then he is not guilty of murder. The onus, of course, is upon the prosecution to prove beyond reasonable doubt that he knew that the force was excessive or that he did not believe that it was necessary. If the prosecution does not do so, it has failed to establish the necessary malice." (At p. 424.)

Butler J. took a different approach; if the accused honestly and primarily intended to defend himself, then he should not be held to have the necessary intention to kill or cause serious injury. Consequently, the moral culpability of the accused is reduced and the killing would amount to manslaughter only.

Notwithstanding the difference in approach between these two opinions, the overall result is clear: in Irish law excessive self-defence will operate as a partial defence, reducing murder to manslaughter. Excessive self-defence may in turn be defined as force used which is greater than that which is objectively necessary, but which the accused honestly believed to be necessary. Clearly, the accused will not be able to establish the necessary honest belief in situations where the victim presented no threat whatsoever. See, for example, *People (AG) v. Commane* (1975) in which the victim was immobilised by a blow to the head with a whisky bottle and subsequently strangled. On those facts, excessive self-defence was held not to be available to go to the jury, since the killing had taken place after the victim had been rendered incapable of further aggression.

It should be noted that there is a debate as to whether this defence has survived the passing of the Non-Fatal Offences Against the Person Act 1997. Section 18 of the 1997 Act puts self-defence on a statutory footing, but is silent as to the case of excessive self-defence, while section 22(2) abolishes common law defences in relation to the use of force in self-defence. From this, it would seem that excessive self-defence is simply done away with by section 22(2). On the other hand, the report of the Law Reform Commission on which the 1997 Act was based (*Report on Non-Fatal Offences Against the Person (1994)*) did not deal with the question of excessive self-defence. In addition, excessive self-defence is limited to the crime of murder and is, therefore, entirely inappropriate to be dealt with in an Act limited in its scope to non-fatal offences. Finally, the decision in *People (AG) v. Dwyer* (1972) is based largely on the statutory definition of the mental element of murder, which the 1997 Act does not alter. (See Bacik, "Non-Fatal Offences Against the Person Act, 1997" [1997] I.C.L.S.A. 26-19, 26-21.)

10.3 Defences unavailable to murder

10.3.1 Duress

The defence of duress is, in some ways, the opposite of the defences of provocation and excessive self-defence. Those defences are only available to a charge of murder, while the defence of duress is available in respect of most crimes, and is only unavailable to a charge of murder. The defence applies in circumstances where a person is compelled to commit a crime by virtue of threats made against him (or perhaps another person); clearly, in these circumstances, the moral culpability of the accused is reduced to the extent that his will is overborne. However, there is no question of the accused not possessing the relevant *mens rea*. He fully intends to commit the offence but his ordinary resistance is overborne to such an extent that the law will not view him as morally responsible for his actions.

The leading Irish case is *People (AG) v. Whelan* (1934). In that case, the accused was charged with receiving stolen property; his defence was that he acted under threats of extreme violence. The jury returned a verdict to the effect that he received the stolen goods, but did so under threat of immediate death or serious violence. The question presented to the Court of Criminal Appeal was whether, on foot of this verdict, the accused was guilty or innocent of the crime charged. The court treated this question as posing a simple issue: was there "such an absence of will as to absolve from guilt"? The prosecution contended that only actual physical force which left the accused no choice of will would absolve from guilt, while anything else would merely go to mitigation of punishment.

This position was, however, rejected by the court, which held that:

> "It seems to us that threats of immediate death or serious personal violence so great as to overbear the ordinary power of human resistance should be accepted as a justification for acts which would otherwise be criminal. The application of this general rule must, however, be subject to certain limitations. The commission of murder is a crime so heinous that murder should not be committed even for the price of life and in such a case the strongest duress would not be any justification." (*Per* Murnaghan J., at p. 526.)

In addition, it is necessary to show that the threats in question were still in effect at the time that the crime was committed, and that the accused did not have an opportunity to extract himself from the effect of the threats:

> "Where the excuse of duress is applicable it must further be clearly shown that the overpowering of the will was operative at the time the crime was actually committed, and, if there were reasonable opportunity for the will to reassert itself, no justification can be found in antecedent threats." (*Per* Murnaghan J., at p. 526.)

(1) Nature of threats - immediacy

People (AG) v. Whelan requires that threats should be immediate. There are, it seems, two reasons for this. First, a threat of future violence will be treated as too remote to overbear the will of the accused in the here and now. Second, a threat of future violence leaves the recipient of the threats free to seek police protection. In light of these reasons, just how immediate must a threat be before it will ground a defence of duress?

This question was dealt with in *R. v. Hudson and Taylor* (1971). The two accused were charged with perjury, having lied about the identification of a man charged with wounding. Their defence was duress: an associate of the man had threatened before the trial to cut them up, and at the trial they could see that associate sitting in the public gallery. Was this threat sufficiently immediate? And could they plead duress where it had been open to them to seek police protection before the threat would be carried out? It was held by the Court of Appeal on the first issue that it was a matter for the jury to decide if the threats were sufficiently immediate, remembering that:

> "the threats of [the associate] were likely to be no less compelling, because their execution could not be effected in the court room, if they could be carried out in the streets of Salford the same night." (*per* Lord Widgery C.J., at p. 207.)

As regards the second issue, the availability of police protection, it was held that this would defeat a defence of duress where it was reasonably open to the accused to neutralise a threat:

> "it is always open to [the prosecution] to prove that the accused failed to avail himself of some opportunity which was reasonably open to him to render the threat ineffective, and that upon this being established the threat in question can no longer be relied upon by the defence. In deciding whether such an opportunity was reasonably open to the accused the jury should have regard to this age and circumstances, and to any risks to him which may be involved in the course of action relied upon." (*per* Lord Widgery C.J., at p. 207.)

This was, however, a question for the jury, and since the defence of duress had not been left to the jury, the convictions were quashed.

(2) Objective or subjective test?

The test laid down by *People (AG) v. Whelan* seems to be objective: an accused cannot avail of the defence unless the threats in question would have overborne "the ordinary power of human resistance" and not merely his personal power of resistance. The weak-willed accused will not, it seems, be able to plead duress. On principle, however, it seems to be right to impose an objective test in this area, notwithstanding that Irish criminal law usually leans towards subjective tests: as Charleton himself points out:

> "Duress ... involves a rational choice between two evils. The threat made to the accused must be of a grave order of magnitude to excuse the commission of a crime. The law might fail to fulfil its objective of ordering society if petty excuses for criminal action were allowed." (Charleton, *Criminal Law - Cases and Materials* (Butterworths, 1992), p. 201.)

(3) Application to murder

It is clear that duress does not apply to murder itself, and *People (AG) v. Whelan* leaves open the question whether there are other, particularly grave offences to which it does not apply. It is unclear, however, whether the defence can apply to the various degrees of participation in the crime of murder. There is no authority from this jurisdiction on this point, and contradictory authority from the House of Lords, which held in *DPP for Northern Ireland v. Lynch* (1975) that the defence was available to a charge of aiding and abetting murder, while in *R. v. Howe* (1987) it overruled *Lynch* and refused to allow the defence on the same charge.

(4) Membership of a violent organisation

Suppose an accused voluntarily joins the IRA, commits a crime, and then claims that had he failed to do so, retribution would have been forthcoming. Can a defendant rely on "self-induced duress" in this way? The answer is no - the person who voluntarily puts himself in a position where duress will be applied is outside the scope of the defence. *R. v. Fitzpatrick* (1977) was a case in which the accused was charged with murder, robbery and membership of a proscribed organisation. He was a member of the Official IRA, but testified that he had attempted to leave but was prevented from doing so by threats of violence to himself and his parents. The trial judge held that the defence of duress was not available on those facts. On appeal, it was contended that duress should be available to members of such organisations, at least where they had made sufficient efforts to disassociate themselves from the organisation. It was held by the Court of Criminal Appeal that duress was a defence having its roots in an absence of moral blameworthiness on the part of the accused and therefore the defence was not available where the accused knowingly and voluntarily joins such an organisation:

> "If a person behaves immorally by, for example, committing himself to an unlawful conspiracy, he ought not to be able to take advantage of the pressure exercised on him by his fellow criminals in order to put on when it suits him the breastplate of righteousness." (*per* Lowry L.C.J., at p. 31)

For the same reason, it was held to be irrelevant that the accused had tried to leave the organisation.

However, it seems that the accused must have some knowledge of the violent nature of the organisation before he joins: "innocent" membership does not make the accused morally culpable so as to defeat the defence of duress. So, in *R. v. Shepherd* (1987), the accused voluntarily joined an organised gang of shoplifters; when he sought to leave, his evidence was that he was threatened with violence. In these circumstances, it was held that the defence of duress should have been left to the jury: it was arguable that the defendant had failed to appreciate the risk of violence, and if that were the case, then the defendant would be entitled to rely on the defence of duress.

(5) Duress and marital coercion

A curious rebuttable presumption existed at common law that a wife who committed a crime in the presence of her husband did so as a result of his coercion and so was immune from punishment, subject to an exception in the case of particularly serious crimes (Charleton, *Offences Against the Person* (Round Hall Press, 1992), p. 165). The Supreme Court, however, in *State (DPP) v. Walsh and Connelly* (1981), held that the presumption reflected a disparity in status between husband and wife which ran counter to the modern concept of equality, and that the presumption did not, therefore, survive the coming into force of the Constitution.

10.3.2 Necessity

The defence of necessity runs parallel to the defence of duress, and is often described as "duress of circumstances". The defence has the same underlying rationale, which is that a defendant ought not to be punished for breaking the law where he has no choice in the matter, whether as a result of threats (duress) or surrounding circumstances (necessity). The defence is also, therefore, subject to some of the same limitations. In particular, the defence of necessity is not available to a charge of murder.

In *R. v. Dudley and Stephens* (1884), the two defendants and the deceased found themselves at sea, in an open boat, without food or water. After several days without food or water, the two defendants killed the deceased, a 17-year-old boy, and survived on his body and blood for four days, at which point they were rescued by a passing ship. Could they rely on the defence of necessity? The jury found that: if the defendants had not fed on the boy, that they would probably have died before the four days were out; that the boy was likely to have died first; that at the time of the killing there was no reasonable prospect of relief; but that there was no greater necessity for killing the boy than either of the two defendants. Even on these findings, the Queen's Bench Division held that necessity was not available as a defence:

"To preserve one's life is generally speaking, a duty, but it may be the plainest and the highest duty to sacrifice it ... It is not correct, therefore, to say that there is any absolute and unqualified necessity to preserve one's life ... It is enough in a Christian country to remind ourselves of the Great Example which we profess to follow ... It is not needful to point out the awful danger of admitting the principle which has been contended for. Who is to be the judge of this sort of necessity? By what measure is the comparative value of lives to be measured? ... We are often compelled to set up standards we cannot reach ourselves, and to lay down rules which we could not ourselves satisfy. But a man has no right to declare temptation to be an excuse, though he might himself have yielded to it, nor allow compassion for the criminal to change or weaken in any manner the legal definition of the crime."

The accused were, therefore, sentenced to death, which was commuted to six months imprisonment.

The parameters of the defence of necessity have been set out by the Supreme Court of Victoria, in *R. v. Loughnan* (1981). In that case, the defendant was charged with escape from prison; he admitted escaping, but claimed that he did so because he believed that he would be attacked and killed by other prisoners. The trial judge refused to allow the defence of necessity to go before the jury, and the defendant was convicted. On appeal, it was held that on the particular facts of the case, the defence did not have to go before the jury. However, the court dealt with the wider issue of necessity and held as follows:

"[T]here are three elements involved in the defence of necessity. First, the criminal act or acts must have been done only in order to avoid certain consequences which would otherwise have inflicted irreparable evil upon the accused or upon others whom he was bound to protect ... The other two elements involved ... can, for convenience be given the labels immediate peril and proportion ... the accused must honestly believe on reasonable grounds that he was placed in a situation of immediate peril ... The element of proportion simply means that the acts done to avoid the imminent peril must not be out of proportion to the peril to be avoided. Put in another way, the test is: would a reasonable man in the position of the accused have considered that he had any alternative to doing what he did to avoid the peril?" (*Per* Young C.J.) and

"The essential conditions, I consider, so far as presently relevant, are that: 1. The harm to be justified must have been committed under pressure either of physical forces or exerted by some human agency so that 'an urgent situation of imminent peril' has been created. 2. The accused must have acted with the intention of avoiding greater harm or so as to have made possible 'the preservation of at least an equal value'. 3. There was open to the accused no alternative, other than that adopted by him, to avoid the greater harm or 'to conserve the value'." (*Per* Crockett J.).

If, therefore, the accused had genuinely escaped with the intention of avoiding a danger to his life, and there was no other alternative open to him, then the defence of duress would have been open to him.

Another example of the defence can be seen in *R. v. Conway* (1988). In this case, the defendant was convicted of reckless driving. His defence was necessity or, as it was termed, duress of circumstances. Two young men in civilian clothes had come running towards the car, in which he had a passenger who had been the target of a shooting shortly before. The passenger shouted at the defendant to drive off, and the defendant did so, believing that the two men were trying to kill the passenger. The car was then chased by the two men in an unmarked vehicle, at which point the driver drove in a reckless manner. The pursuers turned out to be police officers seeking to arrest the passenger. Could the driver plead necessity in those circumstances? It was held that he could. The Court of Appeal held that duress and necessity were different terms for aspects of the one underlying defence, and that the defence, whatever it is termed, should have been left to the jury. This of course illustrates the fact that the threat or danger involved need not be to the defendant himself, but may be to another person.

10.4 General defences

10.4.1 Lawful use of force/self-defence

We have already dealt with the defence of excessive self-defence in the context of murder. More generally, the use of force will be lawful in circumstances including self-defence, the defence of property, the carrying out of an arrest, or the prevention of a crime. The parameters of this defence are now set out in sections 18-22 of the Non-Fatal Offences Against the Person Act 1997, which implement the recommendations of the Law Reform Commission in their *Report on Non-Fatal Offences Against the Person* (L.R.C. 45-1994):

"18(1) - The use of force by a person for any of the following purposes, if only such as is reasonable in the circumstances as he or she believes them to be, does not constitute an offence -

(a) to protect himself or herself or a member of the family of that person or another from injury, assault or detention caused by a criminal act;"

This restates the Irish position that no special relation to the person threatened is required, which departs from the position in other jurisdictions that there must be "some special nexus or relationship between the person relying on the doctrine to justify what he did in defence of another and that other" (*Devlin v. Armstrong* (1971), at pages 35-36.). In that case, the defendant was the activist Bernadette Devlin, charged with incitement to riot and other public order offences in the barricades in the Bogside. She had encouraged others to build the barricade, throw petrol bombs at the police, and so on. Her defence was that she was acting in legitimate self defence and defence of others in the belief that the police, if they entered the Bogside, would commit crimes of assault and unlawful attacks on property. This defence was rejected, on a number of grounds including the ground that she could not act in self-defence of persons with whom she had no special nexus. Even though this ground would not be applicable in this jurisdiction, the other grounds would be, in particular the ground that the alleged danger was not sufficiently specific or imminent to justify the force used, which was, in any event, excessive to the alleged danger.

The position in this jurisdiction was set out in *People (AG) v. Keatley* (1954). In that case, the defendant was charged with manslaughter, having struck and killed another in defence of his brother. The court held that it was not necessary to prove any special relationship between the defendant and the person being defended: the underlying principle of the defence is the right to prevent the commission of an unlawful act, and the question of any special relationship is irrelevant to that principle.

Section 18(1) also provides that the use of force by a person will be lawful:

"(b) to protect himself or herself or (with the authority of that other) another from trespass to the person; or

(c) to protect his or her property from appropriation, destruction or damage caused by a criminal act or from trespass or infringement; or

(d) to protect property belonging to another from appropriation, destruction or damage caused by a criminal act or (with the authority of that other) from trespass or infringement; or

(e) to prevent crime or breach of the peace."

This does not authorise the use of excessive force to prevent *petty* crime. The force must still be "reasonable in the circumstances" and it is debatable whether the use of any force would be reasonable where the offence is trivial. Even where an offence is not trivial, the force used must still be proportionate to the gravity of the offence. Speeding motorists cannot be shot dead.

Section 18 goes on to provide that "crimes" and "criminal acts" include acts which would be criminal but for the fact that an accused would be able to raise a defence of infancy, duress, necessity, involuntariness, intoxication or insanity. In addition, whether an act falls within (a) to (e) of section 18(1) is to be judged by the circumstances as the accused believes them to be, *i.e.* a subjective approach. This has the consequence that a person cannot rely on a defence which was unknown to him at the time of the use of force. It follows that the use of force without apparent justification at the time, which in retrospect turns out to have been justified, is unlawful.

In addition, this section does not provide a defence for the use of force against a person known to be a Garda acting in the course of his duty unless immediately necessary to prevent physical harm to a person. This preserves the position at common law, which can be seen in the case of *R. v. Fennell* (1970). In that case, the accused was convicted of assaulting a police officer who was attempting to arrest his son. His defence was that he believed, on reasonable grounds, that the arrest was unlawful. This was held not to be a defence in these circumstances.

A limitation on this defence is contained in section 18(7) which provides that:

> "The defence provided by this section does not apply to a person who causes conduct or a state of affairs with a view to using force to resist or terminate it:
>
> But the defence may apply although the occasion for the use of force arises only because the person does something he or she may lawfully do, knowing that such an occasion will arise."

A person may not engineer a situation in which he can use force, but may use force notwithstanding that he foresaw that his conduct might give rise to a need for force. This codifies the rule in *R. v. Browne* (1973) that a person may not rely on self-defence where they have deliberately provoked an attack with a view to using force to resist. It also echoes the inability of a defendant to rely on self-induced provocation or intoxication. However, a person remains free to engage in lawful activities notwithstanding that unlawful violence from others may result, following *R. v. Field* (1972). The Law Reform Commission states: "From the point of view of public order, the practical conclusion to be drawn from this is that where a danger arises that the lawful exercise of rights may result in a breach of the peace, the proper remedy is the presence of police in sufficient numbers to preserve the peace, and not the legal condemnation of those exercising their rights". (See *Report on Non-Fatal Offences Against the Person* (L.R.C. 45-1994), page 29.)

Another exception is provided where force is used to carry out an arrest. This is provided for by section 19(1), which states that:

> "The use of force by a person in effecting or assisting in a lawful arrest, if only such as is reasonable in the circumstances as he or she believes them to be, does not constitute an offence."

Section 19 goes on to provide that whether the arrest is to be treated as lawful is to be determined according to the circumstances, as the accused believes them to be, *i.e.* a subjective approach.

A definition of force is contained in section 20(1) of the Act which provides that:

> "For the purposes of sections 18-19 -
>
> (a) a person uses force in relation to another person or property not only when he or she applies force to, but also where he or she causes an impact on, the body of that person or that property;
>
> (b) a person shall be treated as using force in relation to another person if -
>
> (i) he or she threatens that person with its use, or
>
> (ii) he or she detains that person without actually using it; and
>
> (c) a person shall be treated as using force in relation to property if he or she threatens a person with its use in relation to property."

This definition ensures that both direct and indirect assaults are treated as the use of force, as is the threatened use of force.

Section 20, subsections (3) and (4) also set out certain criteria to be followed in deciding whether force used was in fact reasonable. These provide that:

> "(3) A threat of force may be reasonable although the actual use of force may not be.
>
> (4) The fact that a person had an opportunity to retreat before using force shall be taken into account, in conjunction with other relevant evidence, in determining whether the use of force was reasonable."

This restates the common law position, set out in *R. v. McInnes* (1971) that there is no absolute duty to retreat, but whether the defendant had an opportunity to retreat is relevant to determining whether he acted reasonably. In that case, the accused was charged with murder arising out of a fight between greasers and skinheads, which ended in the stabbing of one of the skinheads. The trial judge directed the jury that there was a duty to retreat as far as possible before self-defence could be relied upon, but this direction was held to be incorrect by the Court of Appeal.

10.4.2 Other defences preserved

The 1997 Act, although it provides new statutory defences for the use of force, does not rule out the use of other defences which might be available also. This is clear by section 22(1), which provides that:

> "The provisions of this Act have effect subject to any enactment or rule of law providing a defence, or providing lawful authority, justification or excuse for an act or omission."

The Act does, however, do away with the common law defence of the lawful use of force, as made clear by section 22(2), which states:

> "(2) Notwithstanding subsection (1) any defence available under the common law in respect of the use of force within the meaning of sections 18-19 or an act immediately preparatory to the use of force, for the purposes mentioned in sections 18-19 is hereby abolished."

This subsection abolishes the common law defence of necessary force, and makes it clear that any such defence is now entirely contained in sections 18-19. It does not, however, affect the availability of any other defence. It should be noted that there is a possibility that this subsection does away with the defence of excessive self-defence in relation to murder. This point is discussed earlier in this chapter in relation to excessive self defence.

The effect of this defence is that only reasonable force can be used. At the same time, however, the courts will not demand exact precision in the amount of force which is used. As Holmes J. put it in *Brown v. US* (1921): "Detached reflection cannot be demanded in the presence of an uplifted knife." (at p. 343.).

If a person mistakenly believes he is faced with a threat, then he will be judged according to his genuine judgment of the situation. This was the position at common law: *R. v. Williams (Gladstone)* (1987), where the Court of Appeal held that the appellant was entitled to be judged according to his view of the circumstances, even though he had made a genuine error in believing that a youth was being assaulted when in fact he was being arrested for stealing. The 1997 Act preserves this position: sections 18(1), 18(5), 19(1) and 19(3).

10.4.3 Intoxication

The availability of intoxication as a defence has always been problematic. Moral disapproval of intoxication contributed to a reluctance to admit that it might mitigate guilt: Aristotle recommended that a person who committed a crime while drunk should be punished twice, once for committing the crime and once for being drunk. Moral disapproval aside, the large proportion of crimes which are committed as the result of intoxication leads to a justifiable judicial reluctance to admit intoxication as a defence lest the result should be unduly lenient. The fact that a person's inhibitions and judgment are lowered while drunk is not, therefore, in itself a defence; it may even be an aggravating factor, as in the case of road traffic offences. There is, it follows, no general defence of intoxication.

However, a so-called defence of intoxication does arise in situations where an offence requires *mens rea*, and the defendant claims that he lacked that mental element through the effects of intoxication. For example, murder requires an intention to kill or cause serious injury: if the accused is too drunk to form that intention, then a conviction for murder cannot be forthcoming.

(1) Dutch courage

This defence is strictly limited in scope. In the first place, it does not apply in circumstances where a person took drink or drugs in order to give himself Dutch courage to carry out a crime. So, in *Attorney General for Northern Ireland v. Gallagher* (1961), the accused was charged with the murder of his wife. The evidence showed that he, while sober, had made up his mind to kill his wife. He then downed a bottle of whisky, either for Dutch courage or to drown his conscience after the killing. While drunk, he killed his wife. His argument was simple: at the time of the killing, he was so drunk as to lack the intention to kill or cause serious injury. Although he had, earlier, intended to kill his wife, the *actus reus* and the *mens rea* did not coincide. This was, unsurprisingly, rejected by the House of Lords:

"If a man, whilst sane and sober, forms an intention to kill and makes preparation for it, knowing it is a wrong thing to do, and then gets himself drunk so as to give himself Dutch courage to do the killing, and whilst drunk carries out his intention, he cannot rely on this self-induced drunkenness as a defence to a charge of murder, nor even as reducing it to manslaughter. He cannot say that he got himself into such a stupid state that he was incapable of an intent to kill ... The wickedness of his mind before he got drunk is enough to condemn him, coupled with the act which he intended to do and did do." (*Per* Lord Denning at p. 314.)

(2) Basic/specific intent

The second major limitation to the availability of the defence is imposed by the distinction between specific and basic intent. This is an artificial distinction, best explained in terms of *intention to carry out an action* and *intention to achieve a result*. If a crime merely requires intention to perform a particular act, then it is a crime of basic intent. An example is the crime of assault, which simply requires an intention to inflict force on another without their consent. If, however, a crime requires an intention to achieve a particular result by that act, then the crime is one of specific intent. An example is the crime of murder, which requires both a particular act, and an intention as a result of that act to cause serious injury or death.

This distinction was elaborated in the context of intoxication by the House of Lords in *DPP v. Majewski* (1976). In that case, the accused was charged with assault occasioning actual bodily harm and assault on a police officer in the course of his duty. He was a drug addict, and had taken a large quantity of drugs and alcohol before the offences. He claimed to have blanked out and not to know what he was doing, and there was some medical evidence to the effect that this was possible. The trial judge directed the jury not to treat intoxication as being in any way a defence to the charges. On appeal, this direction was upheld. The basic position was expressed as being that voluntary drunkenness is never an excuse, to which an exception existed only in the limited class of offences which require proof of a specific intent. Where a person becomes voluntarily drunk, then the *mens rea* required is in effect supplied by his conduct in becoming drunk:

"A man who by voluntarily taking drink and drugs gets himself into an aggressive state in which he does not know what he is doing and then makes a vicious assault can hardly say with any plausibility that what

he did was a pure accident which should render him immune from any
criminal liability." (*per* Lord Salmon at p. 157.),

This approach has not met with universal approval. The distinction
between basic intent and specific intent is admitted to be arbitrary, and
for that reason the High Court of Australia has adopted a different
approach in *R. v. O'Connor* (1979-1980), holding that evidence of
intoxication, however caused, was admissible to show absence of
intent. The basic intent/specific intent dichotomy has also been
rejected in New Zealand and South Africa. The law in Ireland is
unclear on this point. (See Law Reform Commission, *Consultation
Paper on Intoxication as a Defence to a Criminal Offence (1995)*,
p. 20.)

(3) Includes intoxication by other drugs

The operation of the *DPP v. Majewski* distinction can be seen in *R v.
Lipman* (1970), which also demonstrates the application of the defence
in the case of intoxication by drugs other than alcohol. In this case, the
accused took LSD and, in the course of hallucinating that he was being
attacked by snakes, killed his girlfriend. Charged with murder, he
claimed that he had no knowledge of what he was doing and no intention to harm her. He was found guilty of manslaughter, and appealed. It
was held by the Court of Appeal that where a killing results from an
unlawful and dangerous act, that no specific intent is required for the
crime of manslaughter: consequently, self-induced intoxication is no
defence to a charge of manslaughter.

An interesting case on intoxication by drugs is *R. v. Hardie* (1984).
In this case, the accused was upset after the breakdown of his relationship with his girlfriend and took several valium pills to calm his nerves.
In fact, he ended up starting a fire in her flat. Could he rely on the
defence of intoxication? It was held that he could, as though he was
involuntarily intoxicated. He did not know, nor should he have known,
that valium in that quantity could produce aggressive effects. He reasonably believed that it would merely have a sedative effect. Had he
known that it might produce aggression, then he would not have been
able to rely on his self-induced intoxication, but since he did not, he
was not morally blameworthy in simply taking the drug, and the issue
of intoxication should have been left to the jury, who should have been
directed to consider whether he was being reckless in taking the drug.

(4) Involuntary intoxication

The parameters of the intoxication defence are set, consciously or otherwise, by judicial disapproval of those who voluntarily drink to excess or indulge in drugs. This disapproval obviously has no place in situations where a person is involuntarily intoxicated, and intoxication is, therefore available as a defence in those situations, even to crimes of basic intent. This has been accepted since the case of *R. v. Pearson* (1835) in which Parke B. stated that "if a party be made drunk by the stratagem or fraud of another, he is not responsible" (at p. 145). However, involuntary intoxication is given quite a narrow ambit. Where a person knows he is drinking alcohol, but is not aware of how strong it is, his intoxication is not involuntary: *R. v. Allen* (1988).

In addition, the defence only applies where the involuntary intoxication is such as to negative intent. It does not apply where the accused, though intoxicated through no fault of his own, still has the capability to form an intention, although his inhibitions might be lowered. This can be seen in *R. v. Kingston* (1994), in which the accused was a man with paedophiliac tendencies. Another man, in order to blackmail the accused, lured a boy to his flat and drugged him. He then (the defendant alleged) laced the defendant's drink. The defendant, involuntarily intoxicated, but aware of what he was doing, sexually abused the boy. The defence of intoxication was rejected, even on the assumption that without the spiked drink the accused would not have given way to his paedophiliac tendencies. The jury, the House of Lords held, had been properly directed that even a drugged intention was still an intention. The fact that the defendant's self-control had been lowered by deception was a factor which went to mitigation of penalty only.

Further reading: O'Malley, "Intoxication and Criminal Responsibility" [1991] I.C.L.J. 86; McAuley, "The Intoxication Defence in Criminal Law" (1997) 32 *I.r. Ju.r (n.s.)* 243; Law Reform Commission, *Consultation Paper on Intoxication as a Defence to a Criminal Offence* (1995); Law Reform Commission, *Report on Intoxication* (1995).

10.4.4 Mistake

Mistake, like intoxication, is not a general defence. Like intoxication, however, mistake may neutralise an element of the *mens rea* of the offence in question. This is subject to one obvious limitation: if the offence in question is one of strict liability, then any mistake will be of no effect, since there is no *mens rea* requirement to be defeated. An example of mistake as a defence can be seen in *R. v. Morgan* (1976), where an honest though unreasonable belief in consent was held to be a defence to a charge of rape. Similarly, the shooting of a person mistaken for a deer will not amount to murder, nor will the taking of an article believed to be the accused's own amount to larceny.

A mistake must go to an element relevant to the offence: if A thinks that he is killing B when in fact he is killing C, then the offence of murder is still committed. Mistake of law is not ordinarily a defence: so if I believe it is legal to kill a person who burgles my home, I may nevertheless be guilty of murder. However, mistake of law will be relevant in some cases. In larceny, for example, an essential part of the offence is that the defendant should act without claim of right *made in good faith*. If a person holds a mistaken view of the law, leading him to the belief that he has a legitimate claim to a particular piece of property, then he will have a claim of right sufficient to defeat the charge of larceny.

At common law a mistake, in order to constitute a defence, had to be reasonable. So, in *R. v. Tolson* (1889), the defendant believed on reasonable grounds that her husband was dead, having been lost at sea. She remarried, only to be charged with bigamy when her husband reappeared several years later. She was acquitted, but only on the ground that her belief was reasonable. (And, indeed, the minority would have held the offence to be one of strict liability.) However *R. v. Morgan* expresses a more modern view, and makes it clear that in some circumstances an unreasonable mistake will amount to a defence. Similarly, *People (DPP) v. Murray* (1977) makes it clear that assessment of criminal responsibility in this jurisdiction is normally to be conducted on subjective standards. It follows that the defence of mistake is to be judged on subjective grounds.

There are, however, exceptions to this. If the *mens rea* of a crime is negligence, then clearly a negligent mistake will afford no defence. So, in the case of *R. v. Foxford* (1974), the accused was a soldier on patrol in Northern Ireland who shot and killed a twelve-year-old boy when firing at a gunman. His defence was that he had mistook the boy for the gunman, but it was held that since this mistake was in itself grossly negligent it could not afford a defence to a charge of manslaughter.

Whether a mistake was reasonable may be taken into account by a jury in deciding whether it was in fact made. This is set out by statute in the particular case of rape, in section 2(2) of the Criminal Law (Rape) Act 1981:

> "It is hereby declared that if at a trial for a rape offence the jury has to consider whether a man believed that a woman was consenting to sex-

ual intercourse, the presence or absence of reasonable grounds for such a belief is a matter to which the jury is to have regard, in conjunction with any other relevant matters, in considering whether he so believed.".

However, this section merely restates the existing law, by which the reasonableness of a belief may be taken into account in deciding whether it was honestly held.

10.4.5 Consent

When will consent be a defence? This varies, as we have seen, from offence to offence, and from victim to victim. For example, consent is no defence to a charge of murder, while children under 15 and the mentally impaired are incapable of consenting to acts which would constitute sexual assaults, and a girl under 17 cannot consent to sexual intercourse. Equally, it appears from *R. v. Brown* (1993) that consent will not be a defence to a charge of causing serious harm contrary to section 4 of the Non-Fatal Offences Against the Person Act 1997.

10.4.6 Infancy

"Criminal law is essentially an adult business. Prisons are designed to punish and rehabilitate mature offenders. Children have no place within a system which may corrupt them further or which may break an undeveloped spirit." (Charleton, *Criminal Law - Cases and Materials* (Butterworths, 1992), p. 271.)

The criminal liability of children is governed at common law by the doctrine of *doli incapax*. This has two parts. First, a child under the age of seven years is conclusively presumed to be incapable of committing a crime. While this is phrased in the form of a presumption, it is important to note that it has the effect of a substantive rule of law: a crime cannot be committed by a child under seven years. Second, a child aged between seven and fourteen years is presumed to be incapable of committing a crime, but this presumption can be rebutted if it can be shown that the child realised that what he was doing was wrong, or, as some older cases put it, that the child had a "mischievous discretion".

This is quite a high standard, and it is not enough to show that the child knew that his conduct was merely naughty or mischievous. In *KM v. DPP* (1994) Morris J. accepted that it must be shown that the child knew what he was doing was gravely or seriously wrong. In that case, a child was charged with sexual assaults on other children when he was aged thirteen. It was accepted, however, that his threats to kill the children if they told anyone what he had done could establish that he knew his conduct was seriously wrong.

(1) Infancy: the special case of rape

At common law, a conclusive presumption existed that a boy under the age of fourteen years could not commit rape. This presumption was limited to cases of rape (or other offences involving intercourse) and did not extend to any other forms of sexual offence. The presumption was therefore an anomaly, and a boy under fourteen could be charged with indecent assault on facts which would otherwise amount to rape. The presumption was removed by section 6 of the Criminal Law (Rape) (Amendment) Act 1990 and a boy under the age of fourteen can now be charged with rape, subject to the normal doctrine of *doli incapax*.

(2) Procedural matters

Where a person under the age of 21 is found guilty of a crime, special rules apply to the institution to which that person may be sent. These rules apply regardless of whether a defence of infancy would be available to that person, and apply having regard to the age of the offender at the date of trial, not at the date on which the offence was committed.

A child offender under the age of 12 must be sent to industrial school if a custodial sentence is to be imposed. Offenders under the age of 15 may be sent to industrial school; and this upper age limit may be extended to the age of 17. A reformatory school is also available to offenders between the age of 12 and 17. An offender may be detained here until the age of 19 or (in certain limited circumstances) 21.

Formally known as a borstal, St. Patrick's Institution and two other centres of equivalent status (Loughan House and Shanganagh Castle) are available for offenders between the ages of 17 and 21. Persons over 17 years of age may be sent to prison. Below that age, persons may only be sent to prison where they are certified as being of such an unruly and depraved character that they cannot be detained elsewhere.

People (DPP) v. W (1998) illustrated problems with this approach. In that case, the accused was a 16-year-old girl who pleaded guilty to murder before the Central Criminal Court. A sentence of 7 years imprisonment was imposed on her. On appeal the Court of Criminal Appeal found that no suitable detention facilities were available for the appellant (who was still aged 16); the only option available to the court would be to direct that she be detained in the women's prison in Mountjoy, which was clearly not a suitable environment for her. For that reason, the court directed the remainder of her sentence be suspended.

(3) Reform

Problems with the criminal justice system as it relates to juveniles are readily apparent. At a basic level, the age at which a child faces criminal responsibility is strikingly low: compare Canada, another common law jurisdiction which has chosen the age of 12, or England which applies an age of 10. It is striking to realise that the common law originally set the age of criminal responsibility at 12, during a time when childhood was not as protracted as it is today.

An interesting comparison can be made with the English position, which has been modified in stages by legislation. First, the age at which criminal responsibility begins was raised to 10: Children and Young Persons Act 1933, amended by the Children and Young Persons Act 1963. More recently, the Crime and Disorder Act 1998 abolishes the presumption of *doli incapax*. As a result, English law now takes the straightforward approach that children under the age of 10 are not criminally responsible, while those over that age are criminally responsible in the ordinary way.

The low age of responsibility in Irish law is to some extent mitigated by the presumption of *doli incapax*. However, this presumption presents difficulties of its own. The most significant of these is the paradox noted by Glanville Williams (*Criminal Law: The General Part* (1961), page 818) that the child whose moral standards are warped, so that he believes crimes to be right, is to be found innocent; as a result, the child most in need of help falls by definition outside the scope of the criminal law. But the presumption also causes difficulty by reason of being a blunt instrument: it presents criminal responsibility in black and white terms, failing to recognise that in the case of a child there are varying degrees of awareness, maturity and thus responsibility.

The Children Bill 1999 proposes to reform the age of criminal responsibility. Children under twelve years of age will benefit from a conclusive presumption of *doli incapax*. The rebuttable presumption of *doli incapax* up to fourteen years of age will be placed on a statutory footing.

Further reading: O'Malley, *Sexual Offences - Law, Policy and Punishment* (Round Hall Sweet & Maxwell, 1996), pages 51-52; Charleton, *Criminal Law - Cases and Materials* (Butterworths, 1992), pages 271-275; Davis, "A Brief Outline of the Juvenile Justice System in Ireland" *(July 1998) Bar Review* p. 427; Hanly, "The Defence of Infancy", (1996) 6 I.C.L.J. 72; Hanly, "Child Offenders: The Changing Response of Irish Law" (1997) 19 D.U.L.J. 113.

10.4.7 Entrapment

(1) Introduction

Suppose that A approaches B with the suggestion that they commit a crime together. After some time, A persuades B of the merits of the plan. They carry out the crime, only to find the police waiting as they make their exit. It emerges that A is an undercover policeman who was acting with the intention of luring B into committing a crime. Has B committed a crime and, if so, does B have any defence?

Clearly B has voluntarily carried out a particular act with the necessary intention. The fact that this intention was procured by another does not make a difference, so long as the intention was formed freely. (The situation would, of course, be different if there was any question of duress.)

The question therefore remains whether B has a defence in respect of the crime which otherwise he has committed. The traditional answer was that entrapment was no defence, and this was the approach taken by the House of Lords in *R. v. Sang* (1980). In that case, the defendant was charged with conspiracy to utter counterfeit U.S. bank notes. He claimed that he had been induced to commit the offence by an informer acting on the instructions of the police, and that he would not have committed any crime but for the inducement. The House of Lords accepted earlier Court of Appeal authority, and held that:

> "it is now well settled that the defence called entrapment does not exist in English law ... A man who intends to commit a crime and actually commits it is guilty of the offence whether or not he has been persuaded or induced to commit it, no matter by whom." (At 443, *per* Lord Salmon.)

Of course, even under this view, an entrapment-type situation may be relevant as a mitigating factor when sentence is being passed, a point which was explicitly made in *R. v. Sang*.

Other jurisdictions have not taken the same view as is taken in England: for example, in the United States the courts have held that entrapment is a substantive defence which is available to an accused person who can show that he was not predisposed to commit a crime, but only did so as a result of the persuasion of agents of the state. This position was adopted in *Sherman v. United States* (1958). In that case, the defendant was a drug addict who attended a drug treatment clinic. Another patient at that clinic was an undercover police agent. The agent repeatedly told the defendant that he needed a fix, and contrived opportunities to bump into the defendant and ask the defendant to supply him with drugs. The defendant refused on several occasions, but eventually agreed to buy heroin for the agent. When he did so, he was arrested.

On those facts, the Supreme Court held that a substantive defence of entrapment was open to the defendant. The court indicated that stealth and strategy were acceptable parts of police procedure, but only when they were directed towards the prevention and detection of crime: they ceased to be acceptable when they were directed towards the manufacture of crime. Accordingly, the Supreme Court held that the defence was available to a person who had no pre-disposition to commit the crime alleged, but did so only as a result of police persuasion.

What is the position in Ireland? It remains unclear how the Irish courts would adjudicate on a case where a substantive defence of entrapment was advanced. The case of *Dental Board v. O'Callaghan* (1969) suggests that the English approach would be followed. In that case, the Dental Board, a regulatory body, suspected the defendant of practising as a dentist despite being unqualified to do so. To obtain evidence, it sent an inspector to have the defendant carry out work which was reserved for dentists, which he did. An issue arose as to whether, in the circumstances, the evidence obtained by an *agent provocateur* was admissible. The High Court (Butler J.) held that it was, and approved of English authority to the effect that the methods used by the police in obtaining evidence should not be grounds on which a conviction could be quashed, although the element of entrapment could be taken into account in determining sentence.

On the other hand, the recent case of *Quinlivan v. Conroy* (1998) seems to suggest the contrary. In that case, the extradition of the applicant was sought, on foot of a number of charges, including charges arising out of an escape from prison. The applicant alleged that this escape was facilitated by a prison guard who was acting as an *agent provocateur* in order to gather evidence on the applicant and his associates. The applicant made the case that, in those circumstances, extradition should not be granted since, under Irish law, no offence would have been committed. (That is, that in such circumstances a defence of entrapment would be available in Irish law.) Although the Supreme Court did not explicitly rule on this point, it did seem to have some sympathy for the argument that a state which had facilitated the commission of a crime should be debarred from seeking the extradition of a person in relation to that crime (*per* O'Flaherty J., at page 8 of transcript). Such an argument would, of course, tend to favour the concept of entrapment as a substantive defence.

We have, therefore, seen two possible ways of dealing with the entrapment problem. One, exemplified by the U.S. approach, is to allow entrapment as a substantive defence to a criminal charge. The other, that adopted in England, is to refuse to allow entrapment as a substantive defence, but to take it into account as a factor mitigating any punishment which may be imposed. It should, however, be remembered that other approaches are possible. In particular, the courts could take the view that evidence obtained by way of entrapment was unfairly obtained, and refuse to admit that evidence; or the courts could rule that prosecutions founded on entrapment-type situations amount to an abuse of the process of the courts (which latter approach would be similar to that adopted by the Supreme Court in *State (Trimbole) v. Governor of Mountjoy Prison* (1985), where the court held that the wrongful arrest of a person amounted to a deliberate and conscious breach of his constitutional rights so as to make any subsequent proceedings consequent on that arrest an abuse of the process of the court). The Canadian position is that proceedings in entrapment-type situations can be stayed as being an abuse of process. Whether proceedings will be stayed depends primarily on the outrageousness of police conduct. The prior disposition of the accused towards committing the crime may also be taken into account.

(2) Influence of the E.C.H.R.

To some extent, Irish law has been overtaken by developments at European level. A recent decision of the European Court of Human Rights has determined that the European Convention on Human Rights requires member states to control the use of *agents provocateurs* and in particular requires member states to limit the use of evidence obtained in such circumstances.

This decision is *Texeira de Castro v. Portugal* (1997). In that case, the applicant had been convicted before the national courts of drug trafficking. His name had been supplied to undercover officers by another individual, and the officers, accompanied by that individual, went to his house and indicated that they wished to buy a considerable amount of heroin. The applicant agreed to sell it to them, and shortly afterwards procured it and brought it to the officers. At that point he was arrested. Before the national courts his argument relating to the use of entrapment was rejected: in particular, the national courts found that the use of *agents provocateurs* was not forbidden under domestic law so long as the use was justified by the seriousness of the offence being investigated.

Before the court, the applicant submitted that his rights under Article 6.1 of the Convention had been infringed. That section provides, so far as relevant, that "In the determination of ... any criminal charge against him, everyone is entitled to a fair ... hearing". He submitted that this provision had been infringed in circumstances where, he alleged, he had no previous convictions and would not have committed the offence but for the blandishments of the *agents provocateurs*. In addition, he complained that the activities of the police had been unsupervised by the courts. The respondent made the case that the special circumstances of drug sales, and in particular the secrecy and victimless nature of the crime, made it necessary to use investigative techniques of this kind, which were customary in a number of jurisdictions.

The court took the view that on the facts of this particular case the rights of the applicant under Article 6.1 had been infringed, in that the activities of the undercover agents had prejudiced the fairness of the applicant's trial. The activities of the agents had been unsupervised by the courts: no preliminary investigation had been opened. The authorities had no reason to suspect the applicant, who had no criminal record and who was at the outset unknown to the police officers. The drugs which the applicant ultimately supplied were not held by him; instead he obtained them from a third party. The inference which the court drew from these facts was that the applicant was not predisposed to commit such an offence; rather, the police officers, instead of investigating in a passive manner, themselves incited the commission of the crime alleged. Accordingly, the court held that:

> "In the light of all these considerations, the Court concludes that the two police officers' actions went beyond those of undercover agents because they instigated the offence and there is nothing to suggest that without their intervention it would have been committed. That intervention and its use in the impugned criminal proceedings meant that, right from the outset, the applicant was definitively deprived of a fair trial. Consequently, there has been a violation of Article 6.1." (Paragraph 39.)

The implications of this decision for Irish practice are not yet clear. Obviously, the decision will or should influence the police in their investigative activities. Whether it will be followed by the courts is another matter. The E.C.H.R. is not, of course, directly binding as a matter of domestic Irish law: but is binding at the level of international law. It will, therefore, be necessary for the courts to shape domestic law so as to comply with the requirements of *Texeira de Castro v. Portugal*, or for legislation to be introduced to the same effect. Perhaps it is most likely that the courts will develop the concept of abuse of process, outlined in *State (Trimbole) v. Governor of Mountjoy Prison*, to include situations in which the E.C.H.R. would require that a prosecution not be instituted. However, should the law remain as it appears to be from *Dental Board v. O'Callaghan*, then it is clear that an accused person convicted in such circumstances would have a remedy in Strasbourg.

10.4.8 Automatism

The defence of automatism is available in circumstances where an accused was, at the material time, physically unable to control his actions. As defined by Ritchie J. for the Supreme Court of Canada:

> "Automatism is a term used to describe unconscious, involuntary behaviour, the state of a person who, though capable of action, is not conscious of what he is doing. It means an unconscious, involuntary act, where the mind does not go with what is being done." (*R v. Rabey* (1980) 15 C.R. (3d) 225 at p. 232.)

It is closely intertwined with the defence of insanity, but differs from that defence in two important ways. First, once the foundations for the defence have been laid, it is for the prosecution to disprove the defence, not for the accused to prove it. Second, an acquittal on the ground of automatism is a complete acquittal, unlike an acquittal on the ground of insanity, after which the accused will be held in the Central Mental Hospital until he can demonstrate that he has recovered.

The defence is available only where the accused had no control over his body, as in the case of the sleepwalker, or the driver attacked by a swarm of bees who veers off the road and kills a pedestrian. It is not available in circumstances where the accused had control over his body, but chose to act in a particular way. If a driver sees a swarm of bees ahead, chooses to swerve to avoid them, and kills a pedestrian, his defence (if any) would be necessity. Similarly, the defence is not available where the accused had control over his body, but that control was lessened due to anger, intoxication, disease of the mind, and so forth.

An important point is that where conduct is involuntary, but results from the self-induced intoxication of the accused, then the accused must rely on the defence of intoxication rather than the defence of automatism: *R. v. Lipman* (1970).

In addition, it seems that the defence is available only where the automatism is a transient state caused by *some external factor*, and is not available where the automatism is caused by a factor internal to the accused. It appears that in cases of an internal factor, the courts take the view that the possibility of recurrence of violence justifies the accused being detained rather than completely acquitted.

This point was discussed in *Bratty v. Attorney General for Northern Ireland* (1963). In that case, the accused strangled an eighteen-year-old girl. He stated that at the time he had "a terrible feeling" and that "a sort of blackness" came over him; but he was able to give some account of what had happened. The defences of automatism due to psychomotor epilepsy and insanity were run at trial, and the trial judge left the defence of insanity to the jury, but refused to so leave the defence of automatism. On appeal, the House of Lords held that the trial judge had been correct. The court drew a distinction between insane and non-insane automatism, and held that where the cause alleged for the unconscious act was a disease of the mind (such as psychomotor epilepsy) then the only verdict which could be returned by the jury was one of insane automatism: there was no room for a finding of non-insane automatism. It was also held that the onus of proving voluntariness in cases of automatism is on the prosecution, once the foundations are laid by the defendant, and that the prosecution must prove voluntariness beyond a reasonable doubt.

This can also be seen in *R. v. Rabey* (1980). In that case, the defendant was a student, who was smitten with another student. The day before the attack, he found a letter she had written complaining about him and expressing an interest in someone else. On the day of the attack, he took a rock from the geology laboratory, met the victim (by chance, it seemed) struck her with the rock and attempted to choke her. The defence of automatism was successfully pleaded at trial, on the basis that the accused was in a complete dissociative state. However, on appeal it was held that this defence could not be sustained: any malfunctioning of the mind or mental disorder which has its source primarily in some matter internal to the defendant is a disease of the mind within the meaning of the defence of insanity, and cannot form the basis of the defence of automatism.

This principle has been applied in the case of sleepwalking. In *R. v. Burgess* (1991), the defendant was watching videos with a neighbour. When she fell asleep, he hit her over the head with a bottle and the video recorder, and then grabbed her by the throat. When she screamed, he "came round", appeared to be concerned, and called an ambulance for her. He was charged with wounding with intent, to which his defence was that he was sleepwalking at the time. At trial, this was found to amount to a defence of insanity, and the defendant was ordered to be detained in a secure hospital. On appeal, the defendant contended that the defence was in fact one of automatism.

The Court of Appeal held that the automatism could not be said to be due to an external factor such as a blow on the head: it was caused by an internal factor. The automatism was also liable to recur, though recurrence in the form of serious violence was unlikely. It followed as a matter of law that, although the automatism was far removed from insanity in a colloquial or psychiatric sense, it amounted to a defence of insanity in legal terms:

> "[T]his was an abnormality or disorder, albeit transitory, due to an internal factor, whether functional or organic, which had manifested itself in violence. It was a disorder or abnormality which might recur, though the possibility of it recurring in the form of serious violence was unlikely. Therefore, since this was a legal problem to be decided on legal principles, it seems to us on those principles the answer was as the judge found it to be." (at p. 776.).

This apparently logical distinction, between internal and external factors, breaks down in the case of defendants who suffer from diabetes and who commit crimes while suffering either from high or low blood sugar levels (hyperglycaemia and hypoglycaemia respectively). Are states of automatism resulting from such conditions to be treated as resulting from internal factors (the diabetes) or external factors (failure to take insulin, etc.)? In *R. v. Quick* (1973), the defendant's automatism resulting from hypoglycaemia was held to result from an external factor (self-administered insulin injections). In *R. v. Hennessy* (1989), however, the defendant's automatism resulting from hyperglycaemia due to his failure to take insulin was held to result from an internal factor (the underlying disease of diabetes). *R. v. Quick* (1973) was distinguished, on the ground that the hypoglycaemia resulted from injections of insulin, not from the underlying diabetes. This is, however, a distinction without a difference.

R. v. Hennessy was on stronger ground, however, in dealing with whether automatism resulting from stress and similar situations was to be treated as resulting from internal or external factors. In *R. v. Hennessy*, the defendant was arrested in the process of driving a stolen car. One aspect of his defence has already been dealt with: that he was suffering from hyperglycaemia. Another aspect of the defence was that automatism could also have been triggered by his depression and by his marital and employment problems. This aspect of the defence was also rejected by the Court of Appeal. If automatism had been triggered by these factors, then it would still have been caused by internal factors so as to make the defence of insanity applicable:

> "In our judgment, stress, anxiety and depression can no doubt be the result of the operation of external factors, but they are not, it seems to us, in themselves separately or together external factors of the kind capable in law of causing or contributing to a state of automatism. They constitute a state of mind which is prone to recur. They lack the feature of novelty or accident..." (Lord Lane C.J., at p. 14.).

It is not necessarily fatal to the defence that the automatism was self-induced. If, for example, a diabetic fails to eat following an insulin injection and, as a result, commits a crime while in a hypoglycaemic state, then the defence of automatism can be pleaded unless it can be proved that in failing to eat he acted sufficiently recklessly. In *R. v. Bailey* (1983), the accused suffered from diabetes. His girlfriend left him, and he subsequently attacked the man for whom she had left him, having shortly before drank a sugar and water solution. His defence was that the resulting hypoglycaemia, owing to his failure to take food having drunk the solution, had produced a state of automatism. The trial judge directed the jury not to consider this defence since the state was self-induced. On appeal, this direction was held to be incorrect: self-induced automatism (other than by intoxication: *R. v. Lipman* (1970)) could provide a defence, unless the conduct of the defendant in inducing automatism had been sufficiently reckless to establish the *mens rea* for the offence.

Finally, in respect of automatism, the case of *O'Brien v. Parker* (1997) should be noted. This was a decision of the High Court in a civil matter, where the plaintiff sued in respect of personal injuries suffered in a road traffic accident. The defendant claimed that at the time of the accident he was suffering an epileptic fit by reason of temporal lobe epilepsy, so that he could not have been said to be negligent. The defendant had no history of epilepsy, but claimed that he had, immediately before the accident, experienced heightened sensitivity to light and smells and an "altered state of consciousness", and that the next thing he remembered was the accident itself.

The High Court, Lavan J., held that automatism could amount to a defence in a civil context to a claim based on negligence. However, for that to be the case, it would have to be shown that there was "a total destruction of voluntary control on the defendant's part. Impaired, reduced, or partial control is not sufficient to maintain the defence." (at p. 176.). In this case, therefore, the defendant had not made out the defence, since he had testified that he was capable of making the decision to continue driving, notwithstanding that his ability to make such a decision was impaired.

Similar criteria apply in a criminal context: the loss of control must be total for a defence of automatism to be available.

10.4.9 *Insanity*

(1) Introduction and procedural aspects

The defence of insanity is distinct from the defence of automatism. It does not apply where the defendant's body is acting without conscious control, but instead applies where the defendant is conscious of his actions but his mental state is in some way impaired. The burden of proving insanity lies on the accused, contrary to the normal rule that the prosecution bear the responsibility of disproving any defence raised: *People (DPP) v. O'Mahony* (1985), at p. 522 *per* Finlay C.J.:

> "If it were established, as a matter of probability, that due to an abnor-
> mality of mind consisting of a psychiatric condition the appellant had
> been unable to control himself and to desist from carrying out the acts
> of violence leading to the death of the deceased, he would have been
> entitled to a finding of not guilty by reason of insanity.".

The accused, therefore, must prove his insanity, but only on the balance of probabilities, not beyond a reasonable doubt. It is, however, also open to the prosecution to prove insanity in an appropriate case: *Bratty v. Attorney General for Northern Ireland* (1963).

The effect of a finding of insanity is that the accused is innocent of the crime charged, but is to be held in the Central Mental Hospital until recovered: Criminal Lunatics Act 1800; Lunacy (Ireland) Act 1821 and the Trial of Lunatics Act 1883. This is so even where the disorder which constitutes insanity in law is not such a disorder as would make it appropriate for a person to be detained. If Irish law follows English decisions to the effect that diabetic hyperglycaemia is a disease of the mind within the meaning of the defence of insanity, then it is possible that a person who commits a crime while in such a state will be detained in the Central Mental Hospital, notwithstanding the fact that they have been found innocent of the crime charged and notwithstanding the fact that they pose no danger to themselves or anyone else.

The decision as to whether a person found not guilty by reason of insanity has recovered, is one for the executive: *DPP v. Gallagher* (1991). That case departed from previous case law which had held that the decision to release such a person was a judicial act forming part of the administration of justice. Instead, the role of the court was said to be to order the detention of a person found not guilty by reason of insanity:

> "until the executive, armed with both the knowledge and the resources to deal with the problem, decides on the future disposition of the person." (*Per* McCarthy J., at p. 344.)

However, *DPP v. Gallagher* (1991), made it clear that the executive, in deciding whether a person should continue to be kept in custody, must consider only whether he is suffering from any mental disorder warranting his continued detention in the public and private interests, and must do so in accordance with fair and constitutional procedures. The decision of the executive will be subject to judicial review if necessary.

(2) Fitness to plead

Another procedural aspect related to insanity is that of *fitness to plead*. This is distinct from insanity *per se*, and relates not to whether a defendant understood what he was doing at the time of the crime, but to whether that defendant is capable of understanding the proceedings at his trial. The law takes the view that it is unjust to try a person who is incapable of understanding the trial and therefore incapable of adequately defending himself, and for that reason, a person who is unfit to plead will be detained in the same way as a person found not guilty by reason of insanity.

It is important to note that fitness to plead is entirely distinct from insanity at the time of the alleged offence. The criminal who is insane at the time of his crime may have recovered to the point where he is capable of understanding his trial; and the criminal who is entirely sane at the time of his crime may, pending trial, suffer some illness or injury which leaves him incapable of standing trial.

The test of fitness to plead is set out in the case of *R. v. Robertson* (1968), and looks to whether the accused is able to: understand the charges against him; understand the nature and effect of a plea of guilty or not guilty; challenge a member of the jury to which he might object; instruct counsel; and understand the evidence which is given. If the accused is unable to do one or more of these things, then he will be found unfit to plead. The decision as to whether a person is fit to plead is made by the jury. Where the prosecution raise the issue, then they must prove unfitness to plead beyond a reasonable doubt; where the defence does so, it must prove unfitness to plead on the balance of probabilities.

(3) What is insanity?

The defence of insanity in Irish law is tangled in that there is no one test which is conclusive of whether a defendant pleading insanity will or will not be held criminally responsible for his actions. It is important to note how this differs from the English position. In England, it has been held that the defence of insanity is exclusively encapsulated in the M'Naghten Rules of 1843. Where a defendant does not bring himself within those rules, a defence of insanity cannot succeed.

In *R. v. Windle* (1952), for example, the defendant killed his wife, who, it seemed, was herself of unsound mind. There was evidence to the effect that the defendant knew what he was doing was legally wrong, but believed, due to mental illness, that it was morally right. However, it was held that the defence of insanity could not, on those facts, be put before the jury: once the defendant knew what he was doing was illegal, then he could not avail of the M'Naghten Rules, and there was no wider defence of insanity open to him.

The Irish position is entirely different, and it has been held by the Supreme Court, in *Doyle v. Wicklow County Council* (1974), that the M'Naghten Rules are not the beginning and end of the insanity defence:

> "In my opinion, the M'Naghten Rules do not provide the sole and exclusive test for determining the sanity or insanity of an accused. The questions put to the judges were limited to the effect of insane delusions and I would agree with the opinion expressed by the Court of Criminal Appeal in *Attorney General v. O'Brien* (1936) that the opinions given by the judges must be read with the same specific limitation." (*Per* Griffin J.)

The M'Naghten Rules are, therefore, only one component of the defence of insanity in this jurisdiction. They do, however, form the primary test.

The M'Naghten Rules were formulated in 1843 in response to the *M'Naghten* case, in which the defendant shot Edward Drummond, the private secretary to the Prime Minister, Sir Robert Peel, mistaking him for the Prime Minister. His defence was that he believed himself to be persecuted by the Tory party, and that consequently his life was in danger. The verdict reached in his case, not guilty by reason of insanity, produced public disquiet, leading the House of Lords to summon the judges before it to answer a series of questions on the law of insanity.

To fall within the M'Naghten rules, the following element is necessary: The accused must establish that he suffered from *a defect of reason from disease of the mind.* Disease of the mind does not mean mental illness or brain damage, but includes, as we saw, conditions resulting from diabetes, epilepsy, and so on. In *R. v. Kemp* (1957), therefore, a defendant was found to be suffering from a disease of the mind where he made a senseless attack on his wife with a hammer, which was triggered by arteriosclerosis causing a blood congestion in the brain. He argued that this should be treated as automatism rather than falling within the M'Naghten rules, but this argument was rejected, notwithstanding that this was a transitory and curable physical interference with the workings of the brain. Similarly, *Ellis v. DPP* (1990) involved a defendant who was charged with murder of a man who, he alleged, was blackmailing him. He relied on the defence of automatism, on the basis that he was in an epileptic state at the time of the killing. The trial judge refused to leave the issue of automatism to the jury but did leave the issue of insanity, and the accused was found not guilty by reason of insanity.

There must have been a *causal link* between the defect of reason and the act: if I believe that the Vatican is bugging my phone and I go shoplifting, then there is clearly no such causal link. It is not enough that the defect of reason and the crime should coincide in point of time; there must also be a causal relationship between the two.

Where the defect of reason takes the form of an insane delusion, then the delusion, if it relates to existing facts, must be one which would mean that the act committed was not a crime. If I shoot a person, believing him to be a tree, then the act would not be a crime if the delusion were true. But if I shoot a person, believing him to be Bill Clinton, then this act would be a crime even if the delusion were true, and the defence will not apply.

The accused must establish either that he did not know the nature and quality of his act, or that he did so know but did not know that the act was wrongful. The nature and quality of the act refers to its physical nature only, not its moral nature (*R. v. Codère* (1916)). So, not understanding the nature and quality of an act would encompass situations of shooting a person thinking he was a tree. A defendant knows that an act is wrongful if he knows it is illegal, or, notwithstanding that he does not know it is illegal, he knows it is an act which he ought not to do. It is irrelevant that the defendant thinks that a particular act is morally right if he knows it is legally wrong. So, in *R. v. Windle* (1952), the defendant, who was mentally ill, believed he was acting in a moral way by killing his wife by poisoning, supposing that he was putting her out of her unhappiness. However, it was held that once he knew his actions to be against the law it did not matter whether he believed them to be otherwise justifiable.

(4) Irresistible impulse

It will be seen from this that the M'Naghten rules are quite restrictive. In particular, they do not allow any scope for the defence of volitional insanity. This is a particular form of mental defect covering situations where an accused knows that conduct is wrong (and therefore falls outside the parameters of the M'Naghten rules) but nevertheless has a diminished capacity to act or refrain from acting based on that knowledge. An example of such a situation would be the case where a person claimed to have had an irresistible impulse to commit a specific crime. The defence of irresistible impulse was never accepted under the M'Naghten rules; indeed, as one judge stated:

> "If you cannot resist an impulse in any other way, we will hang a rope in front of your eyes, and perhaps that will help." (*Per* Riddell J., in *R v. Creighton* (1909)).

The defence of irresistible impulse has never been a feature of English law and has also been rejected in Australia. However, it is now clear that Irish law recognises a defence of volitional insanity. This was foreshadowed by *AG v. O'Brien* (1936). In that case the defendant sought to raise the defence of irresistible impulse, but the trial judge refused to leave the defence to the jury on the ground that it was unknown to the law. On appeal, the Court of Criminal Appeal held that there were no facts sufficient to justify leaving the defence to the jury. It went on to hold that the M'Naghten rules were not intended to be exclusive, and left open for later the decision whether Irish law recognised the defence of irresistible impulse.

Later cases saw trial judges adopt a wider test of insanity. Particularly significant was the case of *People (AG) v. Hayes* (1967) in which the defendant was charged with murdering his wife. He had, over a long period, built up an irrational sense of grievance against his wife, and sought redress for imaginary complaints by killing his wife, as he claimed, to clear the name of their children. Although this defence would probably not have fallen within the scope of the M'Naghten rules, Henchy J. directed the jury in terms which were wider than the M'Naghten rules, saying that "if the jury was satisfied that at the time of the attack the accused man's mind was so affected by illness that he was unable to restrain himself, a verdict of guilty but insane should be returned".

Further, Henchy J. gave a detailed judgment regarding the scope of the defence, stating that:

> "The [M'Naghten] rules do not take into account the capacity of a man on the basis of his knowledge to act or to refrain from acting and I believe it to be correct psychiatric science to accept that certain serious mental diseases, such as paranoia or schizophrenia, in certain cases enable a man to understand the morality or immorality of his act or the legality or illegality of it, or the nature and quality of it, but nevertheless prevent him from exercising a free volition as to whether he should or should not do that act."

This approach was then confirmed by the Supreme Court, in *Doyle v. Wicklow County Council* (1974). This was a claim for compensation brought by the owner of an abattoir burnt down by a seventeen-year-old boy. The claim would succeed only if what was done by the boy was a crime, which made it necessary to consider whether the defence of insanity would have been available to the boy. The facts showed that the boy was suffering from some form of mental disorder which led him to believe that setting fire to the abattoir was a justifiable and moral act, based on his love of animals. The boy knew, however, that the act was nevertheless a criminal one. Griffin J. adopted what had been said by Henchy J. in *People (AG) v. Hayes* as being a correct statement of the law, and held that the defence of volitional insanity would have been open to the boy.

The decision in *People (DPP) v. Courtney* (1994) provides an example of the defence of irresistible impulse (albeit an unsuccessful example). In that case, the accused was charged with murder. He had been a passenger in a car driven by the deceased, who had picked him up while looking for directions. She had, he said, taunted him, at which he "blew a fuse and went mad". He punched her several times, then took the car and drove into the mountains. When she regained consciousness, he hit her with a rock, killing her. He took her clothes off her body, then drove back into the city and abandoned the car.

The defence was that the accused had acted in a panic, without any control of himself, and the accused tendered psychiatric evidence to the effect that he was suffering from post-traumatic stress disorder stemming from his tours of duty as a soldier in Lebanon. Based on this evidence, the trial judge left two questions to the jury: was the accused acting under the influence of an irresistible impulse caused by a defect of reason due to mental illness, which debarred him from refraining from killing the victim; and had it been proved beyond a reasonable doubt that the accused intended to kill or cause serious harm to the victim. The trial judge went on to direct the jury that, depending on their answers to these questions, they could find the accused to be: guilty of murder; not guilty by reason of insanity; or guilty of manslaughter (if it had not been proved beyond a reasonable doubt that the accused intended to kill or cause serious injury). The jury found the accused to be guilty of murder.

On appeal, the Court of Criminal Appeal upheld the conviction of the applicant. It rejected the suggestion that the trial judge had "trivialised" his defence; on the contrary, the trial judge had put this defence fully and painstakingly to the jury, which had found that the applicant had not met his burden of establishing, on the balance of probabilities, that his condition at the time in question amounted to insanity in a legal sense.

This defence has not been elaborated upon to any great extent, but the *obiter* comments of Finlay C.J. in *People (DPP) v. O'Mahony* (1986) are interesting. In that case, the defendant appealed his conviction for murder on the grounds that the defence of diminished responsibility existed at common law and should have been left to the jury. This was rejected by the Supreme Court, but Finlay C.J. noted that:

> "Having regard to the definition of insanity laid down by this Court in *Doyle v. Wicklow County Council* (1974) ... it is quite clear that the appellant in *R v. Byrne* (1960) ... a sexual psychopath who suffered from violent perverted sexual desires which he found it difficult or impossible to control [but did not suffer any other mental illness] if tried in accordance with the law of this country on the same facts, would have been properly found to be not guilty by reason of insanity." (at pages 248-249.).

It appears from these comments, therefore, that in Irish law a person might be able to rely on insanity even in circumstances where they might have some control over their actions, provided that their control was significantly diminished by mental illness. This may also encompass cases where, for example, the accused's ability to make decisions is significantly impaired, as in the example of a father who believes that he and his family would be better off dead, and therefore kills the other members of his family. In these circumstances, it is not the defendant's control over his actions which is in issue, but rather his ability to make decisions concerning his actions. The underlying logic of *Doyle v. Wicklow County Council* (1974) would suggest that this would also amount to the defence of insanity.

(5) Diminished responsibility

The above comments suggest that a defence similar to diminished responsibility might already be available in Irish law. A defence of diminished responsibility was introduced into English law by section 2 of the Homicide Act 1957. The defence is confined to cases of murder and reduces the charge to one of manslaughter. For the defence of diminished responsibility to be made out, the defendant must have been labouring under mental impairment such that his ability to control his actions and make decisions is defective. This does not necessarily mean that he acted with an irresistible impulse. The impulse may well have been easily resisted but the defendant lacked the insight into his actions to do so.

(6) Reform of insanity

Insanity is an all or nothing defence: there is, in this jurisdiction, no defence of diminished responsibility such as is in England for a defendant who suffered from such "an abnormality of mind ... as substantially impaired his mental responsibility for his acts or omissions". (This point has been confirmed by the Court of Criminal Appeal in *People (DPP) v. Reddan* (1995) ("flawed intent") and by the Supreme Court in *People (DPP) v. O'Mahony* (1986).) This English defence is confined to murder, in much the same way as the defences of provocation and excessive self-defence.

Because of the lack of an intermediate verdict, juries are faced with a stark choice between guilty and not guilty by reason of insanity; and juries have proved reluctant to bring in the latter verdict ever since the defendant Gallagher successfully pleaded insanity at trial and shortly afterwards mounted a legal campaign to secure his release on the ground that he was now sane.

Legislation has been repeatedly promised in this area. The Criminal Justice (Mental Disorder) Bill 1996 was an attempt to reform the law in this area. It would have removed the concept of insanity and replaced it with that of "mental disorder". "Mental disorder" was defined in the 1996 Bill to include mental illnesses, handicaps, diseases of the mind and personality disorders. Irresistible impulse was placed on a statutory footing and the defence of diminished responsibility was introduced. This was confined, as under English law, to murder and would have reduced such a charge to manslaughter.

Further reading: McAuley, *Insanity, Psychiatry and Criminal Responsibility* (Dublin, Round Hall Press, 1993); Boland, "Diminished Responsibility as a Defence in Irish Law" (1995) 5 I.C.L.J. 173 and (1996) 6 I.C.L.J. 19.

10.4.10 Unconstitutionality

Article 38.1 of the Constitution states that no person shall be tried on any criminal charge save in due course of law. While standards of procedural fairness must be adhered to by the police and prosecution, an accused can also rely on constitutional provisions in a substantive manner to render a criminal provision unconstitutional. This happens only rarely, however, as there is a presumption that legislation is constitutional and the accused must have exhausted all other arguments before relying on unconstitutionality.

The constitutional right to privacy has been relied on several times to render criminally proscribed conduct legal. For example, it was successful in *McGee v. AG* (1974), where it was held that section 17 of the Criminal Law (Amendment) Act 1935 (prohibiting distribution of contraceptives) violated the guarantee of marital privacy protected by Article 40.3.1. More recently, the constitutional rights to life and privacy were relied on in *Re Ward* (1996) to permit medical treatment to be withdrawn from a woman who had been in a persistent vegetative state for over twenty years, conduct which might otherwise have been criminal.

It is clear that legislation creating an offence may be struck down where it creates an offence which is insufficiently clear and precise. The definition of the offence must be certain to enable an accused to prepare a defence; vagueness may prove to be a fatal constitutional defect. So, for example, in *King v. AG* (1981), various offences of loitering under the Vagrancy Act 1824 were struck down as being unconstitutionally vague.

11. DEGREES OF PARTICIPATION IN CRIME

What do we mean by degrees of participation in crime? Suppose two persons set out to kill another. A holds the victim down while B inflicts the fatal wound. B is clearly guilty of murder; but is A? At first glance, the answer is no. A's actions undoubtedly amount to a crime; but they do not amount to the *actus reus* of the crime of murder. (This must be distinguished from the situation where both A and B hit the victim, who dies as a result. On those facts, both would be guilty of murder.) But this result is intuitively unappealing: it is plainly wrong that a person should escape criminal liability merely because he himself did not strike the fatal blow, where he knowingly took part in the crime, so that he bears the same degree of responsibility as the primary perpetrator.

Indeed, A may bear a greater degree of responsibility than B in some circumstances, as where A is the mastermind, and persuades B, a stupid youth, to inflict the wound. As Glanville Williams puts it: "Lady Macbeth was worse than Macbeth." (*Textbook of Criminal Law* (1978), at page 287.). However, if a person acts through an innocent agent, then that person will be a principal rather than an accessory. Suppose I give a gun to a lunatic and tell him to kill another, which he does. The lunatic bears no criminal responsibility. Consequently, the charge to be brought against me will not be that I incited the commission of an offence by him, but rather that I committed the offence of murder myself, albeit via a third party. See *R. v. Cogan* (1975), where it was held that if A procured B to have sexual intercourse with his wife, in circumstances where the wife appeared to consent but did not, then A would be liable for the crime of rape as a principal offender, notwithstanding that B would lack the *mens rea* for rape.

For this reason, the law recognises that a person who does not himself commit a particular crime may nevertheless be convicted of that crime, where he is a *participant* in that crime. This is the concept of secondary liability. Such a person can be charged, tried and punished as if he himself committed the crime. We will use the term "accessory" to describe such a person, although this terminology is no longer used in the legislation. The term "principal" will be used to describe the primary perpetrator: this term does remain in the legislation.

11.1 Criminal Law Act 1997

The law in this area has quite recently been overhauled by the Criminal Law Act 1997. Prior to 1997 the law on this topic was contained in the Accessories and Abettors Act 1861 which created the following categories of participants in crimes: accessories before and after the fact to felonies (punishable in the same way as the principal offender), and abettors in misdemeanours (punishable in the same way as the principal offender). It was not possible to be an accessory after the fact to a misdemeanour. The 1997 Act does away with some of the technicalities which were inherent in the old law, and the law relating to the criminal liability of participants is now entirely contained in sections 7 and 8.

Section 7(1) deals with *assistance and encouragement of offences* (including assistance after a crime is committed). It states:

> "Any person who *aids, abets, counsels or procures* the commission of an indictable offence shall be liable to be indicted, tried and punished as a principal offender." (Emphasis added.)

The terms in italics are carried over from the 1861 Act and relate to two distinct types of participation in crime. To *aid or abet* a crime is to assist in its commission; to *counsel or procure* a crime is to incite its commission. Where a person aids, abets, counsels or procures the commission of a crime, they can be tried as if they themselves committed the crime. For example, A provides a gun to B knowing that B intends to use it to kill C and B does so. A is guilty of murder notwithstanding that A did not pull the trigger.

This section requires that an offence should in fact be committed: if I assist in or incite the commission of an offence, but no offence ultimately takes place (A persuades B to rob a bank; B changes his mind before committing the crime), then section 7(1) does not apply. The distinction between offences of participation and inchoate (or incomplete) offences should be noted at this point. With inchoate offences such as incitement, attempt and conspiracy (discussed further, *infra*) despite the efforts of the defendant, no crime is eventually committed. The inchoate offence does not depend upon the commission of the primary offence as it constitutes an offence in itself. In contrast, offences of secondary liability depend on the crime being committed. In the above example, A is not guilty of an offence under section 7(1) but of incitement.

Section 7(1) does not require, however, that the accessory should be qualified to commit the offence in question. Before rape became a gender-neutral offence, it could only be committed by a man; nevertheless, a woman could be convicted of aiding and abetting the commission of a rape, and be punished as severely as the principal offender.

Section 7(1) is, it will be noted, limited to indictable offences. However, precisely the same principles apply to summary offences by virtue of section 22 of the Petty Sessions (Ireland) Act 1851.

11.1.1 What conduct amounts to assisting or inciting?

As a basic rule, a person does not assist in or incite the commission of an offence merely by being present at the scene and failing to intervene. There is no general duty in Irish law to intervene to prevent the commission of an offence. An exception, where failure to act does give rise to secondary liability, is where the defendant is under a specific legal duty to act. Such situations are dealt with in the chapter on *Actus Reus, supra*.

This point was considered in *Dunlop and Sylvester v. R.* (1980) where the charges against two defendants included a charge that they stood by and watched a rape being committed, therefore aiding and abetting the commission of the crime. This was held to be an incorrect statement of the law by the Canadian Supreme Court, which expressly held that mere presence at the scene of a crime is not enough to ground culpability: there must be something in the way of encouragement of the offender, or something which facilitates the commission of the offence.

An earlier case, *R. v. Coney* (1882), was referred to, which held that those who had gathered to watch a prize fight could not be guilty of aiding and abetting unless they took some part in the proceedings. But in some cases, the court pointed out, there will be encouragement by conduct (as in the case of spectators who urge on a fight) and in some cases the mere presence of spectators to a crime will ensure against the escape of a victim. However, mere presence and passive acquiescence is not enough.

11.1.2 What degree of knowledge is required? The common purpose rule and the doctrine of joint enterprise

It is not necessary that an accessory should be aware in advance of the precise crime which a principal intends to commit. If A lends his gun to B, who has indicated that he intends to kill someone with it, then A cannot escape liability on the ground that he did not know who the intended victim was.

The application of this principle can be seen in *R. v. Maxwell* (1978). Here the defendant was a member of the UVF, who drove four other members to a bar owned by a Catholic. One of the passengers then threw a pipe bomb into the bar. The defendant admitting knowing that some form of "job" was planned against the bar, but argued that since he did not know its exact nature he could not be guilty of aiding and abetting the crime actually committed. This argument was, unsurprisingly, rejected. The court held that the accused knew he was facilitating a military attack of some kind, whether it was a robbery, shooting or bomb attack. He knew that the principal was about to carry out one or more of a number of possible crimes, and he intentionally lent his assistance in order that one of those crimes should be committed. He was, therefore, a party to the crime which was in fact committed by the principal, so long as that crime was in his contemplation as being a possible result.

Suppose, however, that A and B set out to assault C, in a so-called "punishment beating". During the course of the assault, A produces a gun of which B was unaware, and shoots and kills C. Is B an accessory to murder?

A common-sense view would be that B is not, since what happened went beyond the scope of the crime which he intended to facilitate and also went beyond what he could foresee might happen. The law gives effect to this view, by way of the "doctrine of common design". This doctrine was concisely stated, in *R. v. Anderson and Morris* (1966), by counsel and adopted by the court:

> "Where two persons embark on a joint enterprise, each is liable criminally for the acts done in pursuance of the joint enterprise, including unusual consequences arising from the execution of the joint enterprise; but if one of them goes beyond what has been tacitly agreed as part of the joint enterprise the other is not liable for the consequences of the unauthorised act .... [I]t is for the jury in every case to decide whether what was done was part of the joint enterprise."

The above case offers an example of the doctrine in action. Here, two accused, A and M, went together in search of another, intending to attack him, but not to kill or cause serious harm to him. A was armed with a knife, which M denied knowing about. On finding the victim, A stabbed him with the knife, killing him. M seemed to take no part in the fight.

At trial, the jury were directed that they could find M guilty of manslaughter if there was a common design to attack the victim, and if M took some part in the fight, even if the use of the knife was entirely outside the contemplation of M and even if there was no intention on M's part to kill or cause serious bodily harm. In essence, this direction was to the effect that if two persons were engaged in an unlawful act and one suddenly developed an intention to kill, and did so, then that person was guilty of murder while the other participant was guilty of manslaughter.

This direction was held to be improper by the (English) Court of Criminal Appeal. It was held that this form of imputed intention was unacceptable in modern conditions, although there was support for it in earlier authorities. Instead, the position was summarised in the quotation set out above: if the accused did not foresee a certain result as possible, he could not be held criminally liable for that result.

On the other hand, if the accused in *R. v. Anderson and Morris* had foreseen the *possibility* that death or serious bodily harm was a possible outcome of the joint enterprise, then he would have had the necessary degree of *mens rea* to be convicted

This can be seen from *Chan Wing-Siu v. R.* (1985) in which three gang members went to a flat armed with knives intending to rob a victim. In the course of the robbery, the victim received stab wounds from which he died. Each of the three was charged with the murder of the deceased. The defence case was that the use of the knives had not been intended: that they had been brought along simply to frighten the victim, and that their use (in response to apparent self-defence by the deceased) was not foreseen.

The direction to the jury, which was upheld on appeal, was that each defendant would be guilty of murder if that defendant had *foreseen* the infliction of serious bodily harm (or death) *as a possibility* arising out of the joint enterprise, notwithstanding that that defendant did not *intend* that result. Therefore, it need not be shown that the use of the weapon (or whatever conduct is alleged) was foreseen as being *more likely than not*: it is enough for the prosecution to show that the use of the weapon was foreseen by the accused as *being a real possibility, or a genuine risk*.

Another consequence of this approach is that foresight on the part of the accessory is sufficient *mens rea*, *i.e.* the accessory need not intend the ultimate result provided he is aware the ultimate result is a possibility. This can be seen from *R. v. Powell* (1997). In that case the House of Lords explicitly held that *foresight* rather than *intention* is the basis for liability of secondary parties to a killing carried out in the course of a joint enterprise, notwithstanding the anomaly created, that foresight is not sufficient *mens rea* in the case of the actual perpetrator.

The Irish decisions on this point are substantially to the same effect. The first in time is *People (AG) v. Ryan* (1966), in which the applicant was convicted of manslaughter arising from a fight after a dance. The applicant and a number of friends had got into a row with another group; they then armed themselves with car jacks, etc., and attacked the others. One of the applicant's companions ultimately killed a member of the other group, and was convicted of murder. The applicant did not take any direct part in the killing, but was involved in the fracas and was himself armed with a weapon.

The argument put forward on behalf of the applicant was that any common intention was limited to intimidating the others, and that the companion had gone beyond the ambit of the common design. This argument was, however, rejected by the Court of Criminal Appeal, which held that it was a matter for the jury to determine whether there had been a common intention to injure; and there had been ample evidence before the jury to justify such a finding. In particular, the applicant knew that his companion was armed with a lethal weapon, and could *foresee* that the weapon might be used as it ultimately was.

Another Irish case is *DPP v. Madden* (1977), where four men were convicted of the murder of a particular victim, although the prosecution had not been able to establish who fired the fatal shot. The case made against them was therefore that each aided and abetted the killing, in various ways. The Court of Criminal Appeal stated the general principles which applied to each appellant as follows:

> "[M]otives and desires are irrelevant, and ... mere evidence of common association is insufficient. The kernel of the matter is the establishing of *an activity on the part of the accused* from which his intentions may be inferred and the effect of which is to assist the principal in the commission of the crime proved to have been committed by the principal, or the commission of a crime of a similar nature known to the accused to be the intention of the principal when assisting him." (O'Higgins C.J., at p. 341.)

It follows, as we have seen, that there must be some active participation before liability will attach. The conviction of one of the appellants was set aside on this ground: although he knew that a particular car was to be used for some crime of violence, he had not acted either to prepare or commit such a crime, and his conviction consequently could not stand.

On the other hand, another appellant was held to have been properly convicted where, knowing that a particular car was required for the commission of a serious crime of violence against one of a number of people, he took active steps to provide that car. It was held that, in relation to murder, a person who took active steps in the preparation of a crime likely to cause serious injury to another, in the knowledge that such a crime was intended, could be convicted of murder where death resulted.

The most recent Irish decision is *People (DPP) v. Egan* (1989). In this case, the accused was charged with robbery and receiving stolen goods. He had received a telephone call stating that he should make his workshop available to store a van, that he should be available at a particular time, and that "a small stroke" was to take place. The "small stroke" proved to be the robbery of a manufacturing jewellers, and at the appointed hour a van full of armed and masked men showed up with sackloads of jewellery, which he stored for them.

The accused was convicted of robbery, on the basis that he aided and abetted the commission of the robbery. His conviction was upheld by the Court of Criminal Appeal, which held that a person could aid and abet the commission of a crime without being present at the crime scene. It was not a bar to his conviction that he did not know the *exact nature* of the crime to be committed so long as he knew the *general nature* of the intended crime. On these grounds, his conviction was upheld, since he knew that a crime was about to be committed and that it involved the theft of goods, notwithstanding that the theft could be carried out in a variety of ways. (This decision effectively holds that a person can be guilty of robbery where he merely intended to facilitate larceny and had no knowledge that robbery was intended. To this extent it is out of line with the other authorities, all of which require awareness of the essential elements of the crime charged, and is likely to be narrowed in its effect if the matter again comes before the Court of Criminal Appeal.)

11.1.3 Withdrawal from complicity

A defendant may withdraw from complicity in a crime: they may call off the arrangement before the crime is completed. However, whether particular conduct amounts to a withdrawal is a question of fact in each case. In *R v. Whitehouse* (1940), it was held that there should be some communication of the withdrawal to the other participants, while in *R. v. Jensen and Ward* (1980), it was held that an effective withdrawal requires either such communication, or some positive step, such as calling the police.

This issue was considered in detail in *R. v. Becerra* (1976) where the appellant broke into a house with two others, to steal from it. They were surprised by an occupant; the appellant shouted "let's go" and climbed out of a window, while one of his partners took a knife and stabbed and killed the occupant. The appellant had known that the knife was being carried; his defence was not that what happened was outside his contemplation, but rather that he had withdrawn from the joint enterprise before the killing took place. This contention was rejected by the Court of Appeal, which held that withdrawal requires "something more than a mere change of intention and physical change of place": instead, there must be some timely communication with the other parties, to the effect that if they proceed, they do so without the aid and assistance of the person who is withdrawing.

11.1.4 Position of victims

Where a statute is designed to protect a certain class of person, then that person will not be guilty of aiding and abetting the commission of that crime notwithstanding that they do in fact encourage or facilitate the commission of that crime. The victims of a crime are not to be charged with its commission. If, for example, a young girl consents to sexual intercourse with her father, then she has undoubtedly facilitated the commission of incest by him; but she is not therefore liable as an accessory, for the reason that the law in question was designed for her protection: *R v. Whitehouse* (1977).

11.1.5 Other offences of assistance

Section 7(2) of the 1997 Act creates an offence of impeding the arrest or prosecution of a person who has committed an arrestable offence:

> "Where a person has committed an arrestable offence, any other person who, knowing or believing him to be guilty of the offence or of some other arrestable offence, does without reasonable excuse any act with intent to impede his or her apprehension or prosecution shall be guilty of an offence."

This would cover, for example, the destruction of evidence. Punishment depends on the gravity of the primary crime, and is governed by section 7(4).

Section 8(1) then creates a specific offence of *concealing offences* (which will overlap with section 7(2)):

> "Where a person has committed an *arrestable offence*, any other person who, knowing or believing that the offence or some other arrestable offence has been committed and that he or she has information which might be of material assistance in securing the prosecution or conviction of an offender for it, *accepts or agrees to accept for not disclosing that information any consideration* other than the making good of loss or injury caused by the offence, or the making of reasonable compensation for that loss or injury, shall be guilty of an offence and shall be liable on conviction on indictment to imprisonment for a term not exceeding three years."

This is intended to deal with the situation where witnesses are bought off: it is not *per se* illegal to conceal an offence, but it becomes illegal where it is done in return for some form of payoff, other than restitution for injury suffered.

Note the different scopes of each category of offences. Section 7(1) applies to *indictable* offences, while section 7(2) and section 8(1) apply to *arrestable* offences. Section 7(1) applies to assistance in an offence, either or before or after the fact, while section 7(2) and section 8(1) are offences which can only be committed after the fact.

12. INCHOATE OFFENCES

Inchoate offences are offences where the harmful objective intended may not be eventually realised. An attempt is made to commit a crime, but it may not be successful. A encourages B to commit a crime but B may not go on to do so. An agreement is made to commit a crime, but it may not eventually be carried out. In each of these situations, although the objective may not be achieved, the action may nevertheless give rise to criminal liability. Although inchoate offences are often described as incomplete offences, it should be noted that they are complete offences in themselves.

12.1 Attempt

Offenders should not escape punishment simply because they have not been successful in their endeavours to commit a crime. The incompetent criminal cannot be granted immunity because of his bungling. The law of attempt recognises this, and deems to be criminal those acts which are intimately connected with an offence which is desired to be committed, although the attempt to commit the completed offence failed. Consequently, where there is an attempt to commit an indictable offence, the attempter may be fined and/or imprisoned as if he had successfully committed the offence. In practice, of course, the penalty for an attempt will be significantly less than the penalty for the completed offence, reflecting the fact that no harm actually resulted.

12.2 Mens rea

The prosecution must prove intention on the part of the defendant for an attempt, even if recklessness is sufficient for the completed offence. Charleton has put forward a justification of this "on the basis that the requirement for a more blameworthy state of mind than the completed offence is balanced by the fact that the accused need not have done so much, or indeed any, harm in order to be convicted" (Charleton, *Criminal Law*, p. 263.).

In the case of offences requiring a specific result, it is necessary to show an intention to bring about that specific result. This can be seen by considering the case of murder. The *mens rea* for murder is an intention to kill or cause serious injury; but if A attempts to cause serious injury to B, A is not therefore guilty of attempted murder. Instead, A must have intended to bring about the specific result of death and only an attempt intending to kill will amount to attempted murder: *People (DPP) v. Douglas and Hayes* (1985). An attempt intending to cause serious injury amounts only to the *mens rea* of assault with intent to commit serious injury.

In *R. v. Mohan* (1975), the Court of Appeal explained the logic of such a rule. This case concerned a charge of attempting by wanton driving to cause bodily harm to a police constable. The trial judge directed that recklessness as to whether bodily harm was caused would suffice but this was rejected on appeal. While recognising that an attempt to commit a crime may well be a grave offence which is as morally culpable as the completed offence, James L.J. stated that it is preparatory to the commission of the crime and therefore is a step removed from the attempted offence. He held that it would be wrong to strain to bring conduct which was outside the well-established boundaries of the offence within the offence of attempt.

However, although an accused must intend the result in an offence requiring a specific result, it should be noted that he need not have intention as to all the circumstances of an offence. Take the example of attempted rape. Although the accused must have intention to have sexual intercourse, he need only be reckless as to whether the victim consents. This position has caused academic controversy. In the United Kingdom, the Law Commission was originally of the view that a distinction between consequences and circumstances would be unworkable and recommended that intention should be required as to all elements of the offence. The Law Commission subsequently took the opposite position and recommended that recklessness as to a circumstance should suffice where it suffices for the offence itself. This approach was also followed in *R. v. Khan* (1990).

12.2.1 *Actus reus*

The position at common law was explained in *R. v. Eagleton* (1855). In that case, the accused supplied bread to the poor in return for vouchers distributed by the Poor Law Authority. On presenting the vouchers to the authority, he would be paid a certain sum for each loaf. After he had presented the vouchers, and after his account had been credited, but before the money was paid over to him, it was found that the loaves he supplied had been below the agreed weight. If the money had been given to him, he would have been guilty of obtaining by false pretences; was he guilty of any offence on the facts proven?

He was held to be guilty of an attempt to obtain by false pretences. *Per* Parke B:

> "[T]he mere intention to commit a [crime] is not criminal. Some act is required; and we do not think that all acts towards committing a [crime] are [themselves criminal]. Acts remotely leading towards the commission of the offence are not to be considered as attempts to commit it, but acts immediately connected with it are; and if in this case, after the credit with the relieving officer for the fraudulent overcharge, any further step on the part of the defendant had been necessary to obtain payment, as the making out of a further account, or producing the vouchers to the Board, we should have thought that the obtaining credit in account with the relieving officer would not have been sufficiently proximate to the obtaining the money. But on the statement in this case, no other act on the part of the defendant would have been required. It was the last act depending on himself towards the payment of the money and therefore it ought to be considered as an attempt."

This short passage establishes a number of distinct principles, which apply throughout the law of attempt. Intent is not enough, but must be coupled with conduct. Whether an act is criminal depends on whether it is accompanied by the relevant intent and whether it is sufficiently proximate to the completed offence.

There must be proximity between the act committed and the crime which was intended. If A buys a box of matches with the intention to burn down a house, is A at that point guilty of attempted criminal damage or arson? Clearly not. His conduct is too far removed from the completed crime.

However, determining how proximate conduct must be to a completed crime has proven to be difficult. A number of different theories exist on this topic. One is the last act theory, which asks: did the defendant commit the final act before the completion of the offence? This has some merit, but produces strange results, so that I have not attempted arson merely by splashing petrol all over a building and lighting a match, since I have not yet committed the last act of throwing the match onto the floor. But it is clear from *R. v. Eagleton* (1855) that if a person does commit the "last act" then this is in itself sufficient to ground a charge of attempt.

The last act theory depends on whether the defendant has done an act which is more than merely preparatory to the commission of the offence. This is a matter of fact for the jury to decide. In *R. v. Robinson* (1915), the defendant was charged with attempting to obtain money by false pretences. He was a jeweller who had staged a burglary in his shop in order to make an insurance claim. A passing policeman heard him shouting from inside the shop and found him bound and gagged beside an empty safe. The ruse was uncovered before the defendant had a chance to inform his insurers of the robbery. It was held that the defendant had merely prepared for the commission of an offence and not taken a step in its commission as there had been no communication with the insurance company.

Similarly, in *R. v. Ilyas* (1983), the Court of Appeal held that an appellant had not done every act necessary for him to do to achieve a result. He reported to the police that his car had been stolen and telephoned his insurers to obtain a claim form but had never actually filled out the claim. It was held that his acts were merely preparatory and remote from the contemplated offence.

The House of Lords considered the theory in *DPP v. Stonehouse* (1977). The appellant had insured his life for a large sum with five different insurance companies. He faked his death by drowning while in Miami in order that his wife, who was not a party to the deception and believed he was dead, could claim on the insurance policies. The news was rapidly conveyed to England by the media as the appellant was a well-known public figure but his wife did not claim on any policy. Five weeks later he was discovered in Australia. His conviction for attempting by deception to enable another to obtain property was upheld by the House of Lords. He had done all the acts within his power to commit the offence and all that was left for him to do was not to be discovered. Lord Diplock stated that "Acts that are merely preparatory to the commission of the offence, such as, in the instant case, the taking out of the insurance policies, are not sufficiently proximate to constitute an attempt. They do not indicate a fixed irrevocable intention to go on to commit the complete offence unless involuntarily prevented from doing so ... In other words the offender must have crossed the Rubicon and burnt his boats.".

Another theory, popular in the United States, is that of probable desistance: would the particular conduct have resulted, in the ordinary course of things, in the completed crime if there had been no outside interference? Or would the offender probably have desisted from his conduct? This also, however, produces strange results. The man who gets on a train to go to Cork to kill another is engaging in conduct which, in the ordinary course of events would result in the completed crime; but if the train breaks down, can it be said that he is guilty of attempted murder?

The Irish cases appear to take a pragmatic approach to proximity. In *People (AG) v. England* (1947) the defendant was charged with attempting to procure the commission of an act of gross indecency with another man. He was friendly with a young man and one day talked to him about sex, and invited him to go to a nearby "secluded spot"; when the young man agreed, he offered him ten shillings. Could this amount to an attempt? It was held that it could not since it did not "directly approximate to the commission of an offence". It was, instead, mere preparation for the commission of an offence, which is not in itself criminal.

People (AG) v. Sullivan (1964) is another example. In that case, the defendant was a midwife who was paid a salary plus an additional allowance for each woman treated over a basic number of 25. She prepared and handed in claim forms in respect of fictitious patients. The evidence did not disclose whether these related to patients 1 to 25 or subsequent patients. The completed crime, if money had been handed over, would have been obtaining by false pretences. Since the fraud was detected before money was handed over, the issue became whether she was guilty of an attempt to obtain by false pretences. She submitted that her conduct, assuming the forms related only to patients 1-25, could not amount to an attempt, since, even had the forms been processed in the ordinary way, she would not have received any money until patient number 26 was reached, which might not happen. Instead she submitted that her conduct was mere preparation for the crime which would be committed when she handed in a completed form for patient 26 and subsequent patients.

This argument was, however, rejected by the High Court and on appeal the Supreme Court. It was not necessary that there was a possibility of the successful completion of the offence, and what she had done went beyond mere preparation once she had handed in the false forms. Nor was it relevant that she might have changed her mind even after handing in the false forms and desisted from committing the completed offence. The Supreme Court, applying the test of proximity, found that each false claim put in was as a matter of law sufficiently proximate to constitute an attempt to obtain by false pretences.

The law of attempt in England and Wales is governed by the Criminal Attempts Act 1981. The Act does not state a test of proximity but requires that the act be "more than merely preparatory to the commission of the offence".

12.2.2 Impossibility

What happens where a defendant attempts to do something which is not a crime or which is impossible? There are three main types of impossibility – legal impossibility, physical impossibility and impossibility due to inadequate method.

Legal impossibility is where a defendant attempts to do something, believing it to be illegal, when it is not. In this situation there is no attempt. The motive of the defendant cannot criminalise an activity that is innocent in the eyes of the law. In *R. v. Taaffe* (1984), the defendant imported cannabis into the UK believing it to be currency. Since importation of currency was not a crime, then despite his intention to carry out what he thought to be a criminal act he could not be guilty of an attempt.

The alternative Australian position may also be noted. In the case of *Britten v. Alpogut* (1987), the facts were quite similar to *R. v. Taaffe* (1984). Here however the defendant believed he was smuggling cannabis when in fact he was smuggling something the importation of which was not an offence. Could he be guilty of an attempt to import cannabis? Clearly under *R. v. Taaffe* the defence of impossibility would have been open to him, but it was held that under Australian law he could not plead this defence:

> "If the evil intent of the actor can make a sufficiently proximate though objectively innocent act criminal, so as to amount to an attempt, it would seem irrelevant to have to go on to see whether the attempt could or would have succeeded. At common law, if the intent was to commit a recognised and not an imagined crime, and the act done was not merely preparatory but sufficiently proximate, than at that stage an attempt to commit the recognised crime has been committed, and it seems to me that it is not necessary to go further ... Impossibility is also irrelevant, unless it be that the so called crime intended is not a crime known to the law, in which case a criminal attempt to commit it cannot be made." (*Per* Murphy J.)

Physical impossibility is also a defence. Suppose a defendant stabs, intending to kill, a person who appears to be asleep but is in fact dead. Such a defendant could not be guilty of attempted murder.

However, the situation is more complicated where there is impossibility due to inadequate method. Impossibility is not a defence in circumstances where the objective would be a crime, if achieved, but the defendant fails to achieve that objective because the means chosen are inadequate. It is an attempt to obtain by false pretences notwithstanding that the false pretence never had a chance of success; it is an attempt to murder to place into a victim's tea poison which is in fact ineffective.

The general rule is that impossibility constitutes a complete defence. So, in *Haughton v. Smith* (1975), it was held by the House of Lords that a person could not be guilty of attempting to handle stolen goods where the goods were not in fact stolen (since they had passed into police custody on being intercepted by the police). Similarly, it would not be attempted murder to try to kill a corpse.

12.2.3 Abandonment

There does not appear to be any defence of abandonment since abandonment has no logical relevance to attempts. Once the proximate act has been carried out, then abandoning the enterprise will not absolve the defendant from culpability. Similarly, if the activity is abandoned before any proximity is reached, then there is no inchoate offence. In Canada abandonment may be used as evidence that the defendant did not intend to complete the crime attempted. In the United States, however, voluntary desistance not procured from an external source may amount to a defence to an attempt.

12.3 Incitement

We have already seen that if A incites B to commit a crime, and B does so, then A is liable to be punished as if he himself committed the crime. This result follows from section 7(1) of the Criminal Law Act 1997, in the case of indictable offences, and from section 22 of the Petty Sessions (Ireland) Act 1851, in respect of summary offences.

Now suppose that A incites B to commit the same crime, but B for whatever reason fails to do so. In these circumstances, neither the 1851 Act nor the 1997 Act are applicable, since both require as a prerequisite that a crime should have been committed. However, A's conduct will amount to the common law offence of incitement to commit a crime (sometimes known as solicitation), since this common law does not depend on whether B does in fact proceed to commit the crime.

This crime must be distinguished from attempt in this way: it is not necessary to show that the incitement is in any way proximate to the completed crime. The law takes the view that the incitement is sufficiently dangerous in itself to merit punishment, regardless of how close it comes to success.

This crime is punishable at discretion: that is to say, there is no upper limit on the penalty which the court can impose. This leads to the strange result that the punishment for incitement could, in theory, be greater than the maximum punishment for the completed offence.

12.3.1 What constitutes incitement?

Being a common law offence, there is no hard and fast definition of incitement in this context. One prominent textbook states that incitement is committed where a person "counsels, procures or commands" another to commit a crime (Williams, *Textbook of Criminal Law* (1978), page 384), a definition which is in its essentials co-extensive with "counselling or procuring" under the 1851 Act or the 1997 Act. Authorities under those Acts are, therefore, also relevant in this context, and *vice versa*. In *R. v. Fitzmaurice* (1983), it was held that the necessary actus reus was satisfied by a "suggestion, proposal or request ... accompanied by an implied promise of reward". It should be noted, however, that incitement can occur by threatening as well as persuasive behaviour.

The leading Irish authority on what constitutes incitement is *People (AG) v. Capaldi* (1949). In that case, the defendant was a man charged with inciting a doctor to commit the crime of bringing about an abortion. Referring to a girl whom he had brought to the doctor, he asked whether the doctor would "do something for her" in relation to her pregnancy. The doctor replied "do you realise what you are asking me to do, you are asking me to perform an illegal operation" to which the defendant said "Yes. Would you perform; there is ample money to meet your fees". The doctor refused, and the defendant was ultimately charged with incitement.

It was argued for the defendant that this did not amount to incitement, but rather to the mere expression of a desire; and further, that an incitement must include some element of "overcoming the reluctant mind". The Court of Criminal Appeal accepted that incitement must include some element over and above the mere expression of a desire; however, on the evidence, it was clear that the defendant had made a positive request to bring about an abortion, which could not realistically be characterised as the mere expression of a desire. The court rejected the argument that incitement must involve an effort to overcome the reluctant mind: rather, a person may commit incitement by doing something if "but for it, it would not have occurred to the party incited to commit the crime, whether he had any particular reluctance to commit it or not" (Per Black J., at page 97).

It is not necessary that the incitement should be directed to any particular person; instead, it may be "thrown out" for any person to act upon. This can be seen from, for example, *Invicta Plastics Ltd. v. Clare* (1976) where a company advertising "radar detectors" for motorists was convicted of inciting readers of the advertisement to use unlicensed wireless apparatus.

This decision is interesting in another way, since it shows that incitement may extend to a situation where A encourages B to do something which is itself legal (buying a radar detector) but knowing that it is practically certain that B will as a result do something illegal (using it). In this situation, A must be taken to have intended that B commit the illegal act.

The incitor's liability is limited to the act incited. If A incites B to rob a woman and B not only robs her but proceeds to kill her in the process, then A can only be found guilty of inciting the robbery since B has gone further than the offence contemplated by A.

It must be noted that the act incited must itself be criminal before the crime of incitement is committed. Suppose that A incites B, a child who is *doli incapax*, to kill C. If B does so, then A is guilty as principal, as we have seen elsewhere. But if B does not, can A be charged with inciting B to murder C? The answer is no: since B would have committed no crime by killing C, then A cannot be said to have incited B to *commit a crime*. This rule is illustrated by *R. v. Whitehouse* (1977), where it was held that a father could not be convicted of inciting his daughter under the age of 16 to commit incest with him, since, if she did so, she would commit no crime, the legislation recognising that a daughter under 16 would be a victim rather than a perpetrator.

Similarly, if the incitor realises that the incitee has no *mens rea*, then there is no incitement since he is not inciting a criminal offence.

Impossibility may be a defence to incitement. It will depend upon the nature of the incitement. If the object is a very general one, for example to commit a burglary, then impossibility is not a defence. If, however, the object is to burgle a specific building and that building is no longer in existence at the time of the incitement, then impossibility may be a defence: *R. v. Fitzmaurice* (1983).

12.3.2 Prohibition of Incitement to Hatred Act 1989

This is a statutory form of incitement. It is an offence to publish, distribute or broadcast threatening abusive or insulting material that is likely or intended to incite hatred. Preparation and possession of material likely to stir up hatred is also prohibited and the gardaí are given powers of search and seizure in relation to such material.

12.4 Conspiracy

At common law, it is an indictable offence for two or more persons to agree to do an unlawful act or even, in some circumstances, to perform an act which is in itself lawful. The offence of conspiracy is complete once the agreement has been concluded: it is not necessary that the conspirators should thereafter commit the agreed crime. As with incitement, it is unnecessary to show any proximity between the conspiracy and the completed crime: the conspiracy itself is punishable regardless of how close it came to fruition.

The offence, as with incitement, is punishable at discretion, and again we have the anomaly that conspiracy to commit a crime may carry a punishment more severe than that applicable to the completed crime.

12.4.1 What agreements amount to conspiracy?

The scope of the offence of conspiracy is exceedingly wide, and consequently "[a]ny agreement manifested by words or conduct to commit the wrong constitutes a conspiracy" (Williams, *Textbook of Criminal Law* (1978) page 351).

The agreement must be a concluded one: discussions as to whether a crime should be committed will not suffice. *R. v. Mills* (1963) illustrates this point. In that case, the defendant was charged with conspiring with a woman to procure an abortion. She had telephoned him seeking an abortion, and he had told her to come to his flat bringing payment. On reaching the flat, they talked about the proposed abortion. She asked whether there would be a risk involved; he asked whether her pregnancy was too far advanced for the operation to be performed. At this point, the police entered the flat.

It was argued for the defence that there was no concluded agreement; but this argument was rejected by the Court of Appeal, which held that there was a concluded agreement at the stage of the telephone conversation. Although the agreement was certainly subject to reservations or conditions, those reservations did not take away from its nature as a concluded agreement: as the court pointed out, every agreement is subject to conditions, express or implied, and to accept the defence argument would have the result that no-one could ever be convicted of conspiracy.

It follows, therefore, that an agreement to commit a crime if a particular condition is satisfied is sufficient to amount to a conspiracy: if A agrees with B to kill C if C decides to give evidence in a trial, this conditional agreement will ground a charge of conspiracy.

Where a number of persons are alleged to be parties to a conspiracy, it is not necessary to show that each was aware of the existence of the others, so long as each is a party to the same conspiracy. Suppose that A recruits B, C, D and E to bomb a building, and that B, C, D and E have never met and are unaware of each other's identities. Notwithstanding this, each is party to the same conspiracy: that is, the conspiracy to bomb the building. This is sometimes described as a cartwheel conspiracy, with A at the hub and the rest at each spoke. Equally, one can have a chain conspiracy, where A recruits B, B recruits C, and so on.

Each person involved in the conspiracy must realise the criminal objective of the plan but it is not necessary that each knows the precise details. Cussen J., in *Orton* (1922), stated that each party should have a conscious understanding of a common design. It is not unusual, particularly in a cartwheel conspiracy, for the person at the "hub" to deliberately keep information from each of the "spokes" and this will not lead to the acquittal of any of the parties unless it is shown that the lack of information lead to the reasonable belief that the objective was not a crime. Similarly, each party must realise that they are part of a plan, even if they are unaware as to the precise method of execution of the plan or the number of people involved. The law is merely concerned to distinguish a conspiracy from a situtation where a number of individuals coincidentally work towards the same goal. There must be a co-ordination of action towards a common purpose.

12.4.2 Purpose of the agreement

(1) Criminal acts

It is clear that the crime of conspiracy is committed where the purpose of the agreement is to commit a criminal act, or where the purpose of the agreement is itself lawful, but it is agreed to use criminal means to bring it about.

(2) Civil wrongs

It seems that agreements to commit *civil wrongs* (torts, breaches of contract, breaches of fiduciary duties, and so forth) may or may not amount to criminal conspiracies, depending on the precise nature of the wrong. The rationale for this rule was expressed as follows in *R. v. Parnell* (1881) at 520-521:

> "It is obvious that a wrongful violation of another man's right committed by many assumes a far more formidable and offensive character than when committed by a single individual ... The law has therefore, and it seems to us wisely and justly, established that a combination of persons to commit a wrongful act with a view to injure another shall be an offence though the act if done by one would amount to no more than a civil wrong.".

In this case the accused, Charles Stuart Parnell, was charged with conspiracy to prevent tenants paying their rents. The judges set out three categories of conspiracy: where the end to be attained is in itself a crime; where the object is lawful, but the means to be resorted to are unlawful; and where the object is to do injury to a third party or to a class, though if the wrong were effected by a single individual it would be a civil wrong but not a crime.

(3) Tort

In relation to torts, the leading case is *DPP v. Kamara* (1974), where a number of students were charged with conspiracy to commit the tort of trespass, by agreeing to occupy the London premises of the High Commissioner of Sierra Leone. Did this amount to a criminal conspiracy?

The House of Lords took the view that it did, and that an agreement to commit a tort could ground a conspiracy, but only where the execution of the tort was intended to involve either (a) some invasion of the public domain (as in this case, by the occupation of a foreign embassy) or (b) the infliction of more than merely nominal damage on the victim (as where premises were occupied to the exclusion of the owner). The same test was put somewhat differently in a concurring opinion of Lord Cross, who stated that whether an agreement to commit a tort amounted to conspiracy depended on whether the public had a sufficient interest: that is, whether the execution of the conspiracy would have sufficiently harmful consequences to justify penal sanctions.

(4) Breach of contract

Charleton (*Criminal Law Cases and Materials* (1992), p. 119) states simply "There are no recent examples of the successful use of breach of contract as the unlawful element in criminal conspiracy.".

(5) Acts which are neither criminal nor civil wrongs

It is clear that Irish law in some circumstances regards as criminal an agreement by two or more people to do certain things, notwithstanding that those things, performed by one person, would amount neither to a criminal offence or a civil wrong. This is a somewhat murky area of the law of conspiracy, with very little case law to offer guidance. The only recent Irish authority on point is *AG (SPUC) v. Open Door Counselling*, which applied the English case of *Shaw v. DPP* (1962) to find that there existed at common law a crime of conspiracy to corrupt public morals, and that the activities of the defendants, in providing non-directive counselling in relation to abortion, could amount to such a crime, notwithstanding that the counselling was not otherwise unlawful and that the agreement was therefore to assist in the commission of a lawful act. The High Court judgment, however, was appealed and this issue was not dealt with by the Supreme Court.

Whether Irish law might be extended further in this direction is unclear. In Australia, it has been held that an agreement to bring about "sham" marriages for immigration purposes could not be said to be so offensive to public morality as to justify a charge of conspiracy to bring about an unlawful object: *R. v. Cahill* (1978), where Street C.J. warned of the dangers in criminalising conduct based on the uncertain and ephemeral concept of public morality.

12.4.3 Conspiracy and impossibility

Suppose A and B agree to do something which it emerges is in fact impossible to do. Are A and B guilty of conspiracy? The answer to this question will depend upon the nature of the agreement. If it is an agreement to do a particular act, which is in fact impossible, then no crime is committed. The House of Lords dealt with impossibility and conspiracy in *DPP v. Nock* (1978). The accused were charged with conspiracy to manufacture cocaine using ingredients which they believed were the raw materials for cocaine. However, the ingredients were actually incapable of producing cocaine and their conviction was quashed. However, if it is an agreement to carry out a more general purpose, then it remains an offence notwithstanding that a particular means of carrying out the purpose is impossible.

12.4.4 Abandonment

It is unclear whether abandonment of a conspiracy is a defence or merely a mitigating factor. Conspiracy is a completed offence once two or more persons agree to work together towards a common objective. It would therefore seem to be illogical that a subsequent withdrawal from the arrangement is a defence.

Martin Wasik, ("Abandoning Criminal Intent" (1980) Crim.L.R. 785) has argued that abandonment of inchoate crimes should only be relevant in mitigation of sentence. He refers to an argument by Glanville Williams, in favour of excusing such a defendant, that his previous intention is capable of being interpreted as only half-formed or provisional and therefore insufficient to amount to *mens rea*. It could also be argued that abandonment of a conspiracy is evidence that the defendant should be regarded as no longer dangerous. A third argument, based on public policy, is that the law should provide an inducement to people to abandon crimes and therefore prevent the commission of harm.

13. CRIMINAL LIABILITY OF CORPORATIONS

13.1 Introduction

Corporations are legal persons and may, therefore, be found guilty of crimes. However, there are obvious difficulties in applying the ordinary principles of criminal law to corporations, stemming from the fact that these entities have no "bodies to be kicked, nor souls to be damned". The most significant of these difficulties comes from the fact that the principle of *mens rea* breaks down when it is applied to a body which can have no intention of its own. Other difficulties include the fact that the legal capacity of corporations does not mirror that of natural persons: for example, a corporation cannot marry, and therefore cannot be guilty of bigamy. And, from a practical point of view, corporations cannot be imprisoned, creating problems where the only penalty for an offence is imprisonment (as with the offence of murder). How are these difficulties to be resolved?

13.2 Development of the principle of corporate liability

The common law originally did not recognise criminal liability of corporations. This appears to have stemmed from practical difficulties: corporations could not appear in person (and there was, of course, no right to representation under the common law). In addition, felonies were punishable by death: a sanction which had no meaning in the case of a corporation. These practical points lost their force when the right to representation was granted, and when fines were introduced as a penalty, thus leaving the way clear for the development of criminal responsibility.

13.3 What acts can be attributed to the corporation?

These changes did not, however, address the question of what acts were to be attributed to the corporation. Was the corporation to be held liable for every criminal act of an employee? And, if not, how could it be determined which acts should be ascribed to it? No legislation deals with this question, and as a result the courts have, on a case by case basis, developed certain principles to determine when the corporation should be criminally liable.

13.3.1 Controlling mind theory

The early cases in this area originated in the U.K. in the 1940s, and took the view that a corporation could be identified with its principals, *i.e.* that the acts of the main individuals within the company could be treated as the acts of the company itself. *DPP v. Kent* (1944) and *R. v. ICR Haulage Ltd* (1944) both held that the acts of managers within a company could be treated as being the acts of the company itself.

These cases were said to adopt the controlling mind theory: that is, that to determine whether the company would be liable, one had to ask whether the act was committed by a person who could be said to be substantially in control of the company's operations. Thus, the act of a mere employee with little discretion would not suffice: one would have to show that the act was carried out by a person such as a senior manager with the ability to direct the operations of the company.

This test has since been elaborated on. One leading English case is *Tesco Supermarkets v. Natrass* (1972), where the House of Lords considered whether a supermarket chain could incur criminal liability based on the acts of a regional supermarket manager. Lord Diplock explained at page 199 that:

> "What natural persons are to be treated in law as being the company for the purpose of acts done in the course of its business, including the taking of precautions and the exercise of due diligence to avoid the commission of a criminal offence, is to be found by identifying those natural persons who by the memorandum and articles of association or as a result of action taken by the directors or by the company in general meeting pursuant to the articles, are entrusted with the exercise of the powers of the company."

This test is a restrictive one: it requires that any wrongdoing exist at a senior level within the company, effectively excluding liability for criminal offences committed at a lower level. Having said that, it must be remembered that if senior officers are aware of and connive in activities at a lower level, this will suffice.

The restrictive nature of the test can be seen from the Canadian case of *R. v. Safety-Kleen Canada Inc.* (1997). Here the defendant company ran a fleet of waste-oil collection trucks. One of its drivers was found, contrary to Canadian environmental legislation, to have knowingly given false information in a return made to a provincial officer. The driver was the only representative of the company in a wide area, and carried out a variety of roles: he was, in effect, the only point of contact for customers in the area, and was responsible for administration in the area. However, the employee did not have any managerial or supervisory function, and had no power to make policy. The court found no evidence that the truck driver had authority to make corporate decisions which went beyond those arising out of the transfer and transportation of waste. On this basis, the Ontario Court of Appeal felt that the criminal acts of the employee could not be imputed to the company, notwithstanding the wide discretion which he enjoyed in carrying out his duties.

By comparison, in another Canadian case, *R. v. Church of Scientology of Toronto* (1997), the Church of Scientology was found to be liable for the criminal acts of the Assistant Guardian Toronto, who headed the "Intelligence Bureau" within the "Guardian's Office" of the organisation. This finding was made on the basis that, in respect of his functions, the employee was free from accountability: he answered to no-one within the organisation in the exercise of his functions, notwithstanding that he may not have had discretion to set policy in the area.

The inadequacy of the identification approach in certain situations was highlighted in *DPP v. P&O Ferries (Dover) Ltd.* (1991). This prosecution arose from the sinking of the ferry, Herald of Free Enterprise, just outside the port of Zeebrugge. The tragedy was caused by the assistant bosun's failure to ensure that the bow doors had been closed and the company was charged with corporate manslaughter. The Central Criminal Court held there was no conceptual difficulty in charging a corporation with manslaughter. Turner J. noted, at page 84, that "where a corporation, through the controlling mind of one of its agents, does an act which fulfills the prerequisites of the crime of manslaughter, it is properly indictable for the crime of manslaughter". However, the prosecution ultimately failed as it was not possible to identify the assistant bosun with the company and he was the only person possessing the sufficient *mens rea* of recklessness.

13.3.2 Organisational theory

The controlling mind theory, convenient though it may be for particular cases, has obvious limitations. One of these is evident when we consider sins of omission rather than commission. Where a company fails to do something, then it may not be possible to point the finger of blame at any one individual. Instead, the fault may lie with the systems in place within the company, so that the company, rather than any one individual, is at fault. Another fault is that the controlling mind theory allows companies to escape liability for wrongs committed by more junior employees. Yet another is that the theory encourages proceedings to focus, not on the commission of the crime itself, but on the defendants internal management hierarchy. These faults have led in some more recent case law to a theory of organisational liability, under which the courts will look to the structures and decision-making processes within the defendant corporation.

An example of this can be seen in *R. v. British Steel plc* (1995), where the defendant corporation was charged with health and safety offences, such offences being offences of strict liability (subject to a defence of reasonable care having been taken). The defence put forward was that the senior management had taken all reasonable care in the circumstances, and that any fault lay with independent contractors. This defence was not, however, accepted by the Court of Appeal, which took the view that where strict liability had been imposed, it would undermine that imposition if the company could escape liability on the basis that the "directing mind" was not at fault. In reaching this decision, the court was greatly influenced by the fact that practical difficulties had arisen at the trial of corporate offences, with the bulk of trial time being taken on whether or not particular employees were part of senior management.

Similarly, in *Director General of Fair Trading v. Pioneer Concrete (UK) (Ltd)* (1995), the House of Lords held that a company could be liable where employees acted in breach of court injunctions, notwithstanding that they did so contrary to express instructions and without the knowledge of senior management, on the basis that any other position would effectively give companies immunity from action.

It would appear from these two cases, in particular, that U.K. law is moving towards a wider test of corporate responsibility. However, it should be noted that both cases dealt with very specific statutory contexts; it remains to be seen whether a similar approach would be taken in respect of other offences.

13.4 Restrictions on corporate liability

13.4.1 Corporation the victim

A number of restrictions limit corporate liability. The first is straightforward and readily understandable: a corporation will not be criminally liable for the acts of an employee where those acts are directed towards defrauding the corporation, *i.e.* where the corporation is itself the victim. This point was made in *Canadian Dredge & Dock Co. v. R.* (1985), where the Supreme Court of Canada accepted that where a manager set out to "intentionally defraud" a corporation, then it became "unrealistic in the extreme" to identify the manager with the corporation. However, that case also illustrates the difficulties in establishing the defence.

The defendant companies had colluded together to bid at rigged prices in respect of public procurement contracts. The employees in question had benefited from this arrangement, receiving kickbacks for doing so. The defendant companies therefore claimed that they had been defrauded by the collusion, and so could not be held responsible for it. This argument was rejected by the court, which noted that the companies had received benefits from the collusion: the employees were acting partly for their own benefit, but also partly for the benefit of the companies. The companies were not, therefore, true victims of the conduct in question.

13.4.2 Corporation incapable of committing particular crime

It remains the case that a corporation cannot commit certain crimes by reason of its nature: bigamy and perjury being the obvious examples. Equally, a company cannot be convicted of a crime for which the only punishment is imprisonment, such as murder. It is, however, unclear whether a company could be charged with, for example, counselling or procuring the commission of perjury, for which it could be tried as a principal.

13.4.3 Employees acting contrary to instructions

As we have seen, *Director General of Fair Trading v. Pioneer Concrete (UK) (Ltd)* (1995) held that the existence of instructions against a particular course of conduct did not amount to a defence. A similar view has been taken in Canada, in *Canadian Dredge & Dock Co. v. R.* (1985), where the court expressly held that instructions preventing the conduct in question were irrelevant to the question of guilt. Note, however, that such instructions, or a detailed policy in relation to the conduct, may be an important factor mitigating the penalty to be imposed.

13.5 Punishment of companies

The only sanction which can generally be imposed on a company guilty of a crime is a fine. (Although statute does provide for other forms of enforcement in particular cases, see for example the Safety, Health and Welfare at Work Act 1989 which provides for enforcement notices in relation to unsafe workplaces.) These fines will often be derisory in relation to the profits of the company, particularly where the crime is one prosecuted in the District Court. In such cases, the real punishment of the company may come from other sources: unwelcome publicity, increased insurance premia, or exclusion from further opportunities (for example, the tender procedure for government building contracts will ask bidders whether they have been convicted of any health and safety offences).

Consequently, one can ask whether companies should be fined at a higher level than individuals (as is the case in Australia), or whether alternative sanctions should be imposed. One possibility has been adopted in the US, which provides for a form of corporate probation, allowing the court to monitor the ongoing conduct of a company. Indeed, one might go further and argue for a corporate death penalty, allowing the courts a discretion to wind up companies found guilty of serious criminal offences. Alternatively, it has been suggested that regulation of companies should take place in a civil context, and that civil law remedies will ease the burden of proof associated with corporate prosecutions. It should be remembered in this context that civil liability is much easier to establish than criminal liability, since in the civil law a company is generally vicariously liable for the acts of its employee acting in the course of his employment, regardless of the seniority or otherwise of the employee.

Further reading: Clarkson, C.M.V., "Kicking Corporate Bodies and Damning Their Souls" (1996) 59 M.L.R. 557; Conway, G., "The Criminal Character of a Company" (1999) 7 I.S.L.R. 23; McDermott, P.A., "Defences to Corporate Criminal Liability" *Bar Review* Vol. 5 Issue 4 Jan/Feb 2000 p. 170; Wells, C., "Corporations: Culture, Risk and Criminal Liability" (1993) Crim.L.R. 551.

INDEX